Mary and Early Christian Women

Ally Kateusz

Mary and Early Christian Women

Hidden Leadership

Ally Kateusz
Wijngaards Institute for
Catholic Research
Rickmansworth, London, UK

ISBN 978-3-030-11110-6   ISBN 978-3-030-11111-3   (eBook)
https://doi.org/10.1007/978-3-030-11111-3

Library of Congress Control Number: 2018966131

Cover credit: San Gennaro Catacombs, Naples. Fresco of Cerula. © Societá Cooperativa La Paranza - Catacombe di Napoli.

This Palgrave Macmillan imprint is published by the registered company Springer Nature Switzerland AG
The registered company address is: Gewerbestrasse 11, 6330 Cham, Switzerland

For Arielle and Bella
In memory of Michel-Jean van Esbroeck, whose unexpected death in 2003
was followed by the even more unexpected disappearance of his completed
manuscript edition of John Geometrician's Life of the Virgin.

ACKNOWLEDGEMENTS

Years ago, I discovered womenpriests.org with its layered sources about early Christian women clergy, a site that I have since learned has made a deep impression in the lives of many people, especially women seeking to better understand their role in their own church. It is with deep gratitude that I now thank the Wijngaards Institute for Catholic Research in London, which manages the Web site, for assistance in making this book open access.

I have many to thank. Massimiliano Vitiello was my toughest debate partner and due in part to his encouragement, early versions of some of the research in this book have already won awards including the First Prize Elisabeth Schüssler Fiorenza New Scholar Award, *Feminae* Article of the Month, and the First Place Otis Worldwide Outstanding Dissertation Award. Daniel Stramara, Jr., was my first guide to early Christianity. Stephen Dilks helped me dig deep into the critical discourse analysis of the Six Books Dormition narratives, and Jeffrey Rydberg-Cox and Theresa Torres provided sources and other help. Mary Ann Beavis has been supportive in many ways, including as Chair of the National Society of Biblical Literature Consultation *Maria, Mariamne, Miriam*, where some of this research was initially presented. Mary B. Cunningham and Rachel Fulton Brown provided invaluable critiques. Luca Badini Confalonieri initiated and greatly augmented my research on Cerula and Bitalia. Deborah Niederer Saxon was an insightful sounding board from the beginning. Ann Graham Brock unflaggingly inspired me to sharpen my early arguments, especially related to the mother and the Magdalene.

Hal Taussig provided important nuance to my discussion of ritual meals. A decade ago, Stephen J. Shoemaker introduced me to Michel van Esbroeck's 1986 edition of the *Life of the Virgin*, and I wish I had been able to persuade him, during our debates prior to his own 2012 edition, about the validity of Mary officiating in its Last Supper scene. Many other colleagues provided valuable sources, questions, or suggestions related to one or more ideas, sections, or pieces of art, including Jeffrey Bennett, Virginia Blanton, Jelena Bogdanović, Sheila Briggs, Judith M. Davis, Paula Eisenbaum, Hans Förster, Steven J. Friesen, Deirdre Good, Verna E. F. Harrison, Susan Ashbrook Harvey, Cornelia Horn, Susan Humble, Karel Innemée, Robin M. Jensen, Dickran Kouymijian, Maria Lidova, Matthew John Milliner, Linda E. Mitchell, Michael Peppard, Elizabeth Schrader, Kay Higuera Smith, Joan E. Taylor, Harold Washington, and John Wijngaards.

Deborah Brungardt Alani, Chalise Bourquart, and Shirley Fessel aided in making the manuscript more accessible to readers, and Claus Wawrzinek provided excellent technical support for the images. I am especially appreciative of my Palgrave Macmillan editor, who contacted me after reading my 2017 *Journal of Feminist Studies in Religion* article on women priests, Amy Invernizzi.

Finally, I am deeply grateful for Jane Gilbreath, my mother and reader, and for my husband David Edward Kateusz, traveling companion and supporter for this work in too many ways to count.

CONTENTS

ix

LIST OF FIGURES

CHAPTER 1

Background and Perspective

Feminist scholars have rightfully argued that today the Virgin Mary often operates as an unhealthy feminine ideal of obedience and self-sacrifice.[1] The reality of their arguments sank in one morning as I had coffee with a Hispanic friend who had suffered years of domestic violence. As she sipped her coffee, her childhood seemed close to the surface. She talked about growing up and then told me what her priest had taught the girls. She bowed her head and looked down. I barely heard her words. "Sea sumisa, como la Virgen." *Be submissive, like the Virgin.*

My friend's words, and the way her posture changed as she spoke them, deeply affected me. The power those five words had upon her, their influence on a little girl and her expectations for her life, took away my breath. Later, I wondered if her life might have followed a different path had her priest instead taught the girls to be like the early Christian Mary.

What I have discovered is that some early Christians described Jesus's mother as a very different female role model for girls. These authors and artists did not portray Mary as submissive. They depicted her with an upright posture and a direct gaze. They described her as a liturgical leader in the early Jesus movement—a movement in which women were apostles and preached, healed, washed/sealed/baptized, led the prayers, and presided at the offering table.

In 1983, Elisabeth Schüssler Fiorenza proposed that the Jesus movement began as a "discipleship of equals."[2] Evidence of this gender philosophy is first found in Second Temple Judaism, and new evidence—as we shall see—demonstrates that this gender philosophy remained strong

© The Author(s) 2019
A. Kateusz, *Mary and Early Christian Women*,
https://doi.org/10.1007/978-3-030-11111-3_1

into the sixth century in many Jesus communities, including in the liturgy at the offering table of some of the most important basilicas in Christendom. Surprisingly, or perhaps not so surprisingly, Mary, the Jewish mother of Jesus, provides a key to fully understanding this new evidence. Her story, however, like that of Jesus's women disciples, has long been suppressed.

MARY MAGDALENE AND THE MOTHER OF JESUS

In the last decades, feminist scholarship has taken wings restoring the reputation of Mary Magdalene as a leader in the early Jesus movement.[3] By contrast, relatively little scholarship has been dedicated toward restoring the reputation of Jesus's mother as a leader in the movement. Yet, there could have been two women leaders named Mary—two Marys— both of whom were recast as female caricatures, one as a sinful whore and the other as a submissive virgin.

A woman, after all, can be both a mother and a leader, and vestiges of the strong role that Jesus's mother played are in the canonical gospels themselves. The author of Luke/Acts, in particular, closely associated Mary with prophecy in Luke 1:46–55, the *Magnificat*, giving her the longest speech of any woman in the New Testament. This author again associated Mary with prophecy at Pentecost, when the flames of the Holy Spirit descended, and "Mary the mother of Jesus" alone was named among the women gathered in the upper room (Acts 1:14).

The author of John elevated Mary the Magdalene as the first witness to the resurrected Christ and apostle to the apostles. Yet John also elevated the mother of Jesus during her son's adult ministry. The synoptic gospels barely mention Jesus's mother during his ministry[4]—and when they do, Mark and Matthew seemingly denigrate her and Jesus's brothers (Mk 3:21, 31–35; Mt 2:46–50). John, by contrast, three times identifies Jesus's mother as being with her son during his ministry—and each time presents her in a positive light. The first instance is at the wedding at Cana where Mary launches her son's ministry by instigating his miracle of transforming water into wine (John 2:1–11). The second time is when Jesus and his mother, and his brothers, and his disciples—in that order—traveled from Cana down to Capernaum (John 2:12). The third is at the foot of the cross on Golgotha (John 19:25–27). John does not name "Mary the Magdalene" anywhere in the gospel until we see her at the end of the list of women at the foot of the cross—yet that in no way diminishes the Magdalene's subsequent role as the first witness to the resurrection. The author of John did not place Magdalene and mother in competition during Jesus's ministry. This author elevated both Marys, each in her respective leadership role, and elevated both more than any other gospel writer did.

A further indication that the author of John intended to signify that Jesus's mother was a leader during her son's ministry is that the first person in a list is often thought to signify the leader of the other people in the list. For example, Peter is listed first among the twelve disciples at Matthew 10:2–4, Mark 3:16–19, and Luke 6:14–16, and he is considered their leader. In the same way, Mary the Magdalene is listed first among the women who followed Jesus at Luke 8:2–3. In John 19:25, however, Jesus's mother is listed first among the women at the cross. One might argue that she was listed first because she was his mother, but the authors of the three synoptic gospels listed Mary Magdalene first. In addition, at John 2:12, when they traveled with Jesus from Cana to Capernaum, Jesus's mother is listed before "his brothers" and "his disciples." These passages affirm that the author of John was deliberate, both in three times positively affirming Mary's relationship to her son during his ministry and also in twice identifying her leadership among the other disciples, both women and men.

The author of Luke/Acts, thus, signified Mary's prophetic leadership. The author of John signified Mary's leadership role during her son's ministry, including specifying that she was with him, at Cana, Capernaum, and Golgotha. The authors of both John and Luke/Acts appear to have omitted parts of the original story, but each preserved that both Marys—Magdalene and mother—were important leaders.

Mary, a Jew

Historians know with a degree of certainly only a few things about Jesus. He was born. He died. He and his mother were Jews. Almost certainly he learned Jewish culture, traditions, and teachings from his mother. What did Jesus learn about women from her?

Even today, Judaism is not monolithic in its gender ideals—that is, multiple philosophies regarding the proper roles for women compete within modern Judaism, from Orthodox to Reform. In some synagogues today, women are rabbis and leaders, whereas in others they are not permitted. Likewise, there were multiple streams of Judaism during the era in which Jesus and Mary lived. The third-century painted walls of the Dura-Europos synagogue provide an excellent example where archeology has turned upside down our false imagination of a monolithic Jewish past. Prior to the excavation of this synagogue, most biblical scholars argued that scriptural injunctions against making graven images or likenesses—such as in the second of the Ten Commandments—meant Jews never used such images. The idea that paintings of biblical scenes covered the walls of a third-century synagogue was almost unthinkable. Yet the Dura synagogue walls were painted from top to bottom with biblical scenes. Since its excavation, scholars have catalogued even more synagogue art, especially floor mosaics, which survived when frescos did not.[5]

Corresponding to this cultural diversity in Judaism, but related to women specifically, Judaism, after the destruction of the Second Temple, underwent what is often thought of as a structural change from patriline to matriline[6]—that is, from a child being born a Jew only if its father was a Jew to a child being born a Jew only if its *mother* was a Jew. The speed at which this legal shift seems to have taken place, and the lack of understanding with respect to why or how the change came about, provides another potential witness that within Israel at that time, legal philosophies regarding the role of women were diverse, not monolithic. Diversity in the ritual roles of women in various Jewish communities is further suggested by surviving descriptions of male and female groups paired in community ritual, such as a Qumran liturgical text's description of two groups called Mothers and Fathers,[7] and the Jewish historian Philo's report about the Therapeutae Jews in Judea who had a gender-parallel meal ritual with a female leader who stood in for Miriam and a male who stood in for Moses.[8] Bernadette J. Brooten's study of stone epigraphs that memorialized Jewish women with synagogue titles such as "Head of the Synagogue," "Mother of the Synagogue," "Elder," and "Priestess," suggests that traditions of gender-parallel ritual may have continued in some synagogues in the Mediterranean diaspora.[9] Competing Jewish philosophies about the rights of women during this era are witnessed by multiple pieces of evidence, for example, the two creation stories in Genesis 1 and 2, rabbinical debates,[10] and bills of divorce and other documents evidencing that while some Jewish women had the right to divorce their husbands, others did not[11]—a right also witnessed in Mark 10:1–12 when a rabbi named Jesus ruled that the gender parallelism of *elohim* in Genesis 1:27 meant that both sexes had the right to divorce. Did his mother teach him that?

What kind of Jewish woman was Mary? Cleo McNelly Kearns, in *The Virgin Mary, Monotheism, and Sacrifice*, analyzes in depth the priestly symbolism that the authors of Luke and John associated with Mary, especially their parallels between Mary and Abraham. For example, according to Luke, Mary received a divine Annunciation regarding her miraculously conceived firstborn son—just as Abraham did. In John, Mary's son carried the wood for his own sacrifice on his back up the mountain—just as Isaac did. Mary stood on top of Golgotha at her son's sacrifice—just as Abraham stood on top of Mount Moriah. From this and much more, Kearns proposes that these gospel authors saw Mary as "the New Abraham,"[12] with both Mary and Abraham "later invoked as a founding figure in the cultic and sacrificial discourses that follow in the wake of those narratives; Abraham in the priesthood and temple cult of Israel and Mary in the ecclesiastical body and sacerdotal discourse of the Christian church."[13] The authors of Luke and John, thus, appear to have believed that a Judean woman could be both a mother and a leader.

MARY REMEMBERED IN THE EXTRACANONICAL GOSPELS

Consistent with Mary's portrayal in Luke and John as a founding figure like Abraham, the authors of extracanonical gospels—that is, gospels outside the New Testament canon—remembered her as a religious leader. Many Christians today do not know very much about the extracanonical gospels because in the fourth century these gospels usually were not included in the lists of books that became the modern Bible. Around the Mediterranean, however, many Jesus followers considered these gospels sacred and translated them into the same languages that they translated canonical gospels.[14]

Perhaps the most popular of these was the *Protevangelium of James* which was about Mary's own birth and childhood, as well as about the birth of her son. This gospel is usually dated second century although some scholars argue that it may contain first-century traditions, in part due to its lack of anti-Jewish language when compared to the canonical gospels.[15] Its author self-identified with Israel and did not even seem to know the later term "Christian."[16] Recent research demonstrates that although some of this author's descriptions of Jewish customs are not what we might expect given scripture—much like the painted walls of the Dura-Europos synagogue are not what we might expect given scripture—they nonetheless were consistent with Jewish custom as told in the Mishnah and other Jewish texts of that era.[17]

We can additionally detect that Jesus followers considered these books scripture by the fact that some of their narrative motifs are in the oldest surviving Christian art. For example, Michael Peppard recently proposed that a painting in the third-century Dura-Europos church baptistery represented the Annunciation to Mary at a well, a scene from the *Protevangelium*.[18] In a recent article in the *Journal of Early Christian Studies*, I proposed that a third-century fresco in the Priscilla catacomb in Rome portrayed Mary praying in a scene from the Dormition narrative about her death, a motif appropriate to the funeral environment of the catacombs.[19] In another example, the oldest artifacts to depict the birth of Jesus almost invariably depict him as a swaddled infant in a manger with a donkey and an ox nearby, as prophesied in Isaiah 1:3.[20] This prophetic detail of the donkey and ox at the birth of Jesus is not in the canonical gospel accounts. It is only in the *Protevangelium*, which specifies that Mary rode a *donkey* to the cave where she gave birth, and that an *ox*-manger was inside the cave.[21] For the oldest surviving Nativity scene in art (see Fig. 1.1).

Fig. 1.1   Oldest art of the nativity of Jesus. Jesus swaddled in a manger flanked by an ox and a donkey. Third-century sarcophagus lid, Saint Ambrose Basilica, Milan. © Fratelli Alinari Museum Collections, Florence

Perhaps the least understood aspect of the *Protevangelium* is that its author twice specified that Mary had been inside the very Holy of Holies of the Jerusalem Temple.[22] This seems to be our first serious clue that the author was comfortable presenting Mary with the qualities of a high priest, because the Holy of Holies was the innermost sacred place that, according to Leviticus 16 and Hebrews 9:7, only a high priest was permitted to enter. Mary as a high priest also is consistent with her role as a founding figure in Israel, a New Abraham, as Kearns describes, and even more so after the destruction of the Temple and the structural change to matriline Judaism—that is, you were a Jew only if your *mother* was a Jew.

The *Protevangelium* was not the only gospel to depict Mary inside the Jerusalem Temple as if she were a priest. Another, the *Gospel of Bartholomew*, which is sometimes called the *Questions of Bartholomew*, described Mary partaking of bread and wine at the Temple altar just before the Annunciation.[23] This gospel probably was compiled sometime between the second and fifth centuries, and is usually dated third century without much controversy, because its text preserves archaic literary artifacts such as Mary giving birth without pain and Jesus disappearing from the cross, docetic theology usually dated no later than the second century.[24]

In addition to depicting Mary at the Temple altar, the *Gospel of Bartholomew* also describes her standing in front of the male apostles as their liturgical leader[25]—a scene retrospectively suggested by the scene in the upper room at Pentecost in Acts, which named only "Mary the mother of Jesus" among the women who were there. According to the *Gospel of Bartholomew*, Mary said, "'Let us stand up in prayer.' And the apostles stood behind Mary."[26] Mary actually leading their prayer in this gospel, however, ensued only after a debate between her and the male apostles, a debate in which alternatively she, and then they, gave humble reasons why the other had more right to lead the prayer. This gospel's debate is particularly noteworthy because more typically after such debates, Peter ends up leading the prayer.[27] This author, however, took care to describe Mary's liturgical leadership as greater than that of the male apostles, including even greater than Peter's. Most striking, in this debate the male apostles themselves denied the right of Peter, "chief of the apostles," to lead the prayer.[28] They also rebutted a patriarchal argument today still used against women church leaders: "The head of the man is Christ but the head of the woman is the man."[29] Instead, they told Mary: "In you the Lord set his tabernacle and was pleased to be contained by you. Therefore *you now have more right than we to lead in prayer.*"[30] In this debate, thus, the male apostles undermined their own authority—and validated Mary's.[31] Signifying their subordination, they stood behind Mary. Then, after the debate, she "stood up before them, and spread out her hands to heaven and began to pray."[32] And she spoke a long prayer, praising God.

A second debate in the *Gospel of Bartholomew*, this one between Mary and Peter, is of additional interest because it depicts Peter denying his own authority. In this debate, Mary repeatedly rejects Peter's requests that she ask her son a question. She instead tells Peter he should ask—which Peter, seemingly afraid, never does. Instead, he tells Mary that she has more authority than he does, and that *she* should ask. Finally, Mary dismisses Peter, telling him: "In me the Lord took up his abode that I might restore the dignity of *women.*"[33]

Other early Christian writers similarly described Jesus's mother as a defender of women. A discourse attributed to Demetrius, the third-century Archbishop of Antioch, says: "Hail, Mary, through whom and by whom all the *women* in the world have acquired freedom of speech with her Lord!"[34] In the early fourth century, in the same area, the famed poet Ephrem the Syrian (ca. 306–373) wrote: "In Mary there has come hope for the female sex: from the insults they have heard and the shame they have felt *she has given them freedom.*"[35]

Also in the fourth century, and further suggesting the importance of Mary for women leaders, Bishop Epiphanius of Salamis (ca. 310–403) complained that in a wide swath of Eastern Christianity, from Scythia (southern Russia) to Thrace (Bulgaria) to the Arabian peninsula, women priests were sacrificing bread to the name of Mary on the altar Table.[36] This liturgy may have been especially common in churches in Ancient Syria, the territory that ran from beyond Jerusalem to beyond Antioch. In any case, a liturgical manual written in Old Syriac (a dialect of Aramaic) and embedded in the Dormition narrative about Mary's death preserves a liturgy that similarly instructed that bread be sacrificed to the name of Mary on church altars.[37] Both Stephen J. Shoemaker and I have argued that when Epiphanius complained about women priests who sacrificed bread to the name of Mary, he apparently was complaining about this liturgy, or a liturgy like it.[38]

Many of the early views of Mary are quite different from our ideas about her today. Kim Haines-Eitzen points out, "What is surprising is how little the earliest stories of Mary emphasis her virginity."[39] Many attributes that preachers today most closely associate with Mary—such as virginity and purity—were not closely associated with Mary in the oldest narratives about her. For example, a cornerstone feature of the text of the oldest largely complete manuscript of the Dormition narrative—the fifth-century Old Syriac underscript of a palimpsest—is that, unlike later Dormition homilists who repeatedly called Mary "pure," this author did not once call Mary "pure."[40] This author described Mary as a liturgical leader who praised God, preached the gospel, led the prayers, set out the censer of incense to God, healed with her hands, exorcised, sealed, sprinkled water, and gave women evangelists powerful writings, or books, to take around the Mediterranean.[41] Extracanonical gospels such as these, as well as the canonical gospels of Luke and John, reveal that many Jesus followers remembered Mary as a founder of their movement, a woman founder who was, as Kearns argues, a New Abraham.

METHODOLOGY

I use redaction analysis—a philological tool in the critical discourse analysis toolbox—to expose the changes that later scribes and artists deliberately made to texts. Then I analyze what was at stake in their changes. Ideological struggles in particular provide a treasure trove of discursive data for critical discourse analysis, because, as Norman Fairclough explains, an ideological struggle "pre-eminently takes place in language."[42] Scribal changes to a text, thus, can reveal sites of social conflict.[43] My analysis demonstrates that Late Antiquity underwent an ideological struggle over female gender roles, a struggle reflected in the redactions and excisions that later scribes made to the oldest narratives about Mary and other women leaders.

Because literary and iconographic artifacts depicting women leaders eventually fell out of favor with the hierarchy of some Christian communities, and were censored, outliers in the early data are best studied as a pattern across time and geographical locations around the Mediterranean, rather than as unrelated disruptions at specific times and places. I therefore follow the footsteps of scholars like Peter Brown, who followed the path established by the Annales school in demonstrating the merits of a more macro-historical approach.[44] This approach is particularly appropriate for the study of Christianity during Late Antiquity (ca. 250–650) given the relative abundance of travel and trade during those centuries. Books and small pieces of art were easily transported. Jewish and Christian religions spread around the Mediterranean.

This larger data set illuminates larger patterns, for example, a pattern of female and male leaders with equivalent authority among Jesus movements around the Mediterranean. Another pattern exposes a powerful female gender role during the earliest layer of the Jesus movement—a leadership role modeled by the mother of Jesus. Yet another pattern reveals women who were called "apostles"—women who evangelized, preached, sealed, and baptized. And finally, women who presided at the table come into view—women officiants, who, depending upon the era and the community, were variously called president, bishop, priest, presbyter, deacon, and minister.[45]

THE POWER OF BIO-POWER

Michel Foucault's concept of bio-power, which he describes essentially as mapping micro-structures of social control onto the body, helped me construct a framework for my research.[46] The subtext of each of the following chapters is how texts and iconography represent female bio-power. Whether you can raise your arms in prayer as the liturgical leader or not. Whether you stand or kneel. How you speak, if you can speak. Whether you can look directly at someone or whether your gaze must be lowered. Whether you can travel outside your home or if you must stay inside. Whether you can touch the altar, the censer, the Eucharistic bread, or raise the chalice—all are examples of a normative power structure that has been mapped onto your body to control it.

One means of social control over the female body is to provide illustrations of right behavior—both narrative and iconographic. Mary, as "the mother of the Lord," is culturally situated to provide a powerful exemplar for Christian women and girls. Religious authorities as well as women themselves have used, and continue to use, Mary's gendered behavior to validate similar behavior in women and girls. Mary's body performs as a model for Christian women. When scribes and artists gradually changed their portrayal of Mary from an arms-raised liturgical leader to a silent woman who physically expressed her submission by looking at the floor, we may conclude that at least metaphorically, something dramatic had changed with respect to this feminine cultural ideal for women. For an example of the way artists in the city of Rome over time portrayed Mary's bio-power while praying, see Figs. 1.2, 1.3 and 1.4.[47]

The arms-raised posture of prayer leadership seen in Fig. 1.2 became exceedingly rare in the city of Rome during the Middle Ages, while the much more submissive posture seen in Fig. 1.4 was virtually unknown

Fig. 1.2 Leadership. 300s. MARIA on gold glass, Rome. Perret, *Catacombes*, pl. 4:32.101

300s. Leadership.
Catacomb gold glass.

Fig. 1.3 Queenly.
900s. Maria in Pallara
Church, Rome. Wilpert,
Römischen Mosaiken, pl.
226

900s. Queenly.
Maria in Pallara.

for Mary prior to the end of the first millennium CE. Numerous scribes, artists, and their masters participated in this profoundly subtle mode of influencing the way Mary was seen. Mary's image in churches communicated what was morally possible for a woman to do with her arms, her gaze, and her voice. From an early age, a girl learns what is acceptable or socially obligatory for her body. She learns from pictures, from stories told at home or read in Church, and from what others of the same rank or sex do. She also learns from what authorities, such as priests, tell her—priests who themselves learned as children in the same way—priests such as the one who, when he learned of her domestic abuse, told my friend, "Be submissive, like the Virgin."

Fig. 1.4   Passive.
1500s. Antonio Solario
painting, Rome.
CC-BY-SA Jakob
Skou-Hansen, National
Gallery of Denmark

Early 1500s. Passive.
Antonio Solario.

BREAKING THE BOX OF OUR FALSE IMAGINATION OF THE PAST

What we think we know about the past can impede our ability to see what was actually there. I believe that is especially the case for the Marian religious practices, which for many centuries were central in Church iconography, literature, and ritual. Today the study of ancient Marian religious phenomena is fraught with modern Protestant, Orthodox, and Catholic interpretation, not to mention layers of their associated gender theology. Setting aside for the moment the Reformation's ideology of *sola scriptura* and its enormous implications for subsequent historical perspectives on Mary in the West, a modern analogy of a Great Church Council—in this case, the Council of Vatican II, which ended in 1965—illustrates how our false imagination of the past, that is, what we *think* we know about the past, can make it difficult to see what was actually there.

In 1965 after a nearly tied vote, the council of Vatican II demoted Mary. Afterward, in Catholic churches, the old liturgies featuring Mary were mostly replaced. Similarly, over time the old statues of Mary were quietly moved to less conspicuous places.[48] These changes took place over decades, church by church.

What we can see and hear in today's churches, both Catholic and Protestant, has implications for how we imagine Marian religion in churches of the past. Today it is much more difficult, at least in the West, to visualize Mary ever having been a central figure in Christianity. So consider the following scenario: Imagine that centuries from now archeologists dig up the remains of a twenty-first-century church—a church such as the colonial era church in Catemaco, Veracruz in Mexico, which sits on the shore of a volcanic lake.

These future archeologists would discover a three-foot-tall statue of the Virgin of Catemaco inside a window in the wall behind the altar. Seeing this statue, these archeologists might assume that the priest of the Catemaco church had immoderately elevated Mary, perhaps, they might theorize, to satisfy the indigenous people's need for a goddess. These archeologists, however, would not know that, prior to Vatican II, for centuries the same statue of the Virgin of Catemaco was in the *very center of the nave*, elevated on an enormous pedestal that stood beneath the sun-lit cupola that features stained glass scenes from Mary's life. These archeologists would not know that even during Mass, men, women, and children stood in a long line, waiting to climb the steps that encircled the huge pedestal and led up to the Virgin. When the people, young and old, finally ascended to the round platform with its statue of the Virgin, they carefully placed near her their handwritten notes tied with red yarn, photos of their children, and what they called *milagros*—tiny silver replicas of an arm, leg, cow, ear of corn, car, swaddled baby—all asking Mary for help (see Figs. 1.5 and 1.6).

These future archeologists would imagine that the placement of a statue of Mary in the wall behind the altar was a novel elevation of Mary—they had never seen such a thing—but in reality it had been a demotion of Mary, a demotion instigated by a great Church Council, Vatican II. But what if the archeologists dug out the basement of the

Fig. 1.5 Before Vatican II. Mary on huge pedestal. Public domain

Mary on her huge pedestal

church? What if they found the beautiful old columns that had encircled Mary's pedestal, and then, what if they found the huge pedestal itself? Would they be able to imagine the past? Or would they just try to explain away this new evidence? What if they found the little notes carefully tied with red yarn? What if they discovered an old book with a liturgy where women priests sacrificed bread to Mary on the altar table? Who knows what they would discover in the basement of the church. What would it take for these future scholars to break out of the box of their own false imagination?

That is where we are going—to the basement of the Church.

Fig. 1.6 After
Vatican II. Mary
removed. Courtesy
David Edward
Kateusz

Pedestal removed

CHAPTER 2

More Collyridian Déjà vu

One of the most striking phenomena about the early Jesus people is that women appear to have been exceptionally involved in the spread of the movement. Almost all the house churches named in the New Testament are identified by the name of the women who apparently led them: Chloe, Nympha, Apphia, Priscilla, Lydia, and Mary the mother of Mark.[1] In Romans 16, Paul recognized the work of several women—Phoebe, Prisca, Mary, Junia, Tryphaena, Tryphosa, Rufus's mother, Julia, and Nereus's sister.[2] Debunking the idea that only men were apostles, Paul called Junia an apostle.[3] There Junia stands, in plain view: a woman apostle. Paul introduces her as an apostle without comment or explanation, suggesting none was needed, as if everyone knew there were women apostles.[4]

Roman and Greek writers outside the Jesus movement also indicated that its women leaders were in the majority, or at a minimum, that they were more publicly visible than the men. For example, the first Roman to write about "Christians" was Pliny the Younger, the governor of Bithynia and Pontus. Around the year 113, Pliny questioned several Jesus followers—and when he wanted to know even more about their assemblies, he interrogated two women whom he called *ministrae*, or ministers,

This chapter is a follow-up to Ally Kateusz, "Collyridian Déjà vu: The Trajectory of Redaction of the Markers of Mary's Liturgical Leadership," *Journal of Feminist Studies in Religion* 29, no. 2 (Fall 2013): 75–92. First-Place Prize Elisabeth Schüssler Fiorenza New Scholar Award 2013.

suggesting that he believed these women were the leaders from whom he could learn the most.[5] Further indicating that women leaders were in the majority, later in the second century the Greek philosopher Celsus listed seven founders of various Christian groups—and *five* of the seven were women—Helen, Marcellina, Salome, Mariamne, and Martha. Only two were men: Simon and Marcion. The third-century Christian theologian Origen debated Celsus on a number of points, but he did not contradict Celsus' lopsidedly female list of Christian founders.[6]

Elizabeth A. Clark calls the absence of narratives about these important women "disturbing."[7] Where are the narratives, she asks, that depicted these holy women working miracles and performing "cures, exorcisms, and other wondrous feats" such as found in narratives about holy men?[8]

In fact, some long, full narratives depict holy women preaching, teaching, healing, exorcising, and baptizing (or sealing and washing) other people, just like narratives about male apostles depict them.[9] These authors called their female protagonists apostles. Yet there are, as Clark says, *suspicions* about these long narratives about women.[10] Why?

The reason for the suspicion about the long narratives about early Christian women, and the consequent dismissal of these narratives, is that for years, scholars have misapplied an old rule-of-thumb that was applied to NT texts—*lectio brevior potior*—that is, *the shortest reading is the preferred reading*—and applied it to all early Christian texts, including narratives about women. A short narrative, therefore, was thought to be older than a long narrative about the same person. As a result, most scholars, including Clark herself, and Hippolyte Delehaye in his influential work on the lives of early Christian holy men and women a century ago, have assumed that the shortest narratives about holy women were the oldest.[11] And therefore, they have ignored the longer narratives. In this chapter and the next, I will demonstrate that, *au contraire*, the longest, fullest, most detailed narratives about early Christian women leaders are usually the oldest.

By "narrative," I mean a text whose author described the woman leader *doing things* during her ministry—not just lauding her and saying how pure and holy she was, but describing what she said, what she did, who she did it to, and where and when she did it. Fashions in writing styles changed from time to time; some generations preferred short and simple hagiography, others preferred high-style, elaborated, versions, plus later theology was sometimes added to a text in order to sanitize it for reading in a later church. A Marian homily, for example, primarily told about Mary's many virtues as perceived by the later theologian, but a narrative depicted Mary in specific places, with specific people, and doing specific things, for example, entering the Temple, raising her arms and leading the prayer, exorcising demons, preaching the gospel. I restrict my analysis and conclusion—that the longest, fullest, most detailed narratives about early Christian women are the oldest—to *narratives* about these women.

In some cases, the long narratives about women leaders may have biographical content, with the clearest candidate the *Life of Nino*, a long narrative about a woman evangelist who various ancient authors credited with the conversion of ancient Iberia. Yet even the canonical gospels were written at least a generation after Jesus lived, and questions arise about which parts of them are or are not biographical. In my opinion, the most important reason to identify the oldest narratives about early Christian women leaders is not biography. It is because these narratives can be gleaned for kernels of historicity about the gender practices of various Jesus movements.

For example, as I will demonstrate in Chapter 3, each of the authors of four long narratives about a woman evangelist called their female protagonist an "apostle." These four narratives about women apostles are consistent with latent tradition, most expressly with the naming of a woman, Junia, as an "apostle" in Romans 16. Each of these four authors also described the woman apostle baptizing the people she converted—and described her doing this without any explanation, as if no explanation was needed in their community regarding women baptizers. This suggests that these narratives were composed in Jesus communities where women apostles and women baptizing were considered the norm. These narratives, thus, preserve an important historical kernel regarding the gender practices of some Jesus communities. Also of potential interest to the historian is the way that later scribes censored these long narratives.

In this chapter, I will use redaction analysis to demonstrate that later scribes often censored passages that portrayed a woman in a leadership role, which led to shorter and shorter recensions of the original narrative. First, however, it is important to know that some well-respected text critics have recently issued important exceptions to the old rule-of-thumb.

THE OLD RULE-OF-THUMB: *LECTIO BREVIOR POTIOR*

Until recently, most textual critics of early Christian texts used the old NT rule-of-thumb—*lectio brevior potior*—that is, the shortest reading is the preferred reading. This rule was applied to all Christian texts, with the result that longer recensions were assumed to be later than shorter recensions. In recent years, however, influential experts in text criticism have issued strong caveats about this rule-of-thumb. New research has reversed the old assumptions about this rule. The rule can no longer be considered a rule at all, not even for New Testament texts.

In 2018, for example, Jennifer Knust and Tommy Wasserman wrote, "Recent studies of the most ancient copies of the New Testament books have uncovered a striking fact: scribes omitted portions of the texts they were copying more often than they added to them. This finding is especially startling given the by now centuries-old text-critical criterion *lectio brevior potior* (prefer the shorter reading)."[12] In 2016, Larry Hurtado similarly wrote: "At least in the NT papyri from the second and third centuries, contrary to the assumptions of some previous scholars, omission is notably more frequent than addition (calling into question the sometimes rigid use of the 'prefer the shorter reading' canon in assessing textual variants)."[13] In 2012, Mark Goodacre abandoned the old rule-of-thumb when he argued that some short Jesus sayings in the *Gospel of Thomas* were shortened versions of older New Testament sayings. Goodacre argued that some of these short sayings have a "missing middle" and are a truncated version of the older, longer saying.[14] Even earlier, Eldon J. Epp and Gordon D. Fee warned that the old rule should be used "with great caution because scribes sometimes made omissions in the text either for smoothness or to remove what might be *objectionable*."[15] Bruce Metzger also gave several reasons a longer reading should be preferred over a shorter, including if a scribe may have considered what was omitted *"offensive to pious ears."*[16]

A variety of scholars of texts outside the canon also have issued warnings against using the old rule-of-thumb. Aaron Michael Butts recently wrote about his discovery that later copyists purged large sections of Ephrem the Syrian's early fourth-century writings because these writings did not conform to later theology. According to Butts, Ephrem's most complete writings survive only in the very oldest, and longest, manuscripts. The short versions that survived, Butts says, were "not a random

sample but, instead, a deliberate selection."[17] Richard Bauckham, in
his research into Jewish and Christian apocalypses, similarly pointed
out that "the textual tradition tended to abbreviation rather than
expansion."[18]

Scholars working on extracanonical narratives, including narratives
about a woman named Mary, have issued even stronger caveats about
using the old rule-of-thumb. François Bovon, who worked with multiple manuscripts of the *Acts of Philip*—which has a protagonist named
Mariamne who baptizes and is called an "apostle"—explained why the
opposite rule-of-thumb, that is, *longest is oldest*, is more appropriate for
these narratives:

> Contrary to the rule of thumb followed by most New Testament schol-
> ars, the shorter form of a recension is not necessarily the most ancient. It
> seems that apocryphal texts were sometimes perceived by their readers to
> be overly redundant or *even heretical* in places. Consequently these texts
> were often abbreviated.[19]

Bovon listed some of the ancient editors known to have abbreviated
these narratives, such as Gregory of Tours, Nicetas of Thessaloniki, and
Symeon Metaphrastes. He concluded, "The oldest Apocryphal Acts of
the Apostles were very long."[20] Richard Slater added, "The rules learned
for textual criticism of canonical writings may not be relied upon ... for
many apocryphal writings were abbreviated and excerpted for liturgical
and commemorative purposes and edited to reduce or eliminate material
offensive to orthodox editors."[21] Invoking Bovon and quoting Slater,
Shoemaker likewise argued that the longest recension of a narrative
about Mary the mother of Jesus is more likely to be the oldest.[22]

What types of behavior in women might later scribes have found
objectionable, or *offensive to pious ears*, or *even heretical*, and therefore
excised as Epp, Fee, Metzger, and Bovon suggest? The evidence in this
and the next chapter will demonstrate that later scribes excised depictions
of female leadership and authority that did not accord with the later
Christian gender model. Passages about women who did not follow later
Christian gender norms are unusual in the manuscript tradition—both
canonical and extracanonical—and in this chapter, I will demonstrate
that these passages are unusual because later scribes so frequently excised
them. Scribal excision is why later recensions are shorter.

REDACTION ANALYSIS OF MARY'S LITURGICAL LEADERSHIP

The path to viewing how later scribes censored texts about woman leaders is through redaction analysis. For this analysis, I employ Dormition manuscripts about the "falling asleep," or death, of Mary. The Dormition manuscript tradition is particularly useful in a redaction analysis because the text of the oldest largely complete Dormition manuscript is longer than the text of any other Dormition manuscript, and also because the Dormition manuscript tradition is rich in manuscripts. This richness permits us to view changes made to the popular Dormition text as it passed through the hands of later scribes, translators, and copyists.

The traditional view of Dormition narratives is that they were composed after the Council of Chalcedon (451), a position most scholars today have abandoned. Dormition narratives were popular around the Mediterranean, as evinced by their survival in nine ancient languages.[23] The text of some of these manuscripts preserves literary elements that suggest their original composition was relatively early in the Christian era.

In the last decade or so, Shoemaker has taken the lead in arguing that if Dormition texts were dated in the same way that other texts with "gnostic" elements (such as the Nag Hammadi texts) are dated, then the composition of the Dormition narratives could likewise be dated at least to the fourth century, if not earlier—to the third, or possibly the second century.[24] For example, Shoemaker argues that the "gnostic" or Jewish concept of angel Christology, which is preserved in a handful of manuscripts in the *Liber Requiei* or "Palm" Dormition text tradition, is reason for an early dating because later scribes replaced the Great Angel in the text with Jesus. This text tradition is called the "Palm" tradition because while the oldest recension says that the Great Angel gave Mary a book of mysteries and told her to give it to the apostles, many later scribes replaced Mary's book with a *palm branch*.[25] A variety of scholars have concluded an early dating from other archaic literary elements, with some suggesting that the Dormition narrative originated around Jerusalem, perhaps in an Ebionite Christian community or other community in close contact with rabbinic custom.[26]

The oldest largely complete Dormition manuscript is in Old Syriac, a dialect of Aramaic.[27] It is not in the "Palm" text tradition, but in the Six Books text tradition, so-called because its text says the apostles wrote six books about Mary's passing. Worth noting is that some scholars call the

Six Books tradition the Bethlehem tradition, because the text says Mary went from Jerusalem to Bethlehem, and some have called it the incense and censers tradition, because it contains so many instances of censing with incense.[28] Using a philological approach, some scholars conclude that the Six Books text may be even older than that of the "Palm" narrative with the Great Angel.[29] For example, one Six Books passage, which suggests both its antiquity and its composition around Jerusalem, describes a debate in Jerusalem between the "lovers of the messiah" and the "unbelievers," with both factions depicted as ethnic Jews, but neither faction identified as "Christian" or "Jew," epithets seemingly unknown to the author of this passage.[30] In addition, *both* factions call Jesus the "son of Mary," a designation known from Mark 6:3. This passage therefore would appear to have been composed prior to the gradual parting of the ways, quite possibly prior to when the Jesus followers—or the "lovers of the messiah" as this author called them—were first called Christian.[31] Further militating for an earlier rather than a later date of composition, Richard Bauckham notes that the apocalypse at the end of the Six Books preserves the early view that "the dead are conceived as in a state of waiting for the last judgment and the resurrection," and points out that "there seems to be no other apocalypse expressing this earlier view which can plausibly be dated later than the mid-second century."[32]

Finally, as we will see below, the Six Books narrative depicts Jesus's mother with considerable religious authority, including leading men in prayer as well as preaching, activities which Hans Förster and I have argued suggest a composition prior to the late second-century criticism of such female leadership, such as the middle of the second century. I further argue that the composition seems likely to have been based on first-century oral traditions about Mary.[33] Previous research demonstrates that later scribes in fact did not *add* scenes of Mary's leadership, they *excised* them.[34] The second-century dating of the Six Books text, thus, appears to be consistent with other texts that are without much controversy dated no later than the second century, such as the *Protevangelium* and the *Gospel of Mary*.[35] The precise time that the Six Books narrative about Mary's death was composed, however, is not critical for the following redaction analysis, because this analysis focuses on the manuscript tradition, and all of these manuscripts are of course later than the original composition.

Among the rich Six Books manuscript tradition exists a single largely complete Dormition manuscript. When analyzing the impact of later scribal censorship, its text can be profitably compared to that of later recensions. This very early Six Books text was preserved apparently only because a ninth-century scribe scrubbed it and wrote over it, making it the underscript of a palimpsest. Some Old Syriac Dormition fragments, including some Six Books palimpsest fragments, may be older than this palimpsest, which itself is missing some folios, but this palimpsest is around a century older than any other largely complete Dormition manuscript.

Agnes Smith Lewis acquired the palimpsest manuscript in Egypt and edited, translated, and published its underscript in 1902 as *Apocrypha Syriaca* in Studia Sinaitica 11.[36] Smith Lewis is best known for publishing the underscript of another palimpsest, the famous Old Syriac Gospels.[37] She dated the paleography of the Six Books underscript to the second half of the fifth century, no later than the early sixth century, and her fifth-century dating is generally affirmed.[38]

The text of this fifth-century palimpsest is very long—and it presents the mother of Jesus as if she were one of the women leaders about whom the North African apologist Tertullian (ca. 155–ca. 220) complained: "The very women of these heretics, how wanton they are! For they are bold enough to teach, to dispute, to enact exorcisms, to undertake cures—it may be even to baptize."[39] The palimpsest's narrative depicted Mary teaching, disputing, enacting exorcisms, undertaking cures—and maybe even baptizing. Andrew B. McGowan explains, "Baptism is often referred to in ancient texts as a 'seal.'"[40] According to the palimpsest text, Mary "took water, and *sealed* them, in the name of the Father, and of the Son, and of the Holy Spirit. And she sprinkled it upon their bodies."[41] Tertullian's complaint, thus, has remarkable resonance with the way Mary is described in the palimpsest text.

Close readings of the palimpsest text against the texts of two important later Six Books manuscripts illustrate the trajectory of later scribal censorship—especially with respect to Mary's markers of liturgical authority.[42] The first is a late sixth-century Six Books manuscript that William Wright edited and translated. It is the second-oldest Dormition manuscript so far published (other than the small fragments mentioned above) and it is almost complete.[43] Its text was approximately sixty percent as long as that of the fifth century.

The second manuscript is a medieval Ethiopic translation, dated around the fourteenth century, which was first edited and translated into Latin by Marius Chaine, and later into English by Shoemaker, who considers this Ethiopic text a faithful recension most likely translated in the sixth or seventh century.[44] Its text is approximately half as long as that of the palimpsest.

A Scene of Mary Exorcising Demons

Side-by-side parallels of the text of these three Six Books manuscripts demonstrate a pattern of later scribal excision consistent with *longest is oldest*. For example, this pattern is illustrated by a scene in the palimpsest text that depicted Mary exorcising two demons from a woman named Malchū. In both of the later manuscripts, the passage is shorter—but each later scribe appears to have excised different parts (see Fig. 2.1).

Each of the two later scribes excised different parts of the longer text, presumably each in accordance with what they or their masters deemed *objectionable*, or *offensive to pious ears*, or *even heretical*. For example, the scribe behind the sixth-century Syriac retained Malchū's name and most of her family lineage—but excised almost all the elements of Mary's exorcism. By contrast, the scribe behind the Ethiopic text preserved many elements of the exorcism—but excised Malchū's name and family lineage. This scribe in fact excised not just Malchū's name, but the names of all the women who traveled to Jerusalem to see Mary—Malchū, Flavia, Abigail, and Yuchabar.[45]

Redaction analysis both supplements and is supplemented by other research about Christian women leaders during this early era. For example, in excising all these women's names—women whom the author subsequently described as evangelists whom Mary sent out with books around the Mediterranean[46]—the scribe behind the Ethiopic text may have been following a Late Antique scribal practice of anonymizing important women—a practice that essentially removed them from the history of the Jesus movement. This anonymization of women became particularly noticeable in the fifth-century church histories. Anne Jensen has analyzed how the fourth-century church history written by Eusebius, the bishop of Caesaria, in 325, had over twice as many named women as found in Sozomen's fifth-century church history, and *six times* more named women than found in either of the fifth-century church histories written by Socrates and Theodoret.[47] Sometimes not only these women's names, but also what they did, were erased. For example, around the year 330—five years after Eusebius completed his church history—a woman evangelist converted all of the country of Iberia (modern Georgia).

5th c. palimpsest MS	6th c. Syriac MS	14th c. Ethiopic MS
Malchū came also to her,	Came to her Malchū	Came another woman,
the daughter of Sabinus, the Procurator	the daughter of Sabinus,	omitted
in whom were two demons;	who had two devils,	who was beset by many demons
one that tormented her by night; and the other that came upon her by day, and buffeted her;	one that tormented her by night and another that came upon her by day;	omitted
and she entreated the Lady Mary;	omitted	and she cried out to Mary with a great voice, saying, 'Have mercy on me, my master.'
and immediately when she had prayed over her, and had placed her hand upon her, and had spoken thus:	and she prayed over her,	She extended her hand and prayed, saying,
"I adjure thee, in the name of my Master Who is in heaven, at this time concerning this soul, that she may be healed."	omitted	'I adjure you, in the name of the Lord Jesus Christ, come out of this soul, and do not afflict her again.'
And straight away these demons came out of her, and they wailed, and cried out, saying,	and she was healed.	And at that moment, the demons went forth from that woman, crying out and saying,
"What is there between us and thee, O Mother of God?"	omitted	"What do you have against us Mary, the one who bore Christ?"
. . . Then the Lady Mary		. . . Then Mary
rebuked them in the name of our Lord Jesus the Christ.		omitted
And straightaway they departed towards the sea.		plunged them into the depths of the sea.

Fig. 2.1 Mary exorcized demons from Malchū

Both Sozomen and the early fifth-century church historian Rufinus, who added the later chapters to Eusebius's history, mentioned her extraordinary feat—but anonymized her, with Sozomen calling her "a Christian woman," and Rufinus, "a woman captive."[48] Socrates and Theodoret, the same historians who retained one-sixth as many women's names as Eusebius, ignored both her name *and* her missionary activities. This woman's name was Nino, which we know because she was considered so important in Iberia that a history about her survived in that area (a history we address in the next chapter).[49] Jensen points out that men's names generally remained intact in church histories. She asks, "What *male* missionary of an entire land has remained anonymous in church history?"[50]

WOMEN USING CENSERS AND INCENSE

Below are two more close readings of passages across these three manuscripts, passages that portrayed Mary and other women using censers and incense. Luke 1:8–11, Exodus 30, and Leviticus 16:12–14 closely associate the high priest with the ritual of offering incense in the Jerusalem Temple. Suggesting that Six Books author likewise associated Mary with the Temple priesthood, the Six Books describes Mary using incense to make an offering, and setting out the censer of incense to God.

The presence of censers and incense burning is in fact so dominant in the Six Books that sometimes it is called the censers and incense Dormition text tradition.[51] The phenomenon of later scribes excising depictions of female liturgical authority is again illustrated by three scenes that depicted Mary using a censer to make incense offerings.[52] Mary with a censer apparently became problematic, because both later scribes severely cut or redacted these passages, sometimes excising the same passages and sometimes different passages[53] (see Fig. 2.2).

This chart illustrates that even when scribes retained a passage from the longer version, they did not always *fully* retain it. Sometimes they shortened it, significantly changing it, especially if it depicted a woman performing a liturgical activity, such as throwing incense on a censer or setting out the censer of incense to God. An example of shortening is in the first passage shown in the chart. The palimpsest text describes Mary going to her son's tomb, carrying incense and fire, and throwing incense on the censer.[54] The medieval Ethiopic text omits Mary's actions as well

5th c. palimpsest MS	6th c. Syriac MS	14th c. Ethiopic MS
These virgins were with the Lady Mary night and day, that they might minister unto her, and bring to her the censer of sweet spices.	omitted	omitted
Mary told them everything; and they spread her couch and washed her feet, and folded her garments, and arranged sweet spices.	omitted	She told them everything that they wanted to be taught by her. . . And they washed her feet and made her clothes fragrant with incense.
omitted	omitted	The blessed Mary summoned the virgin women and said to them, "Bring incense and clothing so that I may make an offering to God."
And she opened a chest and they took out her garments and the censer, and put everything in order.	omitted	omitted
And on the Friday the Blessed one was distressed, and said to them: "Bring nigh unto me the censers of incense, for I wish to pray" . . . and these virgins brought nigh unto her the censers.	And on the Friday my Lady Mary was distressed, and said to them: "Bring nigh unto me the censer of incense, for I wish to pray" . . . and they brought nigh unto her the censer of incense.	And on Friday at dawn, Mary became ill, and she said to the virgins, "Bring me a censer, because I want to make an offering". . . and they brought her one, and she placed incense in the censer.

Fig. 2.2   Mary with censers and incense

as the censer, yet preserves the *scent* of Mary's incense burning.[55] The sixth-century text omits even the scent of incense.[56]

Another example of this shortening is in the last two passages in the chart. Here the palimpsest text depicts Mary with considerable liturgical authority—first praying while holding a censer in her hand and then preaching the gospel to the Governor of Jerusalem. According to the sermon that Mary preached, after the angel of the Annunciation departed, Mary herself "set forth the censer of incense to God"[57]—an activity that Exodus 30 and Leviticus 16:12–14 say was performed by the high priest in the Jerusalem Temple. Demonstrating that the palimpsest scribe did not create this long passage about Mary's liturgical authority, the same passage is also preserved in an important Six Books manuscript fragment dated around the year 1000.[58] By contrast, the sixth-century scribe preserved that Mary prayed with a censer in front of her, but excised her preaching to the governor and setting out the censer of incense to God.[59] The scribe behind the Ethiopic text, however, excised everything.[60] Another passage, which describes women bringing censers to Mary so that she can make an offering, is in Fig. 2.3.

This passage related to women and incense is of particular interest because not only does the palimpsest preserve a passage which is not in the Ethiopic manuscript, the Ethiopic preserves a passage which is not in the palimpsest. When read together, they suggest that an even older and longer Dormition narrative is behind both. Both describe the women preparing Mary's garments with incense. Only the Ethiopic text preserves Mary telling the women, "Bring incense and clothing *so that I may make an offering to God.*" And, only the palimpsest text preserves that then the women took Mary's special garments out of a chest, and put the censer and everything in order—presumably preparing for that Mary's offering to God.[61]

Further suggesting an even older source narrative, the Ethiopic text twice preserves that Mary used her censer to make an *offering*, while the palimpsest and sixth-century texts instead say that she used her censer merely to *pray*. Mary's prayer itself could be considered an offering, but the action of offering incense implies more liturgical authority than prayer, and Mary offering incense in these two Ethiopic passages is consistent with the liturgical authority suggested by the palimpsest passage where Mary describes herself setting out the censer of incense to God (bottom of Fig. 2.2). It appears, thus, that some scribes sometimes censored Mary's liturgical authority by replacing her more overt liturgical

5th c. palimpsest MS	6th c. Syriac MS	14th c. Ethiopic MS
On the Friday Mary prepared herself to go to the tomb of the Lord	My Lady Mary came forth from her house, and went to the tomb of the Messiah	On Friday Mary came to pray at the tomb of Golgotha,
and she was carrying sweet spices and fire.	omitted	omitted
And while she was praying and had lifted up her eyes and gazed at heaven, suddenly the doors of heaven were opened and a scent of myrrh went up,	omitted	and as she prayed, she raised her eyes to heaven with the fragrant perfume of fine incense.
which the Lady Mary had thrown on the	omitted	omitted
Now the Lady Mary was standing and praying, the censer of incense being placed in her hand.	Now my Lady Mary was standing and praying, and the censer of incense was set before her.	omitted
[The governor] said to her: "I desire to learn from thee, Lady" . . . Mary said: "Hearken and receive my words" [*and she preached the gospel*] "And after the salutation with which he announced this to me, the angel departed from me. And I arose, and set forth the censer of incense to God."	omitted	omitted

Fig. 2.3 Women with censers and incense

activity with the more passive action of praying. This scribal strategy is also witnessed by the way the sixth-century text says Mary *prayed* over Malchū, while the fifth-century palimpsest and Ethiopic texts preserve the detail that she exorcised demons from Malchū (Fig. 2.1). Sometimes scribes remembered and sometimes they forgot to make the changes, but the presence of passages that describe similar female liturgical authority across multiple manuscripts suggests that an older Dormition narrative, the source, depicted Mary with even more liturgical authority than preserved in any single surviving manuscript.

Today women do not use censers liturgically in either the Eastern Orthodox or Catholic churches, and it is often taken for granted that Christian women never used censers liturgically. Yet here we have descriptions of the mother of Jesus using a censer to make an offering of incense. Does any supporting evidence indicate that these passages preserve a kernel of historicity—that Christian women used censers liturgically during this era?

Kernels of Historicity: Women Using Censers Liturgically

Just as later scribes eliminated depictions of women with censers from the Dormition narrative, an extraordinary wall painting recently discovered beneath a layer of plaster in the Deir al-Surian monastery church southwest of Cairo shows that later artists did the same. This painting provides a good example of why art is called conservative—that is, art changes slowly, and therefore sometimes preserves much older traditions. This painting is one of the two very oldest examples of Dormition iconography, that is, the scene of Mary "falling asleep" on her deathbed with disciples around her.[62] The Deir al-Surian painter illustrated Mary on her deathbed surrounded by women swinging censers, almost as if for a funeral liturgy. Three women are at her head and three at her feet, with Mary herself the holy seventh, the chiastic center.[63] Three chains hold each censer, which are most clearly seen swung by each of the three women on the left and the first woman on the right. Three censers swing in the air just above Mary's body, two over her chest and one at her knees (see Fig. 2.4).

The wall painting itself was painted sometime between the early 700s and the year 914.[64] The only older example of Dormition iconography with people around Mary is on a deteriorated pottery token from

Fig. 2.4 Women with censers at Mary's deathbed. Wall painting. Dated between early 700s and 914. Deir al-Surian Monastery, Egypt. Courtesy © Karel Innemée

northern Israel dated sixth century. This pottery token affirms the antiquity of the painting's iconography with women around Mary, because
it also appears to have portrayed three women at Mary's head (the part
with Mary's feet is broken off).[65] The wall painting's dating makes it
older than any example of Dormition art that depicts *twelve male apostles* around Mary's deathbed—and almost all later examples depict men,
not women, around her bed.[66]

Around the year 800, Syrian monks began to arrive at the Deir
al-Surian monastery, hence its name. During the next two centuries, the
monks collected "an exceptionally rich" library of Syriac manuscripts.[67]
One of these may have been a very early Dormition manuscript, perhaps illustrated. In any case, this painting preserves several nearly lost
Dormition motifs: the Great Angel who came to Mary, women around
Mary on her deathbed, the men outside, and the women around Mary
censing with censers.

The early "gnostic" element of the Great Angel, as mentioned above,
is preserved in a few Dormition manuscripts in the Palm text tradition.
In the painting, the Great Angel with its brilliant red-tipped wings stands
in the center of the scene, in the same place where Jesus stands in later
Dormition art. This motif alone suggests that the painting preserves an
old scene.

The women around Mary, and the men outside, is also a very early
literary element of the Dormition narrative. By analyzing several
Dormition manuscripts, Shoemaker demonstrated that the oldest layer
of the Dormition text originally depicted women, not men, around
Mary's deathbed—just like in this painting. In the original narrative, only
women were with Mary because Jesus took the men outside, where the
men fell asleep—and this painting depicts twelve men seated in the background with their chins on their hands as if sleeping. In the original narrative, when Mary died, a woman went out and told Jesus his mother
had died, and then the men awoke. Later scribes, however, redacted the
women's important role and gave it to the men. According to these versions, men surrounded Mary's deathbed. The women were silent. Quite
humorously, a few manuscripts preserve that after the men announced
Mary's death to Jesus, the men woke up![68]

Like the later scribes who changed the original Dormition narrative and replaced the women around Mary's bed with men, artists also
replaced these women with men. A tenth- or eleventh-century ivory
carving is representative of this later Dormition iconography, and it

Fig. 2.5 Men with Mary on her deathbed. Peter swings a censer. Tenth/eleventh-century ivory plaque. The Walters Art Museum, Baltimore, accession no. 71.66. CC0

depicts twelve male apostles around Mary on her deathbed. The apostle Paul, identifiable because he is balding, kisses her feet. Jesus in the center holds a swaddled infant, representing her soul. One element suggests that the changes may have had something to do with a change in who had authority to swing a censer. Not only are the women gone, but Peter, the chief apostle, swings the censer (see Fig. 2.5).

Given the trajectory of redaction with respect to women and censers in both texts and art, it seems possible that the depiction of women swinging censers around Mary in the Deir al-Surian painting may have been part of the original Six Books composition. Women swinging censers, and Mary herself doing so, may have reflected an actual practice of women using censers liturgically in and around Jerusalem. In any case, the text of the fifth-century palimpsest not only described Mary using censers to make offerings, it also described Mary taking a censer of incense to her son's tomb, and that "a scent of myrrh went up, which the Lady Mary had thrown on the censer, and its odour went about all the regions of heaven."[69] Consistent with this tradition, the late ninth- or early tenth-century Typikon, a liturgical book for the Holy Week and Easter Week liturgies in Jerusalem, specified that women did the censing, including entering and censing the holy sepulcher, that is Christ's tomb, inside the Anastasis Church, which is also known as the Church of the Holy Sepulchre.[70] The rather late attestation of women performing this liturgy in the Typikon is affirmed by a variety of sixth- and early seventh-century artifacts from around Jerusalem, which depict two women, usually identified as the two Marys, carrying a censer and walking toward the shrine over Christ's tomb inside the Anastasis rotunda, as if about to enter the shrine and cense the tomb with incense.[71] This scene was especially common on small pewter ampoules for holy oil or holy water, usually dated sixth/seventh century, which pilgrims to Jerusalem carried to their homes around the Mediterranean.[72] For two examples, see Figs. 2.6 and 2.7.

This Six Books scene of Mary praying and offering a cloud of incense at her son's tomb also resonates with the first recorded use of incense in the liturgy, which also took place at Jesus's tomb. The pilgrim Egeria, who visited Jerusalem around 381, described in her diary the early Sunday morning liturgy inside the Anastasis, that is, the Church of the Holy Sepulchre. Egeria indicated that this liturgy was performed each Sunday, but also said that it was similar to the Easter liturgy. She wrote that deacons and presbyters prayed and then "take censers into the cave of the Anastasis, so that the whole Anastasis basilica is filled with the smell."[73]

Is it possible that women could have been among these clergy and that Egeria witnessed an early example of the censing liturgy later

Fig. 2.6 Two Marys
with censer at Anastasis
shrine. Jerusalem
ampoule ca. 600.
Garrucci, *Storia*, pl.
6:434.5

preserved in the Typikon? Women deacons were active in churches in
the East, and funerary epigraphs from around Jerusalem dated as early
as the mid-fourth century attest that women deacons were active in the
Jerusalem area specifically.[74] The female deacon at this time most likely
had a high rank, perhaps higher than the presbyter, because the third-
or fourth-century Syriac *Didascalia apostolorum* ranked deacons ahead of
presbyters. It explains that the male deacon is the type of Christ, while
the female deacon is the type of the Holy Spirit[75]—Holy Spirit was feminine gendered in Ancient Syria until the end of the fourth century[76]—
and, it said, mere presbyters are the type of apostles.[77]

Women, thus, potentially could have been among the censing clergy.
Egeria's diary, however, does not specify that any of these clergy were
women. There are three reasons why Egeria's diary might not reflect that
women were doing the censing. First, ecclesial titles were not necessarily gendered; Valerie A. Karras documents that in the East up through
the tenth century, both male and female deacons had the same masculine gendered title, *diakonos*.[78] The lack of gendered titles may have
been even more widespread earlier, such as in the late fourth century
when Egeria was in Jerusalem. Second, even if Egeria did specify that
some of the clergy were women, a later copyist may have redacted it.
Even modern editors have redacted the presence of women deacons; for
example, Hans Förster recently documented that a feminine title used in

Fig. 2.7 Two Marys
with censer at Anastasis
shrine. Jerusalem
ampoule ca. 600.
Garrucci, *Storia*, pl.
6:434.6

a White Monastery manuscript, which in 1958 was translated as people "who refrain from the use of women," actually reads in Coptic: "women serving as deacons."[79] Third, and most interesting, Egeria may not have specified that women were doing the censing in the Anastasis because everyone knew women did this censing. A round ivory pyx carved just a few decades after Egeria was in Jerusalem depicts two women carrying censers to an altar[80]—an altar that most likely represented the altar in the Anastasis rotunda or its basilica.[81] A gospel book sets on this altar, a lamp hangs above it, and curtains and the spiral columns of a ciborium (or canopy) over the altar flank it. Two women approach it with censers (see Fig. 2.8a, b).

"The Visit to the Tomb" is how this round pyx is titled in the Metropolitan Museum of Art, and its altar is usually identified as the altar inside the Anastasis rotunda shrine or its associated basilica.[82] The two women with censers of incense are the primary reason for this identification, since there are many examples of the two Marys with a censer *outside* the shrine over Christ's tomb at the Anastasis, such as seen in Figs. 2.6 and 2.7. These are thought to represent the gospel scene of the two Marys going to Jesus's empty tomb. Yet, they are part of what appears to be a liturgical procession to the altar, a procession led by two women with censers, followed by three women with their arms raised.

(a)

(b)

Fig. 2.8 **a** Two women with censers flank the Anastasis altar. **b** Women in procession to the altar. Ivory pyx, 500s. Metropolitan Museum of Art, New York
City, CC0

The ivory pyx is dated 500s. A church floor mosaic in Qasr el Lebya dated 539–540 depicts a woman with a censer.[83] This mosaic is older than what is most likely the oldest iconographic artifact to portray a Christian man with a censer, a mosaic in San Vitale in Ravenna dated around 550.[84] To my knowledge, the ivory pyx is the oldest iconographic artifact to portray anyone holding a censer at a church altar. It is also the oldest to portray people at a church altar in Palestine. In making these claims, I considered another fifth-century pyx that depicts two men (without censers) standing on either side of the Anastasis altar, but they were portrayed slightly turned away from the altar because they are part of adjacent gospel scenes.[85] For obvious reasons, I also exclude depictions of angels (also without censers) at the Anastasis altar. The pyx, thus, is the oldest artifact to depict people at an altar in Palestine, the oldest to depict people at an altar with a censer, and it most likely depicts the Anastasis, the most famous church in Palestine, as well as, arguably, the most famous in all of Christendom—and it depicts women there, not men.

There are various reasons to identify this liturgical scene as taking place at the Anastasis itself, including that the ivory pyx is round like the Anastasis rotunda that was built over the shrine above Christ's tomb. The pyx in fact evokes a variety of sixth- and seventh-century artifacts made around Jerusalem, including glass pilgrim vessels, mosaics, a painted reliquary box, and some ampoules, all of which represent the shrine *inside* the rotunda as polygonal, not square.[86] Some artifacts, for example, depict the front view of the shrine's roof with three triangular panels, like the roof over a hexagonal structure[87]—as seen in Figs. 2.6 and 2.7. The round pyx with its impression of columned arcades imitates this polygonal shape, an architectural shape that would aesthetically fit inside the rotunda. Some ampoules and other artifacts portrayed the shrine with spiral columns[88]—as seen on the ampoule in Fig. 2.6—and the pyx's sculptor likewise carved spiral columns.

Not only is this ivory pyx the sole artifact of this era to depict anyone inside the Anastasis processing toward its altar—it depicts only women in the procession.[89] In 431, women swinging censers led the celebratory procession after the Council of Ephesus.[90] Even earlier, in 312, Eusebius of Caesarea described a dedication ceremony for a church in Tyre that apparently involved incense and raised hands in its Holy of Holies[91]— and the ivory pyx depicts women with incense and raised hands, suggesting that the Tyre church, just a hundred miles from Jerusalem, may have had a similar liturgy at the altar during its consecration.

From the beginning in Christian communities, almost certainly women were associated with censers and incense because Tertullian (ca. 155–220) said more incense was used in Christian burials than in Roman temples[92]—and in Mediterranean culture women had the role of preparing and lamenting for the dead, including during the procession to the tomb. Thus the ritual censing that Tertullian described most likely was performed by women carrying censers, just as women with censers led the procession after the Council of Ephesus, just like women with censers led the procession to the altar at the Anastasis, as illustrated in the ivory pyx, and just like women with censers surrounded Mary on her deathbed in the Dormition source narrative, as illustrated in the Deir al-Surian painting.

After the Peace of the Church in the early fourth century, new churches were often built over the tomb of a holy person, such as the Anastasis, which was built over Jesus's tomb in Jerusalem, or Old Saint Peter's Basilica, which was built over Peter's tomb in Rome. Given the association of the body or relics of a saint with these new churches and their altars, the censing and other rituals that women performed appear to have continued quite naturally inside these beautiful new chapels and basilicas, as least as indicated by the depiction of women with censers at the altar on the ivory pyx. The composition of the Six Books narrative was second century at the latest, and we might reasonably conclude that it was based on first-century oral tradition. Its author's description of women using censers seems to have been consistent with what likely was the custom in some Christian communities, especially around Jerusalem where the Dormition narrative most likely was written.

Today these ancient artifacts—both written and iconographic—attest to an era when in some communities women used censers liturgically. Over the following centuries, however, the use of liturgical censers slowly became restricted to men. Quite possibly the reason some later scribes excised Six Books passages that depicted Mary and other women using censers was to create the historical illusion that only male clergy had ever used them. In any case, these passages appear to preserve a kernel of historicity about early Christian women's liturgical use of censers and incense.

Redaction Analysis of the Markers
of Women's Authority

A macro-analysis of twenty-one narrative elements across eight recensions of the Six Books provides additional evidence of later scribal redaction of the markers of Mary's liturgical leadership. This extended analysis further confirms that the fifth-century Six Books palimpsest has the most complete surviving Six Books text, albeit that it is still not the original composition, which was even more detailed and longer. The first three of the eight Six Books recensions that I analyzed are the same three manuscripts used in the close readings above: the fifth-century Syriac palimpsest, the sixth-century Syriac, and the medieval Ethiopic. The other five are described below.

Syriac "S-2" fragments: The fourth entry on the chart is comprised of two large Syriac manuscript fragments translated by William Wright, who published them together because of their archaic text, which, where it survives, is often very long. One fragment contains the beginning of the Six Books narrative and the other the end, although with many missing folios in the middle, as is shown in the chart.[93] The first of the two fragments is dated to around 1000, and the scribe of the second actually dated it 1197.[94] Despite that these fragments were penned relatively late, scholars of the Dormition narratives consider their surviving text archaic and therefore call them "S-2," signifying that their text is considered the second generation in the Six Books text.[95] As an example of its antiquity, the "S-2" text contains even more instances than the fifth-century palimpsest text of people calling Jesus the "son of Mary" in the debate between the "lovers of the Messiah" and the "unbelievers."[96] It also preserves the same long passage preserved in the palimpsest, but omitted in both the sixth-century text and Ethiopic text—Mary preaching to the governor about the Annunciation, including that she set out the censer of incense to God.[97]

Medieval Syriac MS: The fifth entry is a medieval Syriac Six Books manuscript that E. A. Wallis Budge edited and translated, which comprises the ending to a history of Mary's life.[98] Again, despite that it is from a much later manuscript, its text is relatively long and preserves old narratives elements. For example, it preserves a scene in the fifth-century palimpsest which was often expurgated or redacted—the scene of Mary giving women small books to take back to their homes around the Mediterranean.[99]

Medieval Arabic MS: The sixth entry is a medieval Arabic Six Books manuscript that was translated from the Syriac. It is titled "Transitus of John, the Evangelist," but after a short preamble, contains a rather long Six Books text.[100] For example, its text preserves the *fullest* passage about Mary giving books to women evangelists, even fuller than that of the palimpsest.[101]

Greek Homily: The seventh entry on the chart is a short Greek homily in the Six Books tradition. This short text is usually attributed to "John the Theologian," although occasionally it is attributed to the seventh-century patriarch John of Thessalonica.[102] It is translated from Constantin von Tischendorf's Greek edition of the text, which he compiled from five manuscripts, none older than the eleventh century.[103]

Georgian *Life of the Virgin*: The eighth and final entry is from a long narrative about Mary called the *Life of the Virgin*. This book told the history of Mary's life, from her birth, through her son's ministry, to her death. It was originally composed in Greek, but survives only in an old Georgian manuscript tradition, with its oldest manuscript Tbilisi A-40.[104] Both Michel van Esbroeck and Shoemaker argued that its ending about Mary's death was derived at least in part from the Six Books.[105] The analysis here demonstrates that the texts of the *Life of the Virgin* and the fifth-century Six Books palimpsest in fact have narrative elements in common—including elements not in the sixth-century Six Books, nor in the Greek homily.[106] These include Mary raising her hands to bless people other than just apostles,[107] Mary teaching women,[108] Mary sending out evangelists,[109] and Mary preaching.[110] We will return to the *Life of the Virgin* in Chapter 6.

Most of the twenty-one archaic narrative elements I analyze are markers of liturgical authority associated with Mary or other women.[111] The designation "omitted" can reflect either complete excision or severe redaction; for example, if the text said Mary offered incense at her son's tomb, whether with a censer or with fire, then I consider the narrative element "Mary offering incense" to be present—but if all that remains is Mary and the smell of incense, then I specify the element "omitted." A gap at the relevant place in the manuscript, especially notable in the fragment "S-2," is specified as a "lacuna." Finally, I treat the passage about the "lovers of the Messiah" and the "unbelievers" differently. If the manuscript preserves the passage where Jesus was called the "son of Mary"—a term also found in Mark 6:3, but which later scribes tended to replace with "son of God"—then I specify the *number of times* the term "son of Mary" appears. I also separately note if the scribe changed the term "unbelievers" to "Jews" (see Fig. 2.9).

Each of the narrative elements or motifs on the chart is found in at least two of the manuscripts. Notably, although the text of the fifth-century palimpsest contains nearly all the unusual literary elements found across later manuscripts, again we see that even the palimpsest text is not complete. It does not preserve one element preserved in the Ethiopic, Arabic, and Greek homily texts—Mary instructing the apostles to set out the censer of incense, as if she were their liturgical leader.[112] The Ethiopic text, as mentioned above, preserves the narrative element of Mary putting on special vestments to perform the offering, which the palimpsest text also does not have. Other passages, or fuller passages, were preserved in several of these manuscripts, but they are beyond the scope of the current study. The conclusion to be drawn is that the text of the fifth-century palimpsest is the most ancient, the longest, and the most complete surviving Dormition manuscript—but somewhere in its transmission history was a scribe who omitted certain narrative elements that almost certainly were in the original composition. We know this both because these narrative elements are preserved in other manuscripts, and also because they depict Mary with liturgical authority, and thus are consistent with the palimpsest text.

Based on the trajectory of scribal excision over time, which is illustrated by the Deir al-Surian wall painting, I hypothesize that the oldest version of the Dormition narrative most likely contained elements of both the Six Books and the Palm narratives.[113] The chart in Fig. 2.9 illustrates most clearly how later scribes redacted the Dormition narrative before them, each apparently in accordance with what they or their masters did—or did not—consider objectionable. Philologically that means that archaic narrative elements *can* be preserved in a short text—such as the Greek homily, which preserves Mary instructing the apostles to set out the incense—but, as Bovon pointed out, the longest text of a narrative can be expected to preserve the most.[114]

Perhaps the main reason the Dormition narrative, as well as other texts about women leaders who became known as saints, was sanitized instead of destroyed was that they were traditionally read in church on specific days that commemorated their female protagonist. The liturgical manual embedded in the Six Books, for example, instructed that the Six Books was to be read in the church on the three days of the year that commemorated Mary's passing.[115] By the same criteria, however, the

Narrative Elements	5th c. palimpsest	6th c. Syriac	14th c. Ethiopic	Syr. "S-2" fragments	Medieval Syriac	Medieval Arabic	Greek Homily	Geor. *Life of Virgin*
Mary offers incense at her son's tomb	Yes	omitted	omitted	Yes	Yes	omitted	Yes	omitted
Mary tells virgins to set out incense	Yes	Yes	Yes	omitted	omitted	Yes	Yes	Yes
Preserves names of virgins	Yes	Yes	omitted	Yes	Yes	omitted	omitted	omitted
Mary raises hands, blesses people	Yes	omitted	Yes	Yes	omitted	Yes	omitted	Yes
Mary raises hands, leads apostles in prayer	Yes	Yes	omitted	lacuna	omitted	Yes	Yes	Yes
Mary tells apostles to set censer	omitted	omitted	Yes	lacuna	omitted	Yes	Yes	omitted
After Mary prays, apostles prostrate	Yes	omitted	Yes	lacuna	omitted	Yes	omitted	omitted
Mary teaches women	Yes	omitted	Yes	lacuna	Yes	Yes	omitted	Yes
Mary gives books to women	Yes	omitted	omitted	lacuna	Yes	Yes	omitted	omitted
Mary sends out women evangelists	Yes	omitted	Yes	lacuna	Yes	Yes	omitted	Yes
Mary adjures and exorcises demons	Yes	omitted	Yes	lacuna	Yes	Yes	omitted	omitted
Mary heals people with her hands	Yes	omitted	Yes	lacuna	Yes	Yes	omitted	omitted
Mary seals women	Yes	omitted	omitted	lacuna	omitted	omitted	omitted	omitted
Mary sprinkles water on women	Yes	Yes	omitted	lacuna	omitted	omitted	omitted	omitted
Preserves names of women Mary heals	Yes	Yes	omitted	lacuna	Yes	omitted	omitted	omitted
Mary prays with censer of incense	Yes	Yes	omitted	Yes	omitted	omitted	omitted	omitted
Mary preaches gospel	Yes	omitted	omitted	Yes	omitted	omitted	omitted	Yes
Mary set out censer of incense to God	Yes	omitted	omitted	Yes	omitted	omitted	omitted	omitted
Jesus is called "son of Mary"	6	2	0	8	2	1	omitted	omitted
"Lovers of the Messiah" & "Unbelievers"	Yes	Yes	Yes	Yes	Yes	"Jews"	omitted	omitted
Liturgy for offering bread to Mary	lacuna	Yes	Yes	lacuna	omitted	omitted	omitted	omitted

Fig. 2.9 Trajectory of redaction across eight manuscripts

public reading of these texts probably made them even more susceptible to having passages excised, particularly if a bishop or patriarch considered the passages objectionable. This is why so many Dormition manuscripts are merely short homilies.

Some scribes apparently were under pressure to explain to their readers why their new shorter recension of the old Dormition narrative was so short. One scribe, who identified himself as the seventh-century bishop John of Thessalonica, explained his excisions as removing "heretical" stones in the path of the faithful so that they would not stumble.[116] Another, known as pseudo-Melito, justified his excisions by claiming that a "heretic" had added so many lies to the account of Mary's passing that "it is unlawful not only to read but even to hear it in the church of God."[117] These scribes, thus, blamed "heretics" for the very passages they wanted to excise. Their defensiveness suggests that they may have been under some pressure from their church audiences, people who did not like the fact that the narrative traditionally read in the church was now much shorter.

Yet, as Fig. 2.9 illustrates, a few copyists of old manuscripts continued to faithfully, or nearly faithfully, copy passages that described Mary with markers of liturgical leadership. Perhaps by the time the older narrative was copied, earlier concerns about a woman depicted with liturgical authority had disappeared, especially, perhaps, for monk copyists residing in all-male monasteries. Alternatively, certain communities, including some female monasteries, may have remained more open to the depiction of a woman with liturgical authority; in any case, occasional descriptions of actual women who had some level of such authority, whether as abbess or in some other role, continued into the turn of the millennium.[118]

One of the most interesting archaic narrative elements in the Six Books is a passage that describes Mary sending out women evangelists with books, a passage that again suggests an even older shared source behind both the Six Books and the Palm Dormition text traditions, because according to the Palm narrative, the Great Angel gave Mary a book of mysteries and told her to "give it to the apostles."[119] According to the palimpsest text, Mary gave these women writings, or small books, and sent them to their home cities around the Mediterranean: Rome, Alexandria, Athens, Beirut, and Thessalonica.[120] The fullest passage is in the medieval Arabic manuscript, which says Mary gave these women "powerful writings" to take with them to their countries "so that their people might believe and they might serve as testimony."[121] Women coming to Mary from around the Mediterranean to learn from her and Mary sending them out to serve as testimony are remarkably similar to several passages in the *Life of the Virgin*, which I argue in Chapters 6 and 7 was compiled from very early sources, and which, as can be seen in Fig. 2.9, shares other archaic narrative elements with the palimpsest text. The *Life of the Virgin* says that Mary sent out disciples, both male and female, to preach near and far, that she supervised their preaching, and that they always returned to Jerusalem to report what they had been doing and to receive her teachings.[122]

The Six Books appears to preserve a cultural memory that women had been apostles around the Mediterranean—a cultural memory consistent with latent tradition and the earliest evidence regarding the prominence of women in the Jesus movement, including in particular the woman apostle Junia, whom Paul said was in Christ before he was (Romans 16:7). The case studies in the next chapter reveal four ancient authors who preserved the same cultural memory—the memory of women apostles.

CHAPTER 3

Women Apostles:
Preachers and Baptizers

Relying upon the shorter recensions of texts about women in the early Jesus movements has distorted our modern imagination of the past with respect to the gendered role of women in those movements. In actuality, the longest surviving narratives about these women almost uniformly depict them with far greater religious leadership than do shorter recensions. As a result, an intertextual analysis of the longest narratives about women turns upside down our imagination of the past as a time when only men were apostles and church leaders.

The long biographies of four women whose biographers remembered them as active in the spread of the Jesus movements contain remarkable synchronicities. Each author called their female protagonist an "apostle." Each described her baptizing (or sealing and washing) other people. Each described her performing various other activities that today are associated with male apostles—preaching, healing, exorcising demons, and other wondrous feats, even raising the dead. These four women apostles were Mariamne, Irene, Nino, and Thecla.

This chapter uses three studies to focus on the long narratives about these four women. The first study follows Bovon's restoration of the narrative about the evangelist Mariamne from manuscript fragments of the *Acts of Philip*, a text compiled sometime between the second and fifth centuries.[1] The second study analyzes a long narrative about the first-century evangelist Irene of Macedonia, and also parallels it to a long history about Nino, the woman who reportedly converted all of ancient Iberia in the early part of the fourth century. The third study analyzes

© The Author(s) 2019
A. Kateusz, *Mary and Early Christian Women*,
https://doi.org/10.1007/978-3-030-11111-3_3

depictions of Thecla in two related narratives, the short Greek *Acts of Thecla*, which is usually dated second century, and the longer work, the Greek *Life of Thecla*, which is usually dated fifth century.

From different angles, each study illustrates what should perhaps be called the extracanonical rule-of-thumb for narratives about women leaders: *longest is oldest*, or, *longest is preferred*. This rule is especially true to form when it comes to narratives about women exercising religious leadership. When added to the apostle Junia and the description of Jesus's mother herself sending out women evangelists, these long narratives evince the conclusion that women apostles were rather ordinary during the early era of the Jesus movements.

ASSEMBLING A JIGSAW PUZZLE—THE APOSTLE MARIAMNE IN THE *ACTS OF PHILIP*

Unlike with the rich Six Books manuscript tradition, which includes the long text of the fifth-century palimpsest against which shorter manuscripts can be compared, the *Acts of Philip* survives only in much later manuscripts, mostly short. Even the longest manuscripts have large gaps in the text, either due to missing folios or scribal excision. The process of centuries of scribal redaction in the *Acts of Philip* manuscript tradition was so complex that, according to Bovon, even the longest manuscript, the fourteenth-century *Xenophontos* 32 from Mt. Athos, contains evidence of rewriting, passages omitted, sources added, and individual folios extracted by an unknown hand. Bovon observed that the acts that survived in *Xenophontos* 32 were "considerably larger and less expurgated"[2]—but some of the acts survived only in one of the shorter manuscripts, and Act 10, as well as portions of other acts, remain lost.[3]

Due to missing folios as well as scribal redaction of the text, Bovon and his associates compiled the narrative about the apostle Mariamne using the three most important manuscript fragments of the *Acts of Philip*. They fit sections together like pieces of a jigsaw puzzle. These three manuscript fragments are the fourteenth-century *Xenophontos* 32 in Mount Athos, the eleventh-century *Vaticanus graecus* 824 in Rome, and the fifteenth-century *Atheniensis* 346 in Athens.

Each of these three manuscripts preserves some of the same parts of the narrative about Mariamne's evangelical activity, but more importantly, each also preserves unique narrative elements describing her liturgical authority. If only one manuscript were studied, these individual unique elements might be dismissed as the fanciful additions of a later scribe. As Bovon has demonstrated, the texts of all three manuscripts together provide a complex portrait of Mariamne as an apostle.

Who was Mariamne? The *Acts of Philip* is one of several ancient texts that are not specific regarding which Mary is its protagonist, whether Mary of Bethany, the Magdalene, the mother, or some other Mariamne.[4] This lack of specificity is probably because the manuscript is fragmentary and the text was abbreviated over centuries. Most likely it originally included stronger clues regarding which Mary was meant. According to the surviving text, Mariamne was Philip's sister—but it is uncertain whether this means she was his blood sister or his spiritual sister. Mary Ann Beavis has pointed out that the text says Mariamne "prepared the bread and the salt, and the breaking of the bread," while Martha served the crowds—here Mariamne's association with Martha could signify that Mariamne was to be seen as Mary of Bethany.[5] Recent research, however, suggests that the presence of Martha cannot be considered decisive, because sometimes later scribes added Martha to scenes that originally had a solo Mary, usually to diffuse, or even undermine, Mary's authority.[6] By this analogy, if originally "Martha" was not present, then Mariamne both prepared the bread and also served the crowds. Bovon, who edited the *Acts of Philip*, concluded that Mariamne probably represented Mary Magdalene—but pointed out that the oldest manuscript of the *Protevangelium*, Papyrus Bodmer 5, similarly called Jesus's mother "Mariamne," spelling it the same way, and that "titles, metaphors, and functions applied to the mother [of Jesus] in patristic texts appear here as characteristic of Mariamne."[7] Given the fragmentary state of the medieval manuscripts of the *Acts of Philip*, it seems unlikely we will ever know with certainty which Mary the author intended to signify—Mary from Bethany, Magdala, Nazareth, or somewhere else. For the purpose of this argument, I agree with Ann Graham Brock that Mariamne most likely represented Mary Magdalene.[8] What is most important here, however, is that originally the *Acts of Philip* described Mariamne, like Philip, as an apostle who baptized people.

Vaticanus graecus 824 preserves the ending of Act 8 and part of Act 9, which is where the author repeatedly called Mariamne an "apostle."[9] *Atheniensis* 346 preserves the first half of Act 8, which explains how she became an apostle. Mariamne stood beside Jesus and "held the register of the regions" while Jesus assigned missions, and—because Philip was afraid—Jesus sent Mariamne to evangelize with Philip.[10] *Vaticanus graecus* 824 preserved an exorcism that paired Mariamne and Bartholomew, who was on the same mission, at the ritual: "Philip said to Bartholomew and Mariamne: 'Now rise, lift up your hands with the cup that we hold, and sprinkle in the air the sign of the cross.'"[11] The text of the same manuscript depicted Mariamne preaching to a woman named Nicanora, as well as Mariamne persuading people to enter a house where Philip and Bartholomew were preaching.[12] Bovon argued that since at each step of her missionary journey Mariamne was seen with the duties and privileges of an apostle, and also called an "apostle," most likely the original composition had depicted Mariamne with a preaching load as full as that of the male apostles.[13]

Even more explicit pairings of male and female clergy survived in *Xenophontos* 32, the manuscript which according to Bovon contained the longest and least expurgated text for the few acts which it preserves. For example, according to its Act 14, "Philip was baptizing the men and Mariamne the women."[14]

Act 1 of *Xenophontos* 32 again paired male and female clergy in a passage that depicted blasphemers being tortured in hell. The author wrote that the people being tortured had been condemned to hell because they had "blasphemed against male and female priests, eunuchs, deacons, deaconesses, and virgins with lies about debauchery and adultery."[15] Bovon translated πρεσβυτέρους and πρεσβύτιδας (*presbuterous* and *presbutidas*) here as male priests and female priests, concurring with Maximilien Bonnet that when an ancient author paralleled masculine and feminine church titles, then both titles must be treated in the same way, which was how Bonnet also treated them when he found the gender-parallel church titles of πρεσβύτερος and πρεσβῦτις (*presbuteros* and *presbutis*) paired in the *Martyrdom of Matthew*.[16]

Sexual Slander as Evidence of Women in the Clergy

The *Acts of Philip* demonstrates the way that sexual slander, which was used by both pagans and Christians, was leveled against Christian communities with female clergy.[17] The *Acts of Philip*'s author described people being tortured in hell because they had "blasphemed" male and female clergy—male and female priests, male and female deacons, eunuchs and virgins—"with lies about debauchery and adultery."[18] This passage, which portrayed these blasphemers undergoing awful tortures, was almost certainly the author's literary revenge against opponents who had slandered clergy in the author's own community.

This type of sexual slander often included a charge of deliberately "upsetting the lamp" during an evening service so that an orgy could take place in the dark. Justin Martyr of Rome is the first known to have used this particular sexual slander against other Jesus followers. He described it as "the upsetting of the lamp, and promiscuous intercourse."[19] This kind of "lies about debauchery and adultery" was probably what the *Acts of Philip*'s author was complaining about, and indeed, Justin appears to have had in mind communities which had both men and women clergy. In any case, Justin leveled this slander against the followers of two men, Simon and Marcion, both of whom were known to have evangelized with a woman. Without question Justin knew that Simon evangelized with a woman, because in the same passage that he reported that Simon and Helena evangelized together, he sexually slandered Helena, calling her a prostitute.[20] Although Justin did not mention the woman who worked with Marcion in Rome, he probably also knew about her, because Jerome (374–420), who lived in Rome, knew Marcion had worked with her.[21] Suggesting that Justin Martyr likely knew that women in their community performed priestly duties, including baptism, and that was why he sexually slandered them, only a few decades later, Tertullian, writing in Latin North Africa, apparently knew this.[22]

Sexual slander was arguably most damaging to women, because their reputations were more at stake in an accusation of inverting the gender roles of good wife and mother. Some writers even leveled the charge of blood libel—killing a baby to bake the Eucharistic bread—against Jesus communities known to have women leaders. For example, Augustine of Hippo (354–430) leveled blood libel against New Prophecy, the Jesus movement which Epiphanius recorded ordained woman bishops and priests, or presbyters,[23] and which Bovon suggested could have been the community of the *Acts of Philip*'s author.[24] In a passage where Augustine invoked the names of New Prophecy's three most famous prophetesses— Priscilla, Maximilla, and Quintilla—he complained, "They give such great positions of leadership to women that women even receive the honor of priesthood among them," and said, "They are reported to have gruesome sacraments, for they are said to confect their Eucharist from the blood of a year-old infant which they squeeze from tiny punctures all over its body; they mix it with wheat and make bread from it."[25] Justin Martyr may have been the first to reference this blood libel, for he said that the communities of Simon and Marcion performed "the upsetting of the lamp, and promiscuous intercourse, *and eating human flesh.*"[26]

One thus can understand the social dynamic behind the author of the *Acts of Philip* writing about people who had been condemned to hell because they "blasphemed against male and female priests, eunuchs, deacons, deaconesses, and virgins with lies about debauchery and adultery.[27] Bitter conflict appears to have arisen between communities that had male and female priests, deacons, and other clergy, and those which did not. People who did not have female clergy accused Christians who did of upsetting the lamp, having orgies, and making Eucharistic bread with baby blood—and these Christians in turn said that people who opposed women clergy were blasphemers.

It is uncertain in which century the *Acts of Philip* was composed; most scholars suggest the fourth, but Bovon suggested perhaps earlier, commensurate with his identification of its composition within the New Prophecy movement, which was closely associated with Philip and also very active in the second century.[28] Whenever it was composed, whether second century, third, or fourth, it preserves the favorable memory of a woman named Mariamne who was called an apostle, the commonplace of male and female clergy in the author's community, and also, the witness of a bitter conflict with another community over women clergy.

Irene, Apostle of Jesus

Bovon argued that apocryphal texts were often abbreviated, and he emphasized the importance of searching to find that rarity, a long edition of a saint's life.[29] I found a very long edition of a saint's life in an eighth-century collection of eleven narratives about early Christian women. Most of the narratives in the collection were short, but one was much longer than any of the others. It was about the apostle Irene.

In 778, a scribe named John the Stylite wrote eleven narratives about women leaders over a fourth-century manuscript of the Old Syriac Gospels, thereby creating a palimpsest. Agnes Smith Lewis discovered the famous Old Syriac Gospels in the lower script of the palimpsest, and edited, translated, and published them in what is now her most famous work. She later published the narratives about the eleven women that had been written over these gospels.[30]

The eleven translated narratives ranged in length from six to fifty-four pages. The nine shortest narratives contain few markers of female leadership other than the women's ability to bravely withstand pain when they were tortured. Their torture is so often focused on their female bodies—their breasts pinched, squeezed, or crushed between rocks—that today we might call it violent porn.

The second-longest narrative, about Eugenia, was twice as long as any of the nine shorter ones—and, as might be expected by now, it contained more markers of female religious authority than all of the shorter nine narratives combined. Today both the Roman and the Eastern churches recognize Eugenia as a second-century saint, and according to her narrative, Eugenia read her "book of Thecla," disguised herself as a eunuch, became the abbot of an all-male monastery where she taught the monks, healed with her hands, exorcized demons, and finally, became the leader and teacher of a group of women.[31]

By far, the longest narrative in the collection was about Irene.[32] The narrative about Irene is fifty percent longer than the narrative about Eugenia and comprises over a quarter of the total words in the collection. Moreover, and consistent with the research above, this long narrative preserves many more markers of female religious authority than all the other ten narratives put together.

THE LONG NARRATIVE ABOUT IRENE'S LIFE

Irene is known in the Eastern Church as Saint Irene of Macedonia, who according to Eastern tradition was baptized in the first century by Timothy, after which, she became an evangelist. The long biography about Irene can be compared to a much shorter biography about her—one-tenth as long—that Stephen Janos translated from the *Life of Saint Irene* in the Moscow Patriarchate texts. This short recension preserves that Irene converted 10,000 pagans by traveling to various cities, "preaching about Christ and working miracles, healing the sick."[33] This short recension, while clearly describing Irene as an important evangelist, nonetheless omits a great deal that is in the long narrative. As I detail below, the long narrative additionally calls Irene an "apostle," describes her baptizing people, raising her arms and leading the prayer, exorcizing, sealing, and raising the dead—many of the activities that Mary performed according to the palimpsest text—and also, activities that authors of narratives about male apostles described them performing.[34]

In the long narrative about Irene, the author first described her upbringing. According to this writer, Irene's father was the king of the city of Magedo and made sure she learned to read.[35] Women's literacy does not seem to have been as objectionable to later scribes as some other markers of women's autonomy, because several of the women in the shorter narratives—Eugenia, Marinus, Euphrosyne, and Onesima— were also described as literate.[36]

According to the narrative, just before Irene was to be married, Timothy came with a letter from Paul. He taught Irene and then baptized her with oil and water.[37] Afterward, in a long defiant sermon to her father and other high ranking men, Irene proclaimed herself a bride of Christ.[38] She broke idols and exorcized a demon from her city.[39] When her father was killed, she turned to the East, lifted her hands high, prayed, and—like the male apostles who raised the dead in their acts— she raised her father to life.[40] Afterward, the text says, Irene "remained in the city doing miracles and signs and cures. And she taught the word of truth and instructed many, and baptized them."[41]

MALE RE-BAPTIZERS AND THE APOSTLE NINO

Although the text states that Irene baptized the people in her city, a subsequent passage describes the "holy priest" Timothy coming back and Irene begging *him* to baptize the people in her city—the very people, including her family, whom she had already baptized![42] This pair of seemingly contradictory passages—both Irene and Timothy baptizing the same people in the same city—is similar to contradictory passages found in a manuscript about the life of Nino, the woman who evangelized Iberia (Georgia) in the early fourth century.[43]

Despite the anonymizing tactics of later church historians, Nino was an important saint in Georgia and a manuscript with a long narrative about her mission was preserved in Georgia—*The Conversion of K'art'li*, which includes a long section entitled *The Life of St. Nino*.[44] In this narrative, Nino describes her own ordination by the patriarch of Jerusalem:

My holy father patriarch, my mother's brother, called me and placed me on the steps of the altar and laid his hands on my shoulders. He signed towards the heavens and said, "O Lord, God of fathers and ages, into Your hands I place my sister's orphan child, and I send her to preach Your divinity, so that she may spread the good tidings of Your resurrection" … and he parted me from my mother and gave me a cross and blessing.[45]

Consistent with her ordination by the Patriarch of Jerusalem, the author called Nino "the Apostle and joy of the Son of God."[46]

According to the narrative, Nino baptized forty women in a monastery on her way to Iberia, then preached and baptized with her own hands several tribes in Iberia, as well as their queen.[47] Yet, as with the inconsistent passage about Timothy in the narrative about Irene, which depicted the same people Irene had already baptized re-baptized by Timothy, a later copyist sometimes added a male cleric to Nino's narrative, too. Typically this cleric was a priest, who arrived and baptized the people Nino converted; in those passages instead of the text reading that Nino baptized them with her own hands, the text instead reads, for example, "She baptized the sons of the nobles *through the hands* of Jacob the priest."[48]

According to the much shorter Armenian translation of the history about Nino, Nino did not baptize any of her converts. In this short recension, male clerics baptized all the people Nino converted.[49] Not all scribes, however, were as thorough as the Armenian scribe, for in both the long Georgian narrative about Nino, and the long narrative about Irene, the scribes were inconsistent, as if sometimes they remembered to change the baptizer from a woman to a man, but most of the time, they forgot.

IRENE BAPTIZES AND SEALS

The narrative about Irene contains three more places that describe her baptizing people, for a total of four scenes of her baptizing. The second is another scene of Irene baptizing in her home city of Magedo—where first Irene and later Timothy baptized. After Irene's father finally died, a new unbelieving king came and ruled, after which Irene returned and apparently re-baptized the people whom Timothy had re-baptized. According to the text, she returned to Magedo and, "The blessed lamb of Christ went into the city, and taught many, and baptized them."[50] The third scene of Irene baptizing says: "She was in the city of Callinicus for thirty days doing signs and wonders; and she cured many in the name of Jesus. She made the deaf hear; she opened [the eyes of] the blind; she cleansed the lepers; and she healed all who were in pain; and she baptized many."[51] In yet another city, Tela, a later scribe appears to have redacted that Irene baptized, because the text says that Irene "won many to Jesus"—but then *a priest came and baptized the people that Irene converted*.[52] In the fourth scene that preserves Irene baptizing, she arrived in Nisibis, and "spent a long time in that city, teaching the word of God and making many disciples. And great was the praise of God because of her. And the number of all those who believed in God and were baptized by her hand were a hundred and thirty thousand souls."[53]

This author also described "sealing" in several passages fortunately preserved. For example, Irene, like Paul, had a vision of Christ who "set His seal upon her."[54] Irene herself "sealed" a dying woman—who then died and was taken to heaven.[55] Irene also "sealed" a child to exorcize demons from him, and after the demons left, sealed him again and he was healed.[56] Finally, she twice sealed herself when she thought she was about to die.[57] In one of these passages, "She made the sign of Jesus between her eyes, and on her breasts, and threw herself downwards into the midst of the pit."[58] This language of sealing is likely an archaic reference to the seal of baptism, or perhaps the redemption by oil that Irenaeus of Lyon knew, or the bishop's signing the forehead of the newly baptized after the bishop's hand laying ceremony, or some other chrism or chrismation or anointing by oil, several of which to readers of that time likely would have signified that Irene was a bishop, since these were actions performed by or controlled by bishops.[59] The text itself presents Irene as the overseer of these new Jesus communities.

The narrative concludes with Irene dying in the city of Ephesus, where "she did many cures and miracles in the name of Jesus; and she made disciples of many, for the citizens held her as one of the Apostles of Jesus."[60] Thus, when one follows Bovon's recommendation and searches for the longest edition of a female saint's life, one may discover a long narrative about a woman apostle. One may read about a woman like Irene, a woman called an "Apostle of Jesus"—a woman evangelist, who likes male evangelists, traveled, preached, healed, sealed, exorcized, raised the dead, taught, converted, and baptized many people.

THE "APOSTLE" THECLA BAPTIZES AND SEALS

Thecla, one of the best-known early Christian women, was revered in both the Eastern and Western Mediterranean as a first-century evangelist who had learned from the apostle Paul and then evangelized on her own in Asia Minor. The best-known narrative about Thecla is the short Greek often called the *Acts of Thecla* (hereafter the *Acts*).[61] Fifty manuscripts of the Acts have survived from just the fourth to sixth centuries, with a variety of titles.[62] The Greek *Life of Thecla* (hereafter the *Life*) was far less popular. Although it essentially mirrors the narrative structure of the *Acts*, it is approximately four times longer.[63] In comparison with the shorter Acts, which evidences hundreds of manuscripts, only twelve manuscripts, or important fragments, of the *Life* have survived, none older than the tenth century.[64]

Narratives about Thecla reveal the same pattern seen in other narratives about women leaders—the longest narrative preserves the most markers of female liturgical authority.[65] For example, the *Acts* does not once call Thecla an "apostle." The *Life*, by contrast, five times titles Thecla an "apostle."[66] Similarly, the shorter *Acts* describes Thecla baptizing only herself. It never describes her baptizing other people. Just as the longest narratives about Mariamne, Irene, and Nino depict these women baptizing the people they converted, the *Life* not only depicts Thecla baptizing herself—it three times describes Thecla baptizing other people.

The first time the *Life* describes Thecla baptizing other people is inside Thecla's adoptive mother Tryphaena's home, which the text explains was "more a church than a home"—Thecla "began to catechize and win by the word of faith Tryphaena herself along with a good number of men and girls attached to her service, and *by the seal* she enrolled them for Christ."[67] Andrew B. McGow an explains, "Baptism is often referred to in ancient texts as a 'seal.'"[68] Commentators thus agree that the passage in the *Life* which describes Thecla sealing people in Tryphaena's house means that Thecla baptized them, both men and women.[69]

The text of the *Life* also preserves some other rather archaic language to signify Thecla's baptizing people. For example, Tertullian said the imposition of hands was necessary for baptism—and the *Life*'s author signified Thecla baptizing by Paul saying that Christ put people *into her hands*.[70] Here again, according to the shorter *Acts*, when Thecla met up with Paul in Myra, Paul simply told Thecla: "Go, and teach the word of God."[71] According to the longer *Life*, Paul additionally instructed Thecla that Christ chose her for an *apostolate*. These terms almost certainly signify that Thecla was supposed to baptize the people in these cities.

> Go teach the word, complete the evangelic race, and share with me the zeal for Christ. It is for this reason that through me Christ chose you, to take you up to the apostolate and to *put into your hands* some of the cities that have not yet been catechized.[72]

This comprises the second time that the *Life* depicts Thecla with the right to baptize people. Paul telling Thecla that she was in the "apostolate," and that Christ "put into your hands" cities not yet cat-echized, signified that Thecla would go fourth, catechize, and baptize them.

The third time the *Life* describes Thecla baptizing is in the conclusion. Here, the language is explicit. Just before Thecla died, the author summarized her life: "She had catechized, baptized, and enlisted many people into Christ's army."[73] The conclusion of the shorter *Acts*, merely, says that Thecla died after "enlightening many with the word of God."[74]

The *Life* originally may have contained even more passages that described Thecla baptizing. Alice-Mary Talbot and Scott Fitzgerald Johnson have published an additional fragment of the Thecla narrative, and according to this passage, Thecla told a woman, "If you want your daughter to be healed, receive the seal of Christ. ... After they renounced the devil and submitted themselves to our Lord Jesus Christ, Thekla gave them instruction, teaching them the Gospel of God and, anointing them with the oil of gladness, she baptized them."[75]

DATING CONTROVERSY: WHEN WAS THE *LIFE OF THECLA* COMPOSED?

The composition of the *Acts* is dated prior to the end of the second century because Tertullian complained about a narrative about Thecla.[76] The *Life* is dated later in part because it is longer and therefore is assumed to be later. Yet there are two other reasons it is dated later. Here, I contend that neither these reasons are a valid reason to date it later either.

The first reason the *Life* is assumed to be fifth century is because in three manuscripts of the Life are followed by a second text called the *Miracles of Thecla*, which includes some fifth-century personages. Yet the *Life* itself does not reference any personages after the first century. Gilbert Dagron and Johnson, both of whom have translated the *Life*, agree that the *Life* was written before the *Miracles*.[77]

The second reason the *Life* is assumed to have been composed later than the *Acts* is because some of Thecla and Paul's speeches, which are longer in the *Life* than in the *Acts*, contain fourth-century Trinitarian formulae.[78] During the centuries of the contentious Trinitarian doctrinal debates and councils, scribes sometimes inserted creedal formulae into texts, including even the New Testament. For example, a Latin translator of the letter 1 John inserted the Trinitarian formula into 1 John 5:6–7—which is where it remains in my family's King James Bible, despite that mainstream Bible commentators agree that the Greek manuscript tradition for 1 John makes it clear that the Trinitarian formula was not original.[79] Similarly, the sole place that the phrase "Father, Son and Holy Spirit" appears in our modern Bible editions is at Matthew 28:19, yet, according to Jane Schaberg, even this use may have been a dogmatic insertion made after Nicaea. No pre-Nicaean manuscript of Matthew with that verse has survived, but other evidence indicates that before the Trinitarian debates, Matthew 28:19 read like the similar verse Mark 15:16, that is, it did not contain the Trinitarian formula. For example, prior to the Council of Nicaea, Eusebius of Caesaria sixteen times quoted Matthew 28:19 as Jesus commanding the disciples to baptize "in my name." Only in writings *after* the Council of Nicaea did Eusebius begin to use the Trinitarian formula for Matthew 28:19[80]—"in the name of the Father and of the Son and of the Holy Spirit" (RSV). If scribes could insert a Trinitarian formula into a NT text, why would it be a stretch to believe that they would do the same thing to a popular narrative about Thecla, thereby using her story to carry the new theology to the masses? In any case, these Trinitarian formulae do not account for the *Life's* long length. At almost every point in the narrative, the *Life* is considerably more detailed than the *Acts*.

More significant in my opinion, is the fact that the *Life's* scribe actually *warned the reader* in the preface that extra public speeches had been inserted![81] While warning the reader, this scribe claimed that the text itself was: "received from another history, the oldest, which was followed step by step in the composition. We know only this: we have not undertaken this work in the hope of adding something to what has been said in the past, to write better, or to be more exact."[82] In short, the *Life's* scribe both warned the reader about the insertion of the new language, and also assured the reader that, despite these additions, the narrative itself was taken from the oldest history of Thecla.

Peter Turner suggests with respect to ancient authors: "If authors were sincere in their guarantees of truthfulness then this clearly constitutes a reason at least to give the contents of their works a serious hearing."[83] In warning the reader about these theological insertions instead of trying to pass them off as original to the text, the *Life's* scribe appears to be sincere. For this reason, when the scribe claimed that the narrative about Thecla was "received from another history, the oldest," we should give that claim a serious hearing.

THE THECLA TERTULLIAN KNEW

The most important reason to conclude that the long *Life of Thecla* is much older than the fifth century is that the *Life* is the sole writing about Thecla that comports with Tertullian's complaint about the writings about Thecla. The shorter *Acts* does not. Tertullian, therefore, must have been complaining about a composition like the *Life*, not the *Acts*.

Tertullian's complaint, in his treatise *On Baptism* 17, was that women were using Thecla's example as a license to justify their own teaching and baptizing:

> But the woman of pertness, who has usurped the power to teach, will of course not give birth for herself likewise to a right of baptizing, unless some new beast shall arise like the former; so that, just as the one abolished baptism, so some other should in her own right confer it! But if the writings which wrongly go under Paul's name, claim Thecla's example as a license for women's teaching and baptizing [*exemplum Theclae ad licentiam mulierum docendi tinguendique defendant*], let them know that, in Asia, the presbyter who composed that writing, as if he were augmenting Paul's fame from his own store, after being convicted, and confessing that he had done it from love of Paul, was removed from his office.[84]

Tertullian claimed that Thecla's example in this text provided a license for women's teaching and baptism. The short *Acts* depicts Thecla baptizing only herself—*and no one else*. How could other women have used Thecla's example in the *Acts* as a license to baptize other people? The obvious answer is that they could not.

Various scholars have noted the inconsistency between the text of the *Acts*, which only depicts Thecla baptizing herself, and Tertullian's complaint, which assumes she was baptizing other people. Stevan L. Davies states the problem:

> The Acts lack the very point about which Tertullian and his opponents argue. Paul does give Thecla the right to teach, but this is not Tertullian's main concern in *De baptismo*. Indeed the very fact that Thecla in the Acts is clearly given the right to teach by Paul and does go forth teaching

provides a strong contrast to the fact that she is not given the right to baptize and does not go forth baptizing. No one could claim on the basis of the [Acts of Thecla] Thecla's example as a license for both teaching and baptizing. *It is incredible that Tertullian and his opponents would engage in argument over a text which does not mention the point in disagreement.*[85]

Thecla baptizing only herself and no one else in the *Acts* has led other scholars to conclude that Tertullian was not talking about the *Acts*. Davies, for example, proposes that a different text, not the *Acts*, was probably behind Tertullian's complaints.[86] Anthony Hilhorst alternatively argued that the *Acts* "may well have undergone an abridgement."[87] The longer *Life* satisfies both of their hypotheses. The *Life* is a different text than the *Acts*. The *Acts* is an abridgement of the *Life* or of their shared source.

If the *Acts* is an abridgement, as Hilhorst proposes, that would explain what Johnson calls "syntactical difficulties" in the *Acts*, which he notes that the text of the *Life* "erases."[88] These syntactical difficulties in the short *Acts* suggest that some scribes indiscriminately butchered the long literary *Life*. Evincing the way that later scribes of the Dormition narrative independently made massive cuts to the text, even the texts of the two most important manuscripts of the *Acts*—one a fourth-century Greek and the other a late fifth- or sixth-century Coptic—barely overlap. These two manuscripts' texts are, according to Hal Taussig, "stunningly different in their content."[89] The short *Acts* appear most comparable to the Dormition homilies—short versions of a much longer narrative, which various scribes sanitized in accordance with what they or their master thought was suitable for reading in churches on a special day, which in this case would have been the special day commemorating Saint Thecla.

The most important factor in dating the composition behind the *Life of Thecla* is its portrayal of Thecla baptizing other people. Thecla baptizing other people is consistent with Tertullian's second-century complaint about women using Thecla's example as a license to baptize other people. The witness of Tertullian itself leads to the conclusion that Tertullian must have been complaining about a second-century narrative like the *Life*, not the *Acts*, which only describes Thecla baptizing herself. The witness of Tertullian also explains why scribes so widely distributed their short *Acts*. Women could not use Thecla's example in this shortened narrative as a license to baptize other people.

CULTURAL CONTEXT

These five long narratives about women—the mother of Jesus and four women called apostles—Mariamne, Irene, Nino, and Thecla—were all composed in the Eastern Mediterranean where Christianity initially was the strongest. Given the matter-of-fact way that the authors of these narratives presented their protagonists' activities, as well as the way several were translated into other languages, these narratives must have reflected the gender norms in a significant number of Jesus communities.

Later decrees such as the so-called Gelasian Decree[90]—which anathematized the Dormition narrative, the *Acts of Philip*, and the *Acts of Thecla*—condemned these texts. Perhaps such condemnations were one of the motivating forces behind some editors who excised the long narratives. In other cases, such as the Dormition narratives attributed to John of Thessalonica and pseudo-Melito, the scribes appear to have been trying to sanitize the text in order to permit it to continue to be read in their church on days that commemorated Mary. Thecla, Nino, and Irene each became identified as saints, which may be why later scribes shortened their narratives—to make them suitable for reading in their church. Based on what scribes excised, one reason for this shortening was to bring the older, longer text into conformity with later gender norms—or *desired* norms.

When we follow the *wrong* rule of thumb for interpreting texts about women leaders, we become inundated with numerous sanitized short manuscripts. These later editions then become used as "evidence" to undergird a false imagination of the early Christian era as a time when only men were fully active.

One advantage of looking across multiple long narratives about women leaders in the Jesus movements is the ability to recognize correspondences between texts. This intertextuality strengthens the argument that none of these authors was unique, for example, in calling a woman an "apostle," because, as we have seen, all four called their women protagonists an "apostle." This intertextuality likewise strengthens the argument that women who washed, sealed, or baptized other people were common when these texts were written.

Each of the four long narratives about these women apostles describes them "sealing," "washing," or "baptizing" other people. In addition, the palimpsest text says Mary "took water, and sealed them, in the name of the Father, and of the Son, and of the Holy Spirit. And she sprinkled (it) upon their bodies; and straightaway they were healed."[91] Given that the seal "was at first simply a way of talking about baptism itself," Mary sealing women with water suggests that she, too, was described performing a type of baptismal ritual.[92] All five authors therefore depicted their female protagonist baptizing. We would not realize how common this depiction was if we did not examine multiple narratives.

Tertullian not only complained about Thecla giving women a license to baptize. He complained about women preaching, exorcizing, healing, and sacrificing.[93] Each of the five authors described a woman performing many of these leadership activities. Quite possibly the original compositions described these women performing all the activities about which Tertullian complained. Let's continue our search for this nearly lost evidence.

CHAPTER 4

Mary, High Priest and Bishop

The descriptions of the women apostles in the last chapter help illuminate a second-century conflict over gender roles that is evinced in the New Testament letter 1 Timothy. Mainstream scholars agree that 1 Timothy was falsely attributed to Paul—that is, the real Paul did not write it. It was written by someone whom I call *faux-Paul*. Whoever the author of 1 Timothy was, he first specified that men should pray with their arms raised: "Men should pray, lifting up holy hands" (2:8 RSV). He then specified that a woman should "learn in silence with all submissiveness. I permit no women to teach or have authority over men. She is to stay silent" (2:11–12 RSV).

Almost certainly when writing these new rules, *faux-Paul* had in mind women leaders in some communities of Jesus followers, women like the women apostles of the last chapter. According to the authors who wrote the long narratives about Thecla, Irene, Mariamne, Nino, and Mary, these women lifted their holy hands to pray. They were not silent. They spoke, including when they prayed in front of crowds, when they cast out demons, and when they baptized people. They taught men as well as women. They were not submissive. Sometimes they had authority over men.

The author of 1 Timothy also may have wanted to contradict the reputation of the historical Timothy as a disciple of Paul who appointed women leaders who did all the things that 1 Timothy said they could not do. According to 1 Timothy, Paul himself wrote to Timothy and gave him those gendered rules. According to the narrative about Irene,

© The Author(s) 2019
A. Kateusz, *Mary and Early Christian Women*,
https://doi.org/10.1007/978-3-030-11111-3_4

however, Paul sent Timothy to teach and baptize Irene! Irene, of course, did not follow the gendered rules in 1 Timothy. She did not accept male authority over her. She was not silent. She preached and taught people, including men. For example, one passage describes her leading a crowd in prayer: "She turned to the whole crowd and said, 'My fellow believers, offer a prayer to God with me.' And she stretched out her hands and looked towards heaven, and prayed [out loud]."[1] Three more passages specify that Irene raised her hands to pray, including one that says she raised her arms to pray in front of the king and his army, ultimately teaching them.[2] The author of the narrative about Irene and the scribe today known as *faux-Paul* not only had opposing views on gender roles for women—they also had opposing views on whether the historical Timothy and Paul had sanctioned women leaders.

JESUS'S MOTHER VERSUS 1 TIMOTHY

The authors of the Six Book narrative and 1 Timothy also had opposing views on gender roles for women. According to the Six Books author, Mary acted in direct conflict with the type of gendered rules specified in 1 Timothy. Perhaps most telling is a scene that takes place when Mary is about to die. The twelve male apostles—the original eleven *plus the apostle Paul*—return from their missions around the Mediterranean to see her one last time in Jerusalem. When they arrive, they gather around her. Mary lifts her holy hands and leads the prayer:

> And when my Lady Mary heard these things from the Apostles she stretched out her hands to heaven and prayed, saying, "I worship and praise and sing and laud that I am not a mockery to the nations of the Gentiles ... and I will praise His gracious name for ever and ever. And I cannot glorify His grace sufficiently; that He hath sent His holy disciples to me." And after Mary had prayed, the Apostles set forth the censer of incense, and knelt with their faces down and prayed.[3]

The entire passage is in opposition to the rules in 1 Timothy—Mary raises her arms to pray, speaks the prayer, and has authority over men. The final line states that after Mary raised her arms and praised God, the men prostrated themselves. This describes Mary much as Sirach

50:19–21 describes the Temple high priest: raising hands, praising God, and then the people prostrating themselves.

According to Leviticus 9:22, Deuteronomy 10:8 and 23:20, 1 Chronicles, and Sirach 50:20–21, high priests raised their hands and *blessed* people. In Luke 24:50, Jesus lifts his hands and blesses a crowd. The Six Books narrative also preserves scenes where Mary lifts her hands and blesses people. For example, the fifth-century Six Books palimpsest, the medieval Arabic, the medieval Ethiopic, and the Georgian *Life of the Virgin* all contain at least part of a scene where Mary lifts her hands and blesses a crowd of both men and women.[4] The Ethiopic text preserves the fullest detail:

> Many men and women came to Mary, and they prostrated themselves before her, saying, "Have mercy on us and forgive us, and do not cast us away, O master."[5] And the blessed one, having extended her arms, blessed them and said, 'May the Lord receive your prayer and your petition …'[6]

Most likely, readers of the Six Books were aware of the scriptural resonance between such descriptions of Mary and descriptions of the Temple high priest.

The palimpsest text depicted Mary with authority over the male apostles, "serving in essence as their liturgical leader,"[7] essentially serving as the high priest of the men in the line of apostolic succession, that is, serving as the bishop of bishops. This depiction of Mary apparently became problematic for some scribes because it underwent various forms of scribal redaction. For example, the sixth-century scribe excised that the apostles prostrated themselves before Mary.[8] The scribe behind the Ethiopic translation preserved that they "prostrated themselves on the earth"—but excised that Mary raised her hands to pray and further changed the text so that Mary was seen as prostrate like the men.[9]

Mary raising her hands to pray, which 1 Timothy associates with men, appears to have become a significant concern for later scribes. For example, the homilies attributed to Theoteknos of Livias, Modestus of Jerusalem, Andrew of Crete, Germanus of Constantinople, John of Damascus, and Theodore the Studite, all omit that she raised her hands.[10] Mary as the liturgical leader of the male apostles appears to have been more of a concern to some Dormition scribes than even the presence of the Great Angel. The Palm text of an eleventh-century Greek manuscript, which preserves the Great Angel, nonetheless replaces Mary as the prayer leader with Peter. According to its text, after the apostles arrived to see Mary, Peter raised his arms and prayed. And, after Peter "exhorted the crowd until dawn, the sun rose, Mary got up and went outside, and she recited the prayer that the angel had given her."[11]

The scribe of a Gaelic Dormition manuscript similarly used Peter to silence Mary. In the original text, both Peter and Mary ask Jesus questions. In the redacted scene, Peter asks both Mary's questions and his own.[12] Here Mary is silenced, just as 1 Timothy specifies she should be.

If scribes silenced Jesus's mother by replacing her authority with Peter's, did they do the same thing to other women leaders? Of course, they did. For example, one fragment of the Thecla narrative says that Thecla asked *Peter* to send a priest to baptize a man that she herself had taught and converted. It says, "She wrote to the holy apostle Peter in Antioch and … the priest came from Antioch and baptized the child's father and his whole household."[13] In another example, a Coptic scribe substituted Peter for Mariamne in the manuscript tradition of the *Acts of Philip*. As Ann Graham Brock says, "The replacement of Mary by Peter as Philip's companion in the Coptic version of the Acts of Philip eliminates the authoritative position she held in the original Greek text."[14]

Later scribes, thus, employed a number of strategies to undermine the authority of early Christian women leaders. Art, however, is conservative. Despite that scribes often redacted the scene of Mary raising her arms as the prayer leader of the male apostles, this scene persisted in art. Early Christian art also preserves many images of Mary portrayed as a high priest or bishop.

Mary in Art: High Priest and Bishop

Art historian Alexei Lidov says that the gesture of raising hands "is interpreted in iconographic studies as a liturgical one," and he adds that the symbolic meaning of this gesture can be traced back "to the daily offering of the Evening Sacrifice in the Jerusalem Temple, the Old Testament prototype of the Eucharist."[15] As noted above, many verses described priests raising their arms, and Psalm 141:2 explains, *Let the raising of my hands be as the evening sacrifice.* In the fourth century, Chrysostom similarly wrote, "I am raising up my hands as the Evening Sacrifice."[16] In the West, the Ambrosian Rite specified that whoever celebrated the

Eucharist was to raise their arms at the mystery, and even though the oldest manuscript of this rite is eighth century (like virtually all liturgical manuscripts[17]), its instruction is so similar to the reports in scripture and Chrysostom, that it seems highly likely to be a textual artifact preserved from an ancient Eucharistic liturgy.[18] The intertextuality of the meaning of this gesture across both Jewish scripture and early Christian liturgical practice impacts how we understand depictions of Mary with her arms raised, in both text and art, in the early Christian era.

The Six Books scene of Mary raising her arms to lead the prayer of the twelve male apostles—the eleven *plus Paul*—is preserved in art that corresponds to the Six Books text. Despite the presence of Mary and Paul, until recently this iconography was misidentified as the ascension of Jesus—largely due to the fact that the Six Books text itself was censored to the extent that the scene was nearly lost from view.[19] The best-known example of this iconography is a beautiful full-page illumination bound with the Rabbula Gospels, which themselves were penned near Ancient Syria and dated 586. Suggesting the antiquity of this particular iconography, Jesus was painted with a halo that is not divided to represent his identity with the Trinity. After the fourth- and early fifth-century Trinitarian controversies, the divided halo became virtually obligatory for depictions of Jesus, and the Trinitarian halo is almost always seen on him in art dated after the early fifth century[20] (see Fig. 4.1).

Consistent with the Six Books narrative about Mary's death, this illuminator depicted Mary as the focal point of the scene—she stands in the center with her arms raised. Additionally signifying her headship of the male apostles who stand on either side of her, Mary was painted taller than they. Her posture is erect and powerful, her gaze direct. Signifying her elevated spirituality, she is flanked by archangels, and only she, Jesus above her, and the angels, have halos. The men do not.

According to the Six Books narrative, when Mary had finished her prayer, "it thundered like the sound of wheels rolling over the surface of the sky."[21] Not long afterward, Jesus descended in a "chariot of light" with "wheels of fire" in order to resurrect his mother after she died and take her up to heaven.[22] This illuminator thus painted Jesus's celestial chariot as an orb with flaming wheels spinning off reddish-orange fire.[23] The Six Books also said angels held up his chariot, and the artist included four angels doing just that.[24]

Another key narrative element shown in this illumination, and which identifies it as the Six Books scene, is the apostle Paul. The Six Books

Fig. 4.1   Rabbula Gospels illumination of Mary. © Alinari Archives, Florence

author repeatedly said that the apostle Paul was one of the twelve male apostles who came to Mary.[25] In the Rabbula Gospels illumination, Paul and Peter stand on either side of Mary and they themselves are painted larger than the other men. Peter is on the right and identifiable by his keys and thick bangs. Paul is on the left, identified by his large book and balding pate. Paul was described as bald in the *Acts of Thecla* 2–3, and artists used his baldness, as well as Peter's contrasting thick bangs, to distinguish them. For example, the sculptor of the famous fourth-century sarcophagus of Junius Bassus carved Paul entirely bald and Peter with curly bangs.[26] A fourth-century gold glass from the catacombs of Rome similarly depicts PETRUS on the left with thick bangs, but on the right PAULUS is going bald[27] (see Fig. 4.2).

Just as there is no controversy that the Six Books is about Mary the mother of Jesus, there is no controversy among art historians about this scene depicting her. The Rabbula Gospels illuminator in fact portrayed her with the same halo and dressed in the same dark blue outer garment called a *maphorion* in other scenes that clearly signify she is Mary, the mother of Jesus. For example, in another illumination, she is again portrayed in the midst of male apostles, this time with a dove and flames overhead in the traditional iconography of Pentecost, where Acts 1:14

Fig. 4.2 Peter (*left*) and Paul (*right*). Gold glass ca. 350, catacombs in Rome. Perret, *Catacombes de Rome*, pl. 4:21.3

identifies only "Mary the mother of Jesus" among the women in the upper room.[28]

A sixth-century painted reliquary box likewise illustrates that the arms-raised woman beneath Jesus was intended to represent his mother. This box was painted in or near Jerusalem for the pilgrim trade, and today it is in the Vatican Museum. Like the illuminator of the Rabbula Gospels, this painter included the scene with the arms-raised woman as one of several scenes, including the Nativity, that together identify her as the mother of Jesus[29] (see Fig. 4.3).

The top right frame painted on this reliquary box is the Six Books scene with Mary wearing a black *maphorion*, standing arms-raised directly beneath her son, who is seen in an orb in the sky. She is again flanked by twelve men and a close inspection shows that here again a balding Paul is on the left and Peter, with bangs, is on the right.[30] In this illustration, the men do not seem to have noticed Jesus descending; they stand quietly behind Mary, much as the *Gospel of Bartholomew* describes them standing behind Mary when she prays.[31]

The top left frame of this painted box depicts Mary in her black *maphorion* and another woman dressed in red walking toward the gated entrance to the shrine over Jesus's tomb beneath the Anastasis rotunda; her presence as one of the women at her son's tomb is consistent with her identification at the foot of the cross in John 19:25, and is a dominant motif in both art and text in the East.[32] In the wide center frame, Mary, still in her black *maphorion*, stands on the left at the foot of the cross where she is usually seen in crucifixion iconography. The bottom right frame illustrates the baptism of Jesus, where, in the foreground on the right, two angels hold out Mary's black *maphorion* as if she had given them her outer garment to dry her son; and Mary herself stands watching on the left, behind John the Baptist, her hair in a bun on top of her head. Finally, the bottom left frame depicts the Nativity, with Mary resting in her black *maphorion* after giving birth. Her baby lies in a manger behind her and Joseph sits at her feet. The Nativity scene establishes without question that the woman in the black *maphorion* is Jesus's mother.[33]

The Six Books iconography of Mary with her arms raised in prayer beneath her son in the sky was popular very early, spreading around the Mediterranean. Sixth- and seventh-century artifacts depicting this scene include gold jewelry,[34] a terracotta plaque,[35] frescos in Coptic monastery buildings,[36] ampoules that pilgrims brought home from Jerusalem,[37] and more. Just as some scribes redacted their texts to reduce subtly the

Fig. 4.3 Painted reliquary box ca. 500s, Jerusalem. Mary in five scenes. *Top left*: At Jesus' tomb. *Top right*: Prayer leader. *Center*: Crucifixion. *Bottom right*: Baptism. *Bottom Left*: Nativity. Grisar, *Romische Kapelle*, pl. 59

Fig. 4.4 Mary faces forward, arms-raised. Ampoule ca. 600s, Jerusalem. Monza Cathedral Treasury Museum. Garrucci, *Storia*, pl. 6:435.1

depiction of Mary's liturgical authority, some artists subtly changed Mary's bio-power in this scene. For example, in some cases instead of portraying Mary erect and confidently facing the viewer, with her hands high, artists depicted her semi-profile from the side, with her hands lowered, almost as if pleading instead of praying. Mary in this slightly hunched orante pose became known in the city of Rome as the *Madonna advocata*, for example, in her portrait on perhaps the oldest surviving icon, the sixth- to eighth-century Madonna of San Sisto.[38] Both postures are seen on the small sixth- or seventh-century ampoules that pilgrims to Palestine brought back to Italy, but by far the most popular was Mary facing the front.[39] In both cases, however, Mary remained the central focus directly beneath her son in the sky (see Figs. 4.4 and 4.5).

Fig. 4.5 Mary sideways, *Madonna advocata*. Garrucci, *Storia*, pl. 6:435.2

Various renderings of this iconography during the first millennium suggest the most critical and identifiable feature was the core verticality of Mary, arms-raised, placed directly beneath her son. This vertical pairing of mother and son in part may have been due to artists' familiarity with other Six Books scenes that depicted Mary raising her hands to pray to her son or to praise God when she was by herself, such as while visiting her son's tomb, while on the Mount of Olives, or while offering incense.[40]

Some artists depicted Mary in the middle of more than twelve men. For example, a sixth-century fresco in a Coptic monastery apse depicted her as the liturgical leader of thirteen.[41] A mid-seventh-century mosaic in the altar apse of the Lateran Baptistery chapel of San Venantius in

Rome depicts her as the leader of sixteen (Fig. 4.11).[42] Some of the oldest examples depict her between only two men. One of the oldest ampoules depicted her between the Temple priest Zachariah and John the Baptist.[43] The oldest surviving example decorating a church was carved on the Santa Sabina Basilica wood doors in Rome dated 420 to 430, and this wood carving depicts her between Peter and Paul.[44] Laura Marchiori notes that in subsidiary areas of early medieval churches, "The Virgin is commonly flanked by female saints"[45]—and some artists depicted Mary in this iconography flanked by women. For example, four women flank Mary in the tenth-century altar apse painting in the Santa Maria in Pallara monastery church in Rome.[46] In an early fourth-century fresco in the Cubiculum of the Velata in the Priscilla Catacomb in Rome, two vignettes, both featuring a young woman, flank an arms-raised woman who may have represented Mary beneath a shepherd standing inside a circle.[47] Marchiori notes a tradition of "funerary chapel decoration featuring the Virgin Mary in direct vertical placement with Christ, for whom she serves as primary intercessor."[48] Another early example of their vertical pairing in a funerary environment may be on a fourth-century double tiered sarcophagus from the Christian cemetery outside Arles in ancient Gaul, today in the Arles Cathedral. This sculptor carved a boyish Jesus in the center of the top tier and an arms-raised woman standing directly beneath him in the center of the bottom tier.[49] Scenes of Jesus performing miracles and healings flank them (see Fig. 4.6).

Demonstrating the strong memory of Mary in the arms-raised pose in Gaul even at this early date, the oldest surviving art to explicitly link Mary to the Jerusalem Temple was found sixty miles from Arles where the double sarcophagus is preserved. This stone plaque, along with other late fourth-century sarcophagi, is in a late fourth-century underground crypt, or hypogeum, beneath Sainte-Marie-Madeleine basilica in Saint-Maximin La-Sainte-Baume. According to Michel Fixot, the hypogeum dates to 375.[50] The sculptor of the plaque carved Mary with her hands raised. Inscribed above her head, she is identified as: MARIA VIRGO MINESTER DE TEMPULO GEROSALE, or, "Virgin Mary Minister of the Jerusalem Temple" (see Fig. 4.7).

This inscription is almost certainly a reference to a text like the *Gospel of Bartholomew*, which depicted Mary at the Temple altar, or the *Protevangelium*, which described Mary in the Jerusalem Temple as well as twice described her inside its Holy of Holies.[51] Her portrayal with her arms raised on this plaque, as well as her title, Minister of the Jerusalem Temple, is consistent with her portrayal in the Six Books as a liturgical

Fig. 4.6 Vertical pairing in center of sarcophagus, ca. 350s. Flanked by gospel scenes. Arles Cathedral. Wilpert, *Sarcofagi*, pl. 125

Fig. 4.7 *MARIA VIRGO MINESTER DE TEMPULO GEROSALE.* Stone plaque in hypogeum ca. 375. Sainte-Marie-Madeleine Basilica crypt, Saint-Maximin La-Sainte-Baume, France. Le Blant, *Sarcophages chrétiens de la Gaule*, pl. 57.1

leader within the scriptural memory of the Temple priesthood—raising her arms to bless people, lead the prayer, and praise God. The clear association with the Temple reminds us that Lidov says that the gesture of raising hands "is interpreted in iconographic studies as a liturgical one," and that the symbolic meaning of this gesture can be traced back "to the daily offering of the Evening Sacrifice in the Jerusalem Temple, the Old Testament prototype of the Eucharist."[52] As noted above, many verses described priests raising their arms, and Psalm 141:2 explains, *Let the raising of my hands be as the evening sacrifice.* In the fourth century also, Chrysostom wrote, "I am raising up my hands as the Evening Sacrifice."[53] In the West, where we find this plaque, the Ambrosian Rite specified that whoever celebrated the Eucharist was to raise their arms at the mystery, which, given the other sources, may also be related to ancient practice.[54] This intertextuality impacts our understanding of how fourth-century Christians likely saw this portrait of Mary.

Mary with the Episcopal Pallium

The oldest surviving uncontroversial portrayal in art of a Christian minister officiating at the Eucharist with arms raised high like Mary is depicted in this fourth-century plaque may be an eleventh-century wall painting of Pope Clement. This painting was discovered in the mid-1800s in the underground Basilica of Old Saint Clement's.[55] Pope Clement is depicted with his arms raised, a chalice and a paten of bread on the cloth-covered altar table behind him. The open gospel book, the symbol of a bishop, is in front of him. Clement holds the Eucharistic cloth or handkerchief, which in the West from the ninth century was called the maniple.[56] Most significantly, he wears the episcopal pallium—the long white strip of cloth with a cross on it that was to be worn only when officiating at the Eucharist—See Fig. 4.8.

Fig. 4.8 Pope Clement officiates the Eucharist at the altar. Wall painting ca. 1000, Basilica of Old Saint Clement, Rome. Wilpert, *Römischen Mosaiken*, pl. 240

In the early church, clergy wore the same apparel as the laity, apparel retained by custom over the centuries. Today this lay garb looks rather special. The episcopal pallium, such as Pope Clement wears in the wall painting, eventually became the distinctive episcopal symbol of the bishop's vestment in the West.[57] Pope Gregory the Great (r. 590–604) reportedly gave the pallium only to the bishops of the most important cities, such as Ravenna and Milan, and he prohibited its use except during the Eucharist.[58] Consistent with Mary portrayed in texts as a high priest or bishop, portraits of Mary wearing the episcopal pallium are as old as any that have survived of a man wearing it.

The oldest surviving uncontroversial depiction in art of a male bishop wearing a pallium is mid-sixth century, the same time that we first see Mary wearing it. In this art, this ancient episcopal pallium looks essentially the same as the modern, a long strip of fine white cloth with a black cross on it. Five mosaics in three basilicas depict people wearing this pallium. Two mosaics portray male bishops, two portray Mary, and one portrays Elizabeth, the mother of John the Baptist. All are in the altar apse, where the Eucharist was celebrated below, accentuating the liturgical significance of the pallium.

All three basilicas were completed with many of the same design features. Each was most likely constructed during the reign of Emperor Justinian and Empress Theodora, who dedicated many churches to Mary.[59] The two basilicas with the men are in Ravenna, and the one with Mary and Elizabeth is almost directly east, perhaps a day's sail on the other side of the Adriatic.

Bishop Maximianus of Ravenna was depicted wearing an episcopal pallium standing next to the Emperor Justinian in a mosaic side panel in the apse of the Basilica of San Vitale in Ravenna, completed around 547.[60] The martyr Bishop Apollinaris was depicted arms-raised while wearing an episcopal pallium in the center of the altar apse in the Basilica of Sant'Apollinare in Classe near Ravenna, completed around 549.[61] Within approximately the same decade, Mary was depicted twice and Elizabeth was depicted once wearing the episcopal pallium in the Euphrasiana Basilica in Poreč, Croatia, a church dedicated to Mary.[62] These mosaics of Mary and Elizabeth probably were completed during the reign of Bishop Euphrasius (543–554), but could be as early as 526.[63]

Mary's most visible placement in the Euphrasiana Basilica was in the center of the altar apse, directly above the episcopal throne behind the altar. Here the cross of her episcopal pallium is seen just below the hem of her *maphorion*.[64] (see Fig. 4.9a, b).

(a)   (b)

Fig. 4.9 a Euphrasiana Basilica ca. 550, Poreč, Croatia. b Mary wears episcopal pallium. © Iberfoto/Alinari Archives

An early design feature of this basilica's apse is consistent with Mary's association with women. Her portrait in the altar apse, wearing the episcopal pallium, is framed by round portraits of twelve women, while at the very top, Jesus is flanked by twelve men. Many of the twelve women portrayed around Mary—Thecla, Eugenia, Euphemia, Valeria, Perpetua, Susanna, Justina, Agatha, Agnes, Cecilia, Basilissa, and Felicitas[65]—still today are known as apostles and other leaders in the early Jesus movements. It seems likely that many more long narratives about these women—teaching, preaching, evangelizing, converting, and baptizing—still existed in the middle of the sixth century. Mary wearing the episcopal pallium, as well as these twelve women in the apse, may have been used to guarantee such roles for other women of this era.[66]

The second mosaic that portrayed Mary wearing an episcopal pallium in the Euphrasiana Basilica is on the wall to the right of the altar. Here, Elizabeth, the mother of John the Baptist, also has the episcopal pallium. This mosaic is of the Visitation in Luke 1:39–56, where Mary visited her relative Elizabeth. Each is depicted as being pregnant and wearing the episcopal pallium hanging from beneath her coat.[67] The representation of Elizabeth, as well as Mary, wearing an episcopal pallium, is consistent with Vernon K. Robbins' recent analysis of Luke's portrayal of Elizabeth as a priest. For example, Luke 1:5 specifies Elizabeth's priestly lineage through the daughters of Aaron. Luke 1:42 says that at the Visitation the Holy Spirit filled Elizabeth and in a loud voice she cried out two blessings, one for Mary and one for the child in her womb. Per Sirach 50:20–21, blessing is what a Temple priest did, and Robbins concludes, "Elizabeth, a daughter of Aaron, speaks to Mary like a priest"[68] (see Fig. 4.10).

Mary and Elizabeth were each depicted with an episcopal pallium hanging down in front, from beneath their coats, whereas the two male bishops of Ravenna were depicted with theirs hanging off their left shoulder. Notably, Pope Clement officiating at the Eucharist was also depicted with his pallium hanging down in front. Most likely differences in how the episcopal pallium was worn reflected gender differences, or differences in styles between various communities.

In the past, the interpretation that Mary was depicted with an episcopal pallium was not popular among all scholars, some of whom have tried to explain away that depiction in these mosaics.[69] Recently, however, other scholars have taken the lead in identifying Mary's apparel as what it looks like. Mary M. Schaefer calls Mary's pallium in these mosaics "the unmistakable archiepiscopal pallium."[70] Alexei Lidov calls it a symbol of Mary's priesthood.[71] Ivan Foletti argues that during a time when ordained women were under attack by some men in the hierarchy, portraits of the mother of Jesus as an ordained woman served to position her as the protector and guarantor of women clergy.[72]

The understanding that Mary was a bishop or high priest, like the Six Books, *Protevangelium*, and *Gospel of Bartholomew* portrayed her, was apparently influential around the Mediterranean, but not without controversy even then. For example, during the same century that the mosaic depicting Mary as a bishop was installed in the Euphrasiana Basilica, John of Ephesus (ca. 507–588), a famous Syriac writer in Palestine, wrote a morality tale as a warning for Christians who apparently believed that Mary sat on a bishop's throne and ordained priests.[73]

Fig. 4.10 The Visitation. Mary (*left*) and Elizabeth (*right*) wear the epis-copal pallium. Mosaic ca. 550. Euphrasiana Basilica, Poreč, Croatia. Wilpert, *Römischen Mosaiken*, fig. 313

Nonetheless, the tradition of Mary's role as a bishop who had at least as much, if not more, authority than male bishops seems to have remained steady in some communities, including among those today considered the most orthodox. For example, half a century after John of Ephesus died, Pope John IV (r. 640–642) began installing a mosaic that reprised the vertical Six Books composition in the altar apse of the Lateran Baptistery Chapel of San Venantius in Rome, a mosaic ultimately completed by Pope Theodore I (642–649).[74] In this mosaic, Mary was placed directly above the actual altar. The laity in the nave would have seen her as the Eucharistic leader of sixteen men. Paul (balding) and Peter (bangs) were next to her, then several holy men, and finally bishops who wore the episcopal pallium with a black cross. Mary herself wore an episcopal pallium with a red cross and she also wore red shoes. Both the pallium and the shoes are still insignia of the bishop of Rome, the pope[75] (see Fig. 4.11a, and for detail, Fig. 4.11b).

Schaef er calls Mary in this mosaic *Maria archiepiscopa*.[76] From the perspective of the laity in the nave, Mary was seen above and behind the altar as the chief officiant of the Eucharist. For the laity, Mary's Eucharistic privilege would be signified by her raised arms, her episcopal pallium with its red cross, and by the subordinate position of the bishops who flanked her, as well as her own central position during the rite as mediator with the divine, standing directly beneath Christ, who himself appears to be blessing and authorizing her.

Today not everyone in the Vatican is as comfortable with this mosaic as Popes John IV and Theodore I were almost 1500 years ago. Today this mosaic of Mary is a visual metaphor for the trajectory of redaction around the markers of her liturgical authority. In a city where virtually every other ancient mosaic is on display for pilgrims and tourists, today a huge baroque altarpiece hides this mosaic of Mary. This altarpiece not only hides the episcopal Mary, it features a demure portrait of Mary holding her baby, and thus operates both to conceal and to replace the original image of Mary. From the back of the nave, one can see Jesus's head above the top of this altarpiece, and one can see the men on either side of it—but the massive piece of furniture completely hides Mary. Her image is so well concealed that it took me multiple visits to this chapel searching for her before I finally noticed Christ's head above the altarpiece, and realized that Mary was hidden behind it.[77]

In 1916 the Holy Office forbade depictions of Mary dressed in priestly vestments, and quite likely that was when the huge altarpiece was installed.[78] Perhaps the red tesserae of the cross on Mary's white pallium were removed at the same time. In any case, sometime before 1899, Giovanni Battista de Rossi painted an image of the mosaic with a full red cross on Mary's pallium. All that remains of the red cross today are a few red tesserae. White tesserae have been installed where the rest once were.[79]

Iconography of Mary portrayed as a bishop persisted for several centuries around the Mediterranean.[80] The Saint Demetrios nave mosaics

Fig. 4.11 **a** Mosaics, ca. 650, San Venantius Chapel, Lateran Baptistery, Rome. **b** Mary wears episcopal pallium with red cross, flanked by Paul and Peter. 1890s painting. De Rossi, *Musaici cristiani*, pl. "Abside dell'oratorio di S. Venanzio"

in Thessaloniki, which were destroyed by fire in 1917, portrayed Mary wearing what appears to have been a type of pallium. These mosaics were probably installed between the late fifth and seventh centuries, but during Iconoclasm they were covered with plaster and uncovered again only in 1907. Fortunately photos, though not very distinct, as well as watercolors were made of them before the fire.[81] In one photo, Mary is seated holding her son with a long cloth extending downwards in front of her skirt with three stripes on the end.[82] In a second photo, Mary is portrayed as a side-view orante with a long white cloth hanging from beneath her *maphorion*.[83]

Another artifact, an ivory icon from Egypt or Palestine, carbon dated between 720 and 970, provides an excellent example of how this art was interpreted in some communities.[84] Its sculptor carved it in the Six Books iconography—Mary, arms-raised, directly beneath Jesus inside an orb, with men beside her. Further signifying her elevated liturgical position, a long festival pallium, or omophorion (the comparable insignia in the East), with many crosses on it hangs from beneath her short chasuble-like upper garment. Six men are present—the sculptor may

Fig. 4.12 Mary as bishop of bishops. Ivory icon from Egypt or Palestine, dated 720 to 970. Metropolitan Museum of Art, CC0

have carved more men around the lost back half—and each man carries a large gospel book, the symbol of the bishop, and also wears a pallium hanging from beneath his coat, hanging almost exactly the same as Mary and Elizabeth's were depicted hanging from beneath their coats in the mosaics of the Euphrasiana Basilica[85] (see Fig. 4.12).

An example in the West of Mary wearing a similar long white strip of cloth with many crosses on it, in this case hanging from beneath her *maphorion* on her left side, was originally in the Ravenna Cathedral's altar apse and dated 1112. Today it is in the Archbishop's Museum in Ravenna.[86] Even after that late date, for several centuries, in both East and West, occasionally Mary was depicted wearing liturgical insignia or garments, suggesting that familiarity with the motif of her priesthood continued in some communities.[87]

MARY WITH THE CLOTH OF THE EUCHARISTIC OFFICIANT

Another insignia of the Eucharistic officiant is what Lidov calls the "Eucharistic handkerchief," a narrow white cloth, sometimes plain, sometimes fringed, sometimes with thin embroidered stripes at the bottom, to be worn only during the Mass. Lidov treats this cloth as an important symbol in art of the priesthood of Mary.[88] The significance of this cloth in the West is apparent in the eleventh-century wall painting of Pope Clement in Fig. 4.8, which depicts Clement holding the cloth while performing the Mass.

From the first time we see it in fifth-century church art, this cloth almost certainly represented authority and leadership. Just like the episcopal pallium was probably borrowed from consular garb, this doubled cloth was called the *mappa* and outside the church was associated with the authority of the consul or emperor.[89] When used by someone in association with the altar or the altar area, the cloth represented their authority in that environment. One of the first instances in Christian art where this cloth is seen as a distinctly separate cloth is on a fifth-century ivory diptych from Italy or Gaul, where four men, apparently the four evangelists, are depicted holding the cloth along with a large book that appears to have the four symbols of the evangelists in each corner, that is, a gospel book.[90] A century later the cloth is seen again in the hands of the four evangelists on the front of the mid-sixth-century ivory throne of Bishop Maximianus of Ravenna (r. 546–556), which depicts all four evangelists, three of whom have the fringed cloth over their hand holding their book, along with a fourth who holds his book under his arm, with the fringed cloth doubled in his hand.[91] As demonstrated by the book sculpted on the altar below the hanging lamp in Fig. 2.8, as well as by the open book with Pope Clement in Fig. 4.8, the gospel book was associated with the altar during the liturgy.[92] Indicating the use of this cloth to cover the hand when touching other liturgical objects as well, another ivory plaque on the throne portrays Jesus between two men (one balding and one with bangs), each of whom holds a platter, or paten, with a cloth draped over his hand; one platter is laden with bread and the other with fish.[93]

Around the ninth century in the West, this narrow strip of white cloth, sometimes fringed and sometimes with embroidered stripes at the end, became known as the maniple, the privilege of a Eucharistic offici-ant, by then mostly male. In the East, according to Lidov, "An analogue of the western maniple was the so-called *enchirion* (literally "handy") – a white handkerchief hanging at the girdle of an archpriest, later called *epigonation*."[94] By the time of Clement's painting, the cloth already had been in use for several centuries in some churches in both East and West in one form or another, held in the hand, as Clement demonstrates, or hanging from the girdle.[95] Because of its different names in both East and West—and art depicting women using it was made in both East and West—I refer to it simply as the Eucharistic cloth.

Lidov says that this Eucharistic cloth, or "Eucharistic handkerchief" as he calls it, "carefully introduced the theme of the participation of the Virgin in the Eucharistic sacrifice and of Her priesthood."[96] Mary was portrayed with the Eucharistic cloth relatively frequently around the Mediterranean, sometimes lifting it with her left hand, like Pope Clement at the altar table in the eleventh century, but also, with her arms raised and the cloth hanging from the girdle at her waist. Often she was portrayed in the altar apse, which, given her placement above and behind the altar, accentuated her sacrificial role. Her portrayal with the cloth in the altar apse is consistent with her portrayal with the episcopal pallium in the altar apses of the mid-sixth-century Euphrasiana Basilica and the mid-seventh-century Lateran baptistery chapel in Rome. Both vestments were to be worn only during the performance of the Eucharist itself.

In Rome, the oldest portrait of Mary holding the Eucharistic cloth may be a wall painting, variously dated late fifth to sixth century, in what today is known as the church of Maria Antiqua in Rome, but what originally was a palace anteroom. Mary is seen seated, holding her son on her lap, and holding up the white cloth, a small black cross visible on the fabric.[97] She is similarly painted holding the cloth in a mid-sixth-century wall painting in the Commodilla Catacomb in Rome. In this catacomb portrait, the widow Turtura stands next to her and is depicted using another white fringed cloth to hold what appears to be a book or a platter/paten.[98]

A Coptic apse painting of Mary in Chapel 17 of the Bawit Monastery may be the oldest surviving art portraying her with both arms raised, the cloth hanging from a girdle at her waist. This portrait of Mary was probably painted sometime between the fifth and seventh centuries, although potentially even the fourth century since renovations began then. The painter portrayed Mary in the middle of thirteen men, and as usual standing directly below a young beardless Jesus in the sky, who himself is inside a circle, which is on a mass of scarlet flames. In this Six Books scene in the eastern apse, the leadership symbolism associated with the cloth hanging from Mary's girdle evokes her liturgical authority[99] (see Fig. 4.13a for the apse and Fig. 4.13b for detail of Mary).

Fig. 4.13 **a** Bawit Monastery fresco. **b** Mary wears cloth. Clédat, *Monastère*, pl. 40, 41

A sixth-century altar apse mosaic in a church dedicated to Mary in Livadia, Cyprus, is fragmentary today, but it portrayed Mary standing on a low platform against a gold tesserae background flanked only by two angels, her arms raised and two white strips of cloth hanging from beneath her dark blue *maphorion*.[100] Richard Maguire suggests that her portrait in this mosaic is much like her portrayal in the Rabbula Gospels illumination (Fig. 4.1).[101] Demonstrating the longevity and popularity of this iconography for Mary, both Arthur Megaw, who first studied the Livadia mosaic when a layer of plaster was removed from it, as well as Robin Cormack, favorably compare its sixth-century iconography to that of the eleventh-century altar apse mosaic in Holy Sophia Cathedral in Kiev, which depicts Mary, again standing by herself with her arms raised, wearing the white cloth, shorter, doubled over her belt.[102] This mosaic in Kiev also closely resembles the top right painted frame of Mary, arms-raised, flanked by the twelve men on the early sixth-century painted reliquary box. This painter similarly executed two short white strips at Mary's girdle, seen upon close inspection (Fig. 4.3). The Livadia mosaic is also similar to the mosaic of Mary in the altar apse in the Cefalù Cathedral in Sicily, which the Normans built seven hundred years later, in 1240. In its apse, Jesus and Mary appear in the core vertical composition, with Jesus above as a huge bearded Pantocrator. Mary stands below him flanked by four angels, her arms raised, two red-striped ends of a white cloth hanging from her girdle (see Fig. 4.14a, b for detail).

The sixth-century altar apse mosaic of Mary in the famous Koimesis, or Dormition, church in Nicaea was reportedly restored in the ninth century after Iconoclasm ended.[103] A photo taken of this apse mosaic before the church burned in 1922 illustrates Mary holding her son while also holding the white fringed cloth in almost the same gesture that Pope Clement was painted holding it while performing the Eucharist. The sixth- or seventh-century altar apse mosaic in the Virgin Angeloktisti Church in Kition, Cyprus, depicts Mary holding her son with two narrow strips of fringed cloth hanging from her girdle.[104] The late ninth-century mosaic in the altar apse of the Hagia Sophia in Constantinople was perhaps the most prominent placement in Christendom. It depicts Mary seated and holding her son, the fringed cloth again in her hand.[105]

Fig. 4.14 a Altar apse mosaics ca. 1240, Cefalù Cathedral, Sicily. **b** Mary wears the cloth. © DeA Picture Library, licensed by Alinari

In the West, fifty years before the Hagia Sophia apse mosaic was completed, Pope Paschal (r. 818–822) in Rome oversaw the design of a mosaic in the altar apse of Santa Maria in Domnica, which portrays him with a rectangular halo (indicating he was alive when his portrait was made) and kneeling at Mary's feet.[106] Mary holds both her infant son and the fringed Eucharistic cloth embroidered with two thin red stripes. By this date, the cloth had become known in the West as the maniple, an important clerical privilege and permanent element of the liturgical vestments of a bishop.[107] From the perspective of the laity in the nave, this mosaic portrait of Mary holding both her son and the fringed maniple created an inescapable visual analogy. Above the altar table, Mary held the maniple and offered her son, while below her officiants with the same maniple stood offering his symbolic body and blood[108] (see Fig. 4.15).

Fig. 4.15 Mary holds the cloth. Altar apse, early 800s, Rome. De Rossi, *Musaici cristiani*, pl. "Abside de Santa Maria in Dominica"

WOMEN WITH THE CLOTH OF THE EUCHARISTIC OFFICIANT

The very oldest surviving church decoration dated with certainty that portrays someone holding the Eucharistic cloth is a wall mosaic approximately the same age as the fifth-century ivory diptych that depicts the four evangelists holding their gospel books with the cloth.[109] The mosaic illustrates a woman holding the cloth. This woman is one of two women, each called "church," and each holding a large open book.[110] Both mosaics are in Santa Sabina Basilica in Rome and dated 430 to 440. Originally, mosaics of Peter and Paul were on the wall directly above the two women.[111] One of the women, titled "Church of the Circumcision," holds a large open book that appears to represent the Jewish scriptures, given the square blocks that depict the writing on its pages. The other woman, titled "Church of the Gentiles," also holds a large open book, and it appears to be the Greek gospels, given the squiggly lines with which its writing is represented.[112] Similar to the ivory diptych that depicts the four evangelists using the cloth to hold their gospel book, the woman holding the Greek gospels also holds the cloth.[113] Despite the spread of centuries, the parallel between this woman and Pope Clement in his eleventh-century portrait at the Eucharist in Fig. 4.8 is profound. Both she and Clement are depicted holding the cloth doubled over in their left hand, adjacent a large open book. This iconographic parallel suggests that the meaning of the cloth remained constant over time, whether seen with a woman or with a man. For the mosaics of these two women, see Fig. 4.16.

The gospel book in art typically signified a bishop, and bishops were often depicted holding books. This association seems likely due to the fact that bishops, and bishops only, were ordained with the open gospel book held over their head, the same practice then as today.[114] This ritual of "holding the divine Gospels open upon the head" as part of the episcopal ordination ritual is found in the fourth-century *Apostolic Constitutions*, itself compiled from the older *Apostolic Tradition*.[115] According to the popular preacher and bishop, Severian of Gabala (ca. 380–425), the imposition of the gospel book was an integral part of a bishop's ordination ritual in order that, just as in the upper room at Pentecost, the Holy Spirit's tongues of flame would descend from the book to ordain and inspire the new bishop's preaching.[116]

The proposition that this open gospel book was an allusion to the episcopacy in this mosaic is furthered by another mosaic installed in Rome perhaps ten years later. In the Maria Maggiore Basilica, Peter and Paul, the archetypical bishops themselves, are seen holding out open books on either side of an empty episcopal throne.[117] Peter and Paul holding out their open books toward the empty bishop's throne seem to signify that they are waiting to ordain the new bishop of Rome.[118] This iconography was particularly poignant, because Pope Celestine

Fig. 4.16 The two "Churches." Church of the Gentiles (*right*) holds the cloth. 420 to 430. Santa Sabina Basilica. Wilpert, *Römischen Mosaiken*, pl. 47

(r. 422–432), who most likely started construction on Maria Maggiore, died before that enormous basilica was completed.[119]

The earlier composition of the two women holding open books in Santa Sabina likewise presents them as if authorizing the bishop of Rome—as if authorizing the bishop of Rome *over all other bishops*. The two women held their open books on either side of a large dedicatory inscription that began with these words: "When Celestine held the apostolic eminence shining as the foremost bishop in the whole world …"[120] This was a very early elevation of the Bishop of Rome over all others. One might conclude that the mosaic of these two women, both titled "church," one also holding the Eucharistic cloth, signified women bishops, just as the figures of Peter and Paul holding open books signified bishops. In addition, Mary herself was called "the Church," from at least the time of Clement of Alexandria—who said that he loved to call her "the Church."[121] As we will see in the next chapter, and potentially explaining why there were *two* "churches" in this mosaic, a decade later in the Maria Maggiore mosaics, *two* Marys were present at the Adoration of the Magi.[122]

In any case, ten years later in the city of Rome, Peter and Paul, men in the male line of apostolic succession, were depicted holding an open book. We therefore reasonably may consider the conclusion that two women holding an open book were a symbol of high female episcopal authority. This conclusion is buttressed by two facts. First, one of the two women depicted also holds the Eucharistic cloth. Second, both of the very oldest artifacts to depict someone with the Eucharistic cloth in a liturgical procession depicted *women*, not men, with the cloth.

Three of Theodora's ladies were depicted with the narrow white fringed cloth in one of the two altar apse mosaics installed in the mid-sixth-century Basilica of San Vitale in Ravenna. Almost certainly the ivory throne of Bishop Maximianus, with its carvings of the four evangelists holding a gospel book with the cloth as well as two men using the cloth to hold a platter of bread or fish, was in the Holy of Holies below the mosaic. This mosaic depicted two women with the white fringed cloth hanging from their girdle and one woman holding it doubled over in her hand. Theodora herself, the Augusta, holds the jeweled Eucharistic chalice.[123] I discuss this mosaic in more detail in Chapter 7, but for now, I quote Alexei Lidov, who says: "Let me remind those who are convinced of the lay provenance of the handkerchief that Theodora with her retinue, as well as Justinian, are presented in San Vitale in a liturgical procession in the sanctuary, both holding liturgical vessels – the Chalice and Paten"[124] (see Fig. 4.17).

The second artifact that depicts women in a liturgical procession, in this case wearing the narrow folded cloth hanging from their girdles, is the sixth-century ivory pyx previously seen in Fig. 2.8a, b. This sculptor carved women processing to the Anastasis altar, with two women holding censers approaching the altar from either side. All five women in this procession were sculpted with the cloth hanging from their girdles. The cloth is most clearly represented as two strips on the center arms-raised woman (see Fig. 4.18).

Both the San Vitale mosaic and the ivory pyx substantiate that the cloth was associated not only with Mary's Eucharistic and episcopal

Fig. 4.17 Theodora with the chalice and three women with the cloth. Wall mosaic to the right of the altar. Ca. 550. San Vitale Basilica, Ravenna. © Alinari Archives-Alinari Archive, Florence

authority, but also with women's authority, the same type of authority with which the cloth was associated when used by men. The idea that this narrow white cloth meant something different when used by a woman during the liturgy than when used by a man is a circular argument predicated on the demonstrably false premise that no women during this era were clergy.[125] We are not logically obliged to interpret the authority that this cloth represented differently because it is seen as part of a woman's vestments. The logical conclusion is that this cloth was always associated with power and authority in the church, and only later, much later, became restricted to men.

The *faux-Paul* author of the New Testament letter 1 Timothy challenged the authority of women in the assembly. Various pieces of evidence indicate that this challenge was made because some communities of Jesus followers supported women as well as men in ecclesial leadership roles. The evidence also indicates that these communities ignored 1 Timothy (if they even knew about it). These communities continued to support women as church leaders. Community support for these women leaders

Fig. 4.18 Arms-raised women with two strips of cloth hanging from their girdles. Procession to the altar. Ivory pyx ca. 500s, Palestine. Metropolitan Museum of Art, New York City. Gift of J. Pierpont Morgan, 1917. Accession Number: 17.190.57a, b. CC0

is evidenced in the way that women, including the mother of Jesus, were depicted as church leaders, including in the episcopal role, in church art. Just as women were portrayed liturgically using censers as early as men, these episcopal vestments are seen with women as early as with men.

Around the Mediterranean, Mary was depicted wearing the episcopal pallium as well as wearing, or holding, the cloth used while officiating at the Eucharist. Mary's image in the apse of a church was placed directly above the bishop's throne and the altar table. In this setting, she was variously depicted as bishop of bishops, high priest, and Eucharistic officiant, all of which imbued her image with enormous sacral authority and power. It thus seems quite possible that during this era Mary's image functioned both as a gender ideal for women clergy and also as a guarantor of their office.

CHAPTER 5

Mother and Son, Paired

One of the curiosities of history that suggests the magnitude of hidden early traditions about Mary is that, according to Averil Cameron, until the era of Iconoclasm images of Jesus with his mother "greatly outnumber" images of Jesus by himself.[1] Given the modern pious imagination of Mary, one might assume that all these images of mother and son together depicted him as an infant sitting on her lap. That assumption would be wrong. The pairing of Mary and her infant son was important, but their pairing when he was a young man was apparently just as important or even more so.

As demonstrated in the last chapter, some artists vertically paired Mary with her son in scenes where she was depicted lifting her hands and leading the prayer, praising God, and blessing people, while Jesus was depicted in the heavens above her. This core vertical iconography is best explained as art of the Six Books scene where Mary raised her arms and prayed to her son. Other artists, however, paired mother and grown son horizontally. This horizontal pairing, likewise often depicting Mary arms-raised, is found on silver chalices, censers, processional crosses, gold bishops' medallions (the encolpion), gospel book covers, church decoration, and reliquary boxes, as illustrated in this chapter. Most of this precious art is dated between the year 500 and the end of the seventh century and advent of Islam. Toward the end of this chapter, however, I will demonstrate that in some cases, this dating may be too conservative. Some objects may be older.

© The Author(s) 2019
A. Kateusz, *Mary and Early Christian Women*,
https://doi.org/10.1007/978-3-030-11111-3_5

The pairing of mother and son in early Christian art is consistent with the way some narratives paralleled the importance of mother and son. For example, according to the gospels of Matthew and Luke, Jesus was conceived without a man's seed—and, according to the *Protevangelium*, Mary also was conceived without a man's seed, thusly conceived while her mother's husband was in the wilderness for 40 days. The *Protevangelium* said an angel first went to Mary's barren mother Anna and announced that she *would* conceive and next went to her husband, Joachim, who had been in the wilderness forty days, and announced that Anna *had conceived*.[2] In the late fourth century, Bishop Epiphanius of Salamis treated this scene as gospel, *as it is written*. He did not question that Anna had conceived Mary without a man's seed, but he bitterly complained that some people were using this "to make her God, or to have us make offerings in her name, or, again, to make women priestesses."[3] Perhaps, as Epiphanius complained, the belief that Mary was conceived without a man's seed indeed was used to justify offerings in her name and women priests. If so, that might explain why later scribes redacted the scene to add that Mary had a *human* father. In one popular example, the angel instead announces to Joachim: "Know that she has conceived a daughter from thy seed."[4] Another scribe bluntly added: "Anna conceived from the seed of Joachim."[5] Yet another explained that Mary "was born of a father and a mother even as all men."[6]

In another narrative parallel, the canonical gospels depict Jesus as dead, then resurrected, and the oldest surviving Dormition text depicts Mary as dead—and then her son resurrects her.[7] Likewise, Luke 24:50 depicts Jesus bodily ascending after his resurrection—and the early Dormition text depicts Mary bodily ascending after her resurrection (in her son's chariot).[8] Accordingly, some Greek Dormition manuscripts use the same word for Mary's ascension—*analēpsis*—that Luke 9.51 uses for the ascension of Jesus.[9] Their two ascension scenes are paralleled on two side-by-side wood panels on the Santa Sabina Church doors in Rome dated 420–430.[10] The parallel of their auspicious deaths persisted longer than the parallel of their births—no bones of either Jesus or Mary became relics in the medieval era, because Christians believed that both had been bodily taken up to heaven.

Their sacrificial roles also appear to have been seen as parallel from an early date. Jesus was seen as a sacrifice, and Lily Vuong has detailed how the *Protevangelium* described Mary as a Temple sacrifice.[11] Writers called both mother and son the altar, the incense, the lamb, the ark; he was king, she was queen; he was prophet, she prophetess.[12] The early fourth-century poet Ephrem the Syrian called them brother and sister, as well as mother and son.[13] With these early literary parallels in mind, we examine the way that artists paralleled them on objects used in the liturgy.

MOTHER AND SON PAIRED
ON OBJECTS USED IN THE LITURGY

Early Byzantine silver objects, many of which were used during the Eucharistic liturgy, provide excellent examples of the liturgical pairing of mother and son. It was rare that Jesus was portrayed on one of these sacred utensils without his mother.[14] Mother and son, or scenes from their respective lives, were typically placed on opposite faces. In some cases, each stands alone on opposite faces. Sometimes Mary is flanked by angels, or sometimes by male saints, although she may be flanked by a woman and a man on a silver flask that most likely held oil for anointing.

Some of the most exquisite examples of this mother and son pairing are on chalices found in buried hoards of church silver in the Eastern Mediterranean, primarily in and around Ancient Syria. A few chalices, such as three in the Beth Misona Treasure in the Cleveland Museum of Art, have facial portraits of Jesus and Mary on the opposite sides of each chalice.[15] Most chalices portray their entire body. On these, Mary is almost always depicted with her arms raised.[16] Likewise, Jesus is almost uniformly depicted as a beardless youth[17]—a characteristic of the earliest Christian art, such as in the Christian catacombs of Rome.[18]

A treasure of church silver found in Attarouthi in northern Syria paired Mary and Jesus as counterparts on the opposite faces of eight of the ten chalices found. Neither was depicted on the remaining two chalices.[19] None of these items had silver stamps, but are broadly dated 500–650. On some chalices, Mary was depicted with what appears to be a Eucharistic cloth, or episcopal pallium, or other priestly insignia, hanging from her waist.[20] For one example, see Fig. 5.1. Dora Piguet-Panayotova suggests that this particular insignia, hanging from beneath Mary's *maphorion*, represented a belt such as an Artemis priestess might have worn.[21] It might alternatively represent the insignia of a Christian woman priest. For youthful Jesus holding a large book on the opposite side of the same chalice, see Fig. 5.2.

Censers for incense were used during the liturgy, and many of these also depicted Jesus and Mary on opposite faces, including one of the three unstamped silver censers found with the chalices in the

Fig. 5.1 Mary with priestly insignia hanging from her girdle. Unstamped silver chalice usually dated 500–650. Attarouthi Treasure, northern Syria. Metropolitan Museum of Art, New York City. Purchase, Rogers Fund and Henry J. and Drue E. Heinz Foundation, Norbert Schimmel, and Lila Acheson Wallace Gifts, 1986. Accession no. 1986.3.7. CC0

Attarouthi hoard.[22] Other censers that paired mother and son are in the British Museum and the Bayerisches Nationalmuseum in Munich.[23] A hexagonal censer probably made in Constantinople that portrays Mary,

Fig. 5.2 Boyish Jesus holds a large book (opposite side of chalice)

arms-raised, is also in the Metropolitan Museum of Art in New York City, but from a different hoard. It has silver stamps, which securely date it between 582 and 602.[24]

Other items likely used in the liturgy, or associated with the altar, paired Mary and Jesus. The silver Homs ewer in the Louvre Museum probably was used to hold the wine. It does not have silver stamps and therefore is broadly dated sixth to seventh century.[25] Two silver reliquary boxes have survived that paired mother and son, neither of which depicts Mary with her arms raised. One, in the Kunsthistorisches Museum in Vienna, portrays Mary holding an open book. It was found near Pola, Croatia, and is unstamped, therefore broadly dated sixth or seventh century.[26] The other box, in the State Hermitage Museum in St. Petersburg, shows only Mary's face. It has silver stamps dating it between 527 and 547.[27]

Christians used holy oil continuously from the beginning. The canonical gospels describe women anointing Jesus (Matt 26:7, Mark 14:3, Luke 7:37–38, John 12:3), as well as apostles (Mark 6:13) and presbyters (James 5:14–15) anointing the sick. Some second-century writers described baptismal anointing.[28] This rite appears to be described in a fragment of the Thecla narrative: "Thekla gave them instruction, teaching them the Gospel of God and, anointing them with the oil of gladness, she baptized them."[29] An unstamped silver flask that probably held such oil was excavated in Syria, an area where anointing was prominent as part of the baptismal ritual.[30] Today this silver bottle is in the Walters Art Museum in Baltimore. It has no silver stamps but is dated to the same period as liturgical utensils with stamps, from 500 to 670. Like objects others mentioned above, this flask also depicts Jesus on one side and his mother on the opposite side. Here, a boyish Jesus carries a book. Mary, arms-raised, wears a type of cloth insignia hanging from beneath her girdle. Between them are two arms-raised saints, one with long curly effeminate hair (a female saint?) and one with short hair[31] (see Fig. 5.3a, b).

Mother and son were also paired on silver processional crosses. With respect to these large crosses, Maria Mundell Mango says it is important to distinguish between crosses and crucifixes, because crucifixes, which bear the body of Christ, do not appear until the Middle Byzantine period.[32] Before then, Mary is often found in the center of the cross, and she continues to be even during the transition to crucifixes. For example, a medieval silver cross in the Musée de Cluny has several scenes from Mary's life on it, including Mary holding her infant in the center of it; in another example, a copper cross in the Benaki Museum in Athens depicts Mary arms-raised in the center of the front of the cross and Jesus in a loincloth on the back.[33] A large number of small wearable pectoral crosses in the same style—Mary arms-raised on the front and Jesus on the back—have survived from the Middle Byzantine period.[34]

Another example of an earlier silver processional cross with Jesus and Mary on it is the Čaginkom Cross in the Archeological Museum of

Fig. 5.3 **a** Mary and Jesus paired on silver flask for holy oil. Cloth insignia hangs from Mary's girdle. **b** Boyish Jesus holds gospel book. Unstamped silver flask usually dated 550–600. Hama Treasure from Ancient Syria. The Walters Art Museum, Baltimore, accession no. 57.639. CC0

Istanbul. It has silver stamps that date it between 527 and 547.[35] The portrait of Mary is featured in the center of the cross. A portrait of Jesus is above Mary, at the top. The portrait of a female saint is below Mary, at the bottom. Portraits of archangels are at the ends of both arms of the cross.[36]

Another silver processional cross depicts Mary, arms-raised, inside the center medallion on one side and Jesus, stepping out of his sarcophagus, inside the center medallion on the other side. This is the stational cross of Bishop Agnello in the Archbishop's Museum in Ravenna. It does not have silver stamps to date it, but is usually considered sixth century[37] (see Fig. 5.4).

Fig. 5.4   Jesus in center medallion. **Inset**: Mary on opposite side. Unstamped silver processional cross usually dated 500s. Archbishop's Museum, Ravenna. © Alinari Archives-Alinari Archive, Florence

Two sixth-century sets of ivory book covers, likely used for the gospels, also paired Jesus and Mary.[38] One set, the Saint-Lupicin covers, is today in the National Library of France. The other, called the Etchmiadzin gospel covers, is in the Mantenadaran in Yerevan, Armenia. One cover on both sets has a portrait of Mary holding her baby, which is surrounded by four scenes from her life. The opposite cover has a portrait of Jesus, which is surrounded by four scenes from his life. Two scenes from the *Protevangelium* are on both of the covers with Mary. One scene depicts Mary holding a wide bowl at the Test of Bitter Water. The other depicts Mary holding a spindle for her weaving. The iconography of Mary is similar on both, but on the Saint-Lupicin covers, the artist depicted Jesus bearded like an old man—a later motif. The Etchmiadzin Gospel covers, however, portray Jesus as a beardless youth, which is characteristic of the oldest Christian art. For Mary on the Etchmiadzin gospel covers, see Fig. 5.5a. For Jesus, see Fig. 5.5b.

(a)   **(b)**

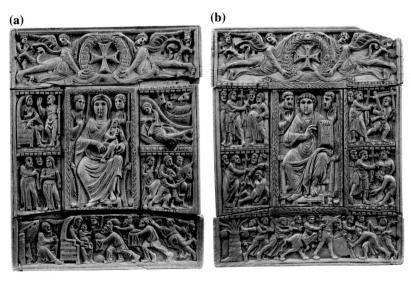

Fig. 5.5 **a** Mary on ivory gospel cover. **b** Jesus on opposite cover. Etchmiadzin gospel covers, usually dated 550–575. Mantenadaran, Yerevan, Armenia. Courtesy © Hrair Hawk Khatcherian

The pairing of scenes from Jesus and Mary's respective lives is also on some gold pectoral medallions. A pectoral medallion like this is called an "encolpion." It signifies episcopal authority and is worn hanging from the neck of the bishop. One encolpion dated circa 600 and unearthed in Adana, near Tarsus, is today in the Archeological Museum of Istanbul. One face has several small scenes featuring Mary—Annunciation, Visitation, Nativity, the ride to Bethlehem, and the Adoration of the Magi (the wise men bearing gifts). The other face has seven small scenes of Jesus's healings, miracles, and ministry.[39] Yet another encolpion, dated 584 and unearthed in Cyprus, is now in the Dumbarton Oaks Collection. One face portrays Mary holding her infant, plus two small scenes of the Nativity and the Adoration of the Magi. The other side comprises a large scene of the baptism of Jesus.[40]

The most interesting gold encolpion is in the State Museum of Berlin. It is nearly identical in shape to the other two, although it has a more ornate setting. Its front face depicts Mary holding a spindle for her weaving in accordance with the *Protevangelium*. Its back face depicts Jesus at the miracle of Cana and is entitled, "The first miracle."[41] The encolpion probably hung from a large, ornate gold pectoral made by the same goldsmith, which has an inscription, "Lord help the wearer"—with the word "wearer" in the feminine gender—and, so, according to Marvin C. Ross, "This pectoral must have been made for a woman."[42] This encolpion is rarely identified as an encolpion, apparently because it hung from a pectoral which was worn around a woman's neck[43] (see Fig. 5.6).

Jesus and Mary sometimes were paired in church decoration. For example, the early fifth-century wood panel on the door of the Santa Sabina Church that depicted Mary with her arms raised beneath Jesus, in the Six Books scene of her death and ascension, was paired with a second, adjacent, wood panel that depicted Jesus's own ascension.[44] In another example, around the year 500, King Theodoric installed monolithic mosaics of Mary and Jesus seated on thrones facing each other across the nave on opposite sides of the altar apse in Sant'Apollinare Nuovo Basilica in Ravenna.[45] Along the walls of the nave, twenty-two women and three magi bearing gifts process toward the portrait of Mary, while on the opposite side, twenty-six men process toward Jesus. The mosaics of these saints date approximately sixty years later than the mosaics of Jesus and Mary and may have replaced older mosaics of earlier saints.[46]

Another pairing of Mary and Jesus on thrones is on the late fourth-century San Nazaro silver reliquary box in Milan, which features

Fig. 5.6 Gold encolpion—Mary at Annunciation. Pectoral inscription: "Lord help the wearer (f)." 600s. Dennison, *Gold Treasure*, pl. 17

a portrait of Mary flanked by two men, each of whom carries a large platter or paten. A portrait of Jesus as a young man is on its lid. Until recently, this silver reliquary box confounded some modern art historians and instigated quite a dispute over its dating. Excavated in 1896 from late fourth-century strata beneath the high altar of the Roman era church of San Nazaro, some scholars refused to concede that the age of

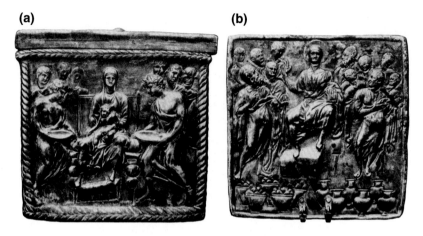

(a)   **(b)**

Fig. 5.7   **a** Mary on front. **b** Jesus on lid. San Nazaro silver reliquary box, ca. 380, Milan. Wilpert, *Römischen Mosaiken*, figs. 338 and 363

the reliquary box could possibly match its strata. On the box, Mary sits on a throne larger than the one upon which her grown son was seated, and these scholars argued that this elevation of Mary meant the box must be much later—some scholars argued it was a late nineteenth-century forgery. A recent technical investigation, however, decisively demonstrated that the box indeed was manufactured around the year 380, the same dating as the strata in which it was discovered under the altar[47] (see Fig. 5.7a for Mary on the front and Fig. 5.7b for Jesus on the lid).

Dividing the Mother-Son Dyad: The Maria Maggiore Mosaics

The dating controversy around the late fourth-century San Nazaro silver reliquary box, which continued until the recent technical investigation demonstrated that, indeed, the box was the same date as its late fourth-century strata. The late fourth-century dating of this silver reliquary box suggests that other Marian artifacts pairing mother and son—many of which have not been technically investigated—may also be older than currently dated. An example of such artifacts that are usually dated sixth century or later—but which could be older—are the unstamped silver chalices for the Eucharist, as well as other unstamped silver pieces associated with the liturgy that paired Mary and Jesus.

Between the years 500 and 670, silver was stamped with the reign of the emperor. If a silver object is stamped, it can be securely dated to the years during which that emperor reigned. Maria Marlia Mango did a study which, remarkably, indicated that only around a quarter of all silver pieces associated with the liturgy have silver stamps. Furthermore, the iconography of the unstamped pieces associated with the liturgy is substantially different than the iconography of the stamped pieces. For example, stamped objects seldom have figural decoration (such as images of Jesus and Mary). *None of the silver chalices that paired Jesus and Mary were stamped.*[48] In addition, unstamped objects tend to have portraits of Jesus as a beardless boy without a cross—much like he was depicted in the Christian catacombs of Rome.[49] Finally, unstamped silver pieces associated with the liturgy rarely have large crosses as part of their design, whereas the stamped silver pieces do.[50] The lack of large crosses suggests that the unstamped pieces could be older, because the cross is virtually never seen in Christian art prior to the end of the fourth century and afterward only slowly became a featured motif.

Could unstamped silver liturgical objects that pair Mary and Jesus be older than the stamped pieces? That is, could they have been made prior to the year 500, when silver stamping began? There appears to be no reason that they could not be older. Yet, as the dating controversy around the San Nazaro silver reliquary box illustrates, modern art historians typically date objects that depict Mary *later*, to the sixth century, and beyond.

This late dating of Marian artifacts began with the old hypothesis that when the church fathers at the Council of Ephesus in 431 called Mary the "Theotokos," they caused a gradual explosion of Mariology.[51] This hypothesis assumes that Mariology would have taken a few decades to blossom and that therefore, with little exception, almost all Marian artifacts must have originated after the year 500. In circular fashion, this late dating of Marian artifacts then becomes evidence used to validate the original hypothesis.

Until recently, most scholars accepted the hypothesis that the bishops at the Council of Ephesus in 431 essentially caused Mariology by using the title Theotokos for Mary. Recently, some scholars have delicately pointed out that this title was already in use for Mary.[52] Long before the Council of Ephesus, at least as early as the Council of Nicaea in 325, some bishops were already calling Mary "Theotokos," and they were calling her that without any definition or explanation. According to Richard Price, "The use of the word is incidental: it is not explained or justified, and no weight is placed upon it. The implication is that by the time of the Council of Nicaea in 325 the term was already in standard use."[53] The earliest undisputed use of Theotokos for Mary is in 319, when Bishop Alexander of Alexandria used Theotokos for Mary.[54] Decades before the Council of Ephesus, some of the most influential people in the Empire—from the famed Trinitarian theologian Athanasius (296–273) to the pagan Roman Emperor Julian "the Apostate" (330–363)[55]—are recorded calling Mary the Theotokos. Additional evidence indicates the title was used for Mary in the third century.[56]

Consistent with the early use of Theotokos for Mary, literature that elevated Mary, such as the *Protevangelium* and the Dormition narrative, which portrayed Mary as someone who, like her son, was born without a man's seed and bodily taken up to heaven, was composed centuries before the Council of Ephesus.[57] Finally, as we saw earlier in Chapter 2, after the Council of Ephesus, some scribes were not elevating Mary, they were demoting her—they were excising passages that portrayed her with liturgical authority.

Recently, some scholars have questioned the validity of the old hypothesis that the Council caused Mariology.[58] A false premise has kept the old hypothesis alive. That false premise is that the triumphal arch mosaics in the huge Maria Maggiore Basilica in Rome elevated Mary. Since these mosaics were completed shortly *after* the Council of Ephesus, they are presented as evidence that, nonetheless, somehow, the Council must have kicked off Mariology. Over the decades, however, some art historians have quietly concluded that the Maria Maggiore mosaics do *not* elevate Mary as the Theotokos.[59]

The first clue that the Maria Maggiore Basilica mosaics were not designed to elevate Mary as Theotokos is that the basilica's dedicatory inscription did not call her Theotokos. Nor did the inscription call Mary by her equivalent Western title, Mother of God. Instead, Sixtus III dedicated the basilica to *Virgo Maria*—the Virgin Mary.[60]

The second clue that the mosaics were not intended to elevate Mary is that Mary was not depicted with a halo in these mosaics. King Herod overseeing the Massacre of the Innocents has a halo—but not Mary. Certainly, a halo for Mary was a design option, because much older fourth-century gold glass from the Christian catacombs of Rome depicted a woman usually identified as Mary[61]—an arms-raised woman with MARIA or MARA written over her head[62]—with a halo. For two examples, see Fig. 5.8.

Fig. 5.8 Mary with halo. Late 300s gold glass from the Christian catacombs, Rome. Perret, *Catacombes de Rome*, pl. 4:21.1 and 7

The third clue that these mosaics were not intended to elevate Mary is that the scene of the Adoration of the Magi (the wise men bearing gifts) was unique, never seen before and never seen again. Instead of elevating Mary's motherhood, as was typical in older scenes of the Adoration of the Magi, the mosaic designer de-coupled mother and son. For the first time, the child was seen seated alone on a huge throne, his mother divided into two women seated on either side of him, neither touching him, much less holding him. This scene is so extraordinarily peculiar that Beat Brenk calls it "the most unusual scene in Early Christian art."[63]

Before viewing the Maria Maggiore mosaic of the Adoration of the Magi, it is important to first view older artifacts of the Adoration of the Magi in Rome, because this iconography was very popular, with dozens of older examples still in existence.[64] The Maria Maggiore mosaics broke with the way earlier artists—as well as later artists—portrayed Mary's relationship with her son. The older iconography almost universally portrayed Mary holding her son on her lap. For example, an early fourth-century fresco in the Petrus and Marcellinus catacomb in Rome portrays Mary holding him on her lap while she is seated on a tall round-backed chair. They are flanked by two men holding out platters[65] (see Fig. 5.9).

Fig. 5.9   Mary holds her son. Two magi bring platters. Early 300s fresco of the Adoration of the Magi, Rome. Wilpert, *Malereien*, pl. 60

Although today we are accustomed to three men bearing gifts, neither Matthew, nor Luke nor the *Protevangelium*, specifies how many magi came. Early Christian artists portrayed two to four magi. These wise men were almost always dressed as Phrygians with colorful tunics, leggings, and floppy, peaked caps. In addition, their gifts were often depicted as large round platters, as if for communion bread, sometimes with tiny pieces on the platter, also seen in Fig. 5.9.

In the context of the scene of the Adoration of the Magi in the Maria Maggiore mosaics, the most important comparative example is a wood panel on the doors of Santa Sabina Basilica dated 420–430—it thus was carved only a few years before the Council of Ephesus. Here, the gifts appear to be round flat loaves of bread, and the one offered by the first magi is even etched with a large four-sided cross, as if for the communion. This wood sculptor literally elevated Mary. She is carved seated atop six steps, holding her infant son, herself the seventh, holy, level (see Fig. 5.10).

Fig. 5.10   Mary holds her son, elevated. Three magi bring platters. 420–430, Santa Sabina Basilica, Rome. Wiegand, *Altchristliche*, pl. 13

Santa Sabina Basilica was constructed under Pope Celestine (r. 422–432), who died almost immediately after the Council of Ephesus, *before* news of the council reached Rome. Clearly, as this wood panel demonstrates, even before the Council of Ephesus he was comfortable with art that elevated Mary. He may have been the pope who began construction of the huge Maria Maggiore Basilica dedicated to Mary. Although two inscriptions identify the next pope, Pope Sixtus III (r. 432–440), as the pope who *completed* Maria Maggiore, archeological evidence related to its construction indicates that Pope Celestine may have *started* it. Maria Maggiore's construction method is the same as Santa Sabina's— and different than any church built in the decade after Celestine died.[66] Thus, if Pope Celestine had lived just a few more years, we might today see an Adoration scene in Maria Maggiore like the one carved on the Santa Sabina wood panel. Instead, we see a completely novel scene— the scene that Brenk calls "the most unusual" in early Christian art[67]—a scene where the infant Jesus sits by himself on a huge throne, a scene that divides his mother into two women seated on either side of him, one dressed in gold, one in black, neither touching him. It is as if the child has two mothers, yet no mother at all. Which of the two parallel women beside the infant represents his mother—and *who* is the second woman?—is still debated[68] (see Fig. 5.11).

Here again, we see the magi dressed as Phrygians with their floppy caps and tunics, carrying large round platters laden with what appears to

Fig. 5.11 *Top*: Adoration of the Magi. Child sits alone. Two women flank him. *Below*: Herod with halo, directing soldiers. 432–440. Maria Maggiore Basilica. © DeA Picture Library, concesso in licenza ad Alinari

be pieces of bread. Yet here Mary does not hold her son. Cleo McNelly Kearns describes mother and son in older scenes of the Adoration of the Magi as a "unity" or "the mother-son dyad."[69] Here, the mosaic designer divided the mother-son dyad. This strange composition of the Adoration of the Magi suggests that the patron of these mosaics did not intend to elevate Mary or her motherhood. Not only is the mother-son dyad divided, but also we cannot even tell for certain which woman is his mother. Further signifying Mary's demotion, neither of these women has a halo. Yet directly below them, King Herod—in the scene where he orders his soldiers to kill all the male children who were under two years old (Matthew 2:16)—has a large yellow halo.

Three more mosaic panels on the triumphal arch depict Mary, always without a halo. One, an Annunciation scene that portrays her weaving, a scene from the *Protevangelium*, naturally does not have her son in the scene with her because he was not yet conceived. The two that do depict her son with her further demonstrate that the patron of these mosaics wanted to symbolically demote Mary's motherhood in the public eye.

Only one mosaic panel shows Mary actually touching her son. That panel is top right, high above the floor of the nave. In addition to the height, it is hard to identify Mary in it because she is off center and smaller than the people who are in the center.[70] In the panel directly below this one, Mary is even further off center. In this scene, as in the scene of the Adoration of the Magi, Mary does not hold her son. Again the mother-son dyad is divided. A man was placed standing *between* Mary and her son. As if that were not enough to convince the laity in the nave that Mary was not all that important, the panel below *again* depicts Herod, with his big halo, directly below Mary—a positioning that appears to be intended to highlight that even compared to Herod the babykiller, Mary herself is not holy enough or regal enough—or Theotokos enough—to have a halo.[71]

One final detail strongly suggests that the patron of these mosaics wanted Mary to literally disappear. In all four registers, Mary is dressed in gold against a gold mosaic background—which makes her disappear into the background, as seen in Fig. 5.11. Some scholars propose that Mary dressed in gold suggests her elevation, either divine or imperial.[72] Yet Mary does not have a halo, nor, as Maria Lidova notes, does she have a crown.[73] Regardless why Mary was dressed in gold, the designer of these mosaics almost certainly knew that dressing Mary in the same gold color as the gold background would make her form disappear.

In conclusion, the premise that the Maria Maggiore mosaics elevate Mary is false. When compared with depictions of Mary in older art—whether on gold catacomb glass or in older scenes of the Adoration of the magi—it is apparent that the design of the Maria Maggiore mosaics was not intended to elevate her. The overall design of the mosaics appears to signify a powerful opposition to Mary as Theotokos—at least in the city of Rome at that moment in time.

This opposition, however, like the pope himself, was transitory. The strange iconography of the Adoration of the Magi is never seen again in art, despite that it was prominently displayed in one of the four largest basilicas in Christendom. Instead, art that elevated Mary continued to be installed in Rome. For example, around the year 700, Pope John VII installed a monumental mosaic cycle of Mary's life in his oratory in Old Saint Peter's Basilica, a cycle which included the Adoration of the Magi. Here, the laity saw the mother-son dyad the same way we see it in catacomb art: Mary seated on a large chair, her son on her lap, the magi bringing gifts.[74]

It is uncertain whether the papal patron behind the Maria Maggiore mosaics was Pope Sixtus III or his archdeacon, the future Pope Leo the Great.[75] Whoever it was, in Chapter 7 below, I provide a plausible reason for his opposition to Mary as Theotokos. For now, suffice it to say that his opposition almost certainly was related to the dispute that led to the Council of Ephesus in the first place—a conflict between Nestorius, the new patriarch of Constantinople, and the Augusta, the Princess Pulcheria, who herself invoked Mary the Theotokos.[76]

THE MOTHER-SON DYAD IN ART PRIOR
TO THE COUNCIL OF EPHESUS

Silver stamps on a handful of liturgical objects, such as some censers, prove that some Christians continued to pair Mary and her son into the seventh century. The late fourth-century San Nazaro silver reliquary box demonstrates that some Christians were already pairing mother and son in the late fourth century. A second fourth-century reliquary box adds to the accumulation of evidence that artists were pairing them well before the Council of Ephesus.[77]

In the early 1970s in Novalje, near the city of Zadar in modern Croatia, someone digging in their courtyard discovered a copper-sheathed reliquary box that was buried along with other objects typical of the fourth century.[78] The Novalje box was covered with thin sheets repetitively stamped with two tiers of frames depicting ten scenes, five from Hebrew scripture and five from the gospels. This iconography is consistent with that of fourth-century frescos and gold glass from the Christian catacombs of Rome, including the way that the letters of names are sometimes in sections on both sides. A boyish shepherd titled with the word for shepherd in Latin, PASTOR, is in the middle of the gospels scenes.[79] On this unquestionably Christian artifact, the shepherd almost certainly represents Jesus, who, in John 10:11–21, said, "I am the good shepherd." Next to the shepherd is an arms-raised woman with Mary's name in Latin on either side of her head, MARIA. Here, Mary as the arms-raised woman and Jesus as the shepherd function as counterparts (see Fig. 5.12).

Fig. 5.12 PASTOR and MARIA. Novalje Reliquary Box, late 300s. Courtesy David Edward Kateusz and Archeological Museum Zadar

The Novalje reliquary box is in the Archeological Museum of Zadar. A recent reconstruction overseen by the museum's director, Jakob Vučić, indicates that this image of MARIA originally appeared ten times around the sides and lid. This stamping presupposes a mold and suggests mass manufacture. Given the amount of trade around the Mediterranean during the fourth century, it is impossible to say where the mold, or the stamped sheathing, or even the box, originated. Nonetheless, the mass production implicit in its mode of manufacture suggests that the pairing of mother and son was common in art.

This secure identification of Mary as the arms-raised woman in this fourth-century pairing means that with some confidence, we can also identify similar pairs of an arms-raised woman and a shepherd as symbolizing Mary and her son. A pairing similar to that on the Novalje box is on a fourth-century sarcophagus found near Arles in Ancient Gaul, today in the Museé de l'Arles antique. On the Novalje box, the shepherd and arms-raised woman named MARIA are side-by side and flanked by frames depicting gospel scenes. On this sarcophagus front, they also are side-by-side and flanked by gospel scenes[80] (see Fig. 5.13).

Fig. 5.13 Paired on sarcophagus. Flanked by gospel scenes. Sarcophagus fragment, second quarter of the fourth century. Courtesy Author and Musée Départemental Arles antique. Sarcophagus of the Good Shepherd, second quarter of the fourth century, Carrera marble, ferous alloy. Inv. No. FAN.92.00.2521

Another pairing is on what may be the oldest known Eucharistic utensil. This lead vessel stamped with early Christian symbols that was found in Tunisia and is dated between 350 and the early 400s.[81] Tertullian, who lived in Tunisia, wrote about Christians who painted the shepherd on their cups and chalices to represent Jesus. This artist seems to have followed that iconographic tradition.[82] This artist paired the shepherd and the arms-raised woman on opposite faces of the utensil, much as later chalices paired them. Other symbols on the vessel, such as two deer drinking from a stream with a cross above, identify it unquestionably as Christian. The vessel was inscribed, "Take the water with joy."[83] Some first-century Jewish communities, such as the Therapeutae, in their gender-parallel meal ritual in Judea, used only water, not wine. Andrew B. McGowan says early Jesus communities also had a variety of Eucharistic rituals, and by the end of the first century, at the latest, some used bread and water, not bread and wine.[84] It seems likely this vessel was used by that stream of Christianity (see Fig. 5.14).

Fig. 5.14 Arms-raised woman and shepherd on a vessel: "Take the water with joy." 350 to early 400s. Tunisia. De Rossi, "Secchia di piombo"

MOTHER AND SON PAIRED
IN THIRD- AND FOURTH-CENTURY FUNEREAL ART

According to Robin Jensen, during the third and fourth centuries the arms-raised woman and shepherd "were extremely popular and appear in Christian art more than any biblical subject."[85] Could they be the mother-son dyad? The fourth-century Novalje box's identification of an arms-raised woman named Mary paired with a shepherd representing Jesus in the midst of gospel scenes provides a new possibility for one of the greatest art history mysteries—who is the arms-raised woman in Christian catacomb art? More than two hundred images of this woman have been found in the Christian catacombs, but scholars have yet to agree who, or what, she represents.[86]

Some scholars call this arms-raised woman, who was so prevalent in catacomb art, a metaphor, an allegory of the church, a symbol of the soul, or some other symbol.[87] Stine Birk says the arms-raised gesture on a woman in catacomb art is "suggestive of some of the social roles that were open to women in early Christian society. She could apparently teach, preach, or act as a spiritual leader—even for men."[88] In the Vatican Museum, the arms-raised woman is almost always called a deceased woman. Nicola Denzey describes the oddity of seeing so many catacomb images of deceased women: "Where are the men and children in these family graves?"[89]

Jensen suggests that the frequent juxtaposition of the arms-raised woman and the shepherd in the Christian catacombs "justifies explaining the pairing as a convention of early Christian funerary imagery. The two balanced each other. Perhaps one represented the deceased's prayers for salvation and the other the one who could fulfill those prayers."[90] Jensen's interpretation mirrors the roles of Mary and Jesus in the Dormition narrative, where Mary raised her arms and prayed, and Jesus came down and took her up with him to heaven, fulfilling her prayers. For the bereaved, this pair served as an illustration of the power of prayer, and especially, of Jesus's promise that the beloved dead would live again. Sculptors often paired the arms-raised woman and the shepherd, sometimes on plaques,[91] sometimes on the opposite ends of sarcophagi, balancing each other, and sometimes, they flanked a portrait of the deceased[92] (see Figs. 5.15 and 5.16).

Fig. 5.15 Arms-raised woman and shepherd paired on catacomb plaque. Third-century, Rome. Vatican Museum. Marucchi, *Monumenti del Museo Cristiano*, pl. 57

In a 2015 article in the *Journal of Early Christian Studies*, I proposed that an anonymous woman, or her family, may have commissioned frescos in the Cubiculum of the Velata in the Priscilla Catacomb with the intent of patterning her portrait after Mary.[93] The association of Mary with women, especially when she was described arms-raised, seems likely to have been an old tradition. In any case, the Six Books originally contained multiple scenes of Mary raising her arms to bless women. For example, the "S-2" fragment says Mary "called the women of her neighborhood," invited them to go to Bethlehem with her, and then "stretched out her hands to heaven, and blessed them."[94] The medieval Arabic preserves that when women came from around the Mediterranean to Jerusalem, Mary raised her arms and blessed them.[95] Yet another scene, partially preserved in both the fifth-century palimpsest and the Arabic, originally depicted Mary raising her hands and blessing the women who lived with her.[96]

Fig. 5.16 Arms-raised woman and shepherd paired on opposite ends of sarcophagus. In the center, the deceased woman holds a scroll. Italian sarcophagus, third century, marble. Detroit Institute of Arts, City of Detroit Purchase, 26.138

The Cubiculum of the Velata contains what appears to be the core vertical composition of the Six Books scene. The large central woman stands with her arms raised directly beneath a shepherd inside a circle. The arms-raised woman is flanked by two vignettes, each depicting a young woman with similar facial features. The right-hand vignette portrays the young woman seated on a large round-backed chair holding an infant in a composition that closely resembles the way Mary looks holding her infant in the fresco of the Adoration of the Magi, above in Fig. 5.9. The left-hand vignette portrays three people, a young woman holding what is usually identified as a book or a scroll, along with a bearded man next to her, and a young, beardless man standing behind her. Some scholars suggest that a woman holding a book wanted to be remembered as literate.[97] A book could also mean that she wanted to be remembered like Mary, because the Dormition narratives associated Mary with books, as did Ambrose (340–397) and Jerome (347–420).[98] The deceased woman's portrait therefore may have been patterned after Mary. If so, these three scenes signified that the deceased woman, like Mary, had been a mother, a literate woman, and a religious leader (see Fig. 5.17).

The oldest surviving example of the core vertical composition *aboveground* is on a wood door panel on the doors of the Santa Sabina Basilica. These are the same doors that preserved the Adoration of the Magi with Mary holding her son while elevated as the seventh step.[99] When the door panel with the core vertical composition and the fresco in the Cubiculum of the Velata are compared side-by-side, the similarities between the two compositions are substantial. In both, a young man stands inside a circle. He holds up his right hand, as if in greeting. Directly beneath him stands an arms-raised woman. On the panel, she is portrayed in the less powerful-looking semi-profile *Madonna advocata* arms-raised pose that became so popular for Mary in Rome. In the catacombs, a peacock, the symbol of eternal life, was painted over her head, while on the church door, a circle with a cross was carved over her head. The biggest difference is that in the Cubiculum of the Velata, she is flanked by two vignettes that feature a woman, whereas on the church door a century later, she is flanked by two men—one balding and one with bangs, Paul and Peter[100] (see Figs. 5.17 and 5.18).

The Santa Sabina wood door panel is adjacent to a second panel that depicts Jesus being lifted by angels into the clouds—a scene very much

Fig. 5.17 Flanked by frescos of a woman. Ca. 300. Cubiculum of the Velata, Priscilla catacomb, Rome. Courtesy J.M. Gilbreath

like one on a famous ivory dated 400, which likewise depicts Jesus being lifted into the clouds, but which also has a second scene below it, which depicts the two Marys at the tomb. The women at the tomb in the composition suggest that that when Jesus is seen lifted into the clouds, it represents his ascension.[101] Thus, iconography depicting the heavenly ascents of both mother and son are seen, side-by-side, on the Santa Sabina doors—just as mother and son were paired in so much other art.

The long cultural durée of Marian religion, a continuity most clearly witnessed in art, is evoked by the images of a woman in modern cemeteries around Rome. The woman portrayed in these cemeteries is never considered the portrait of a dead woman—despite that sometimes her portrait is placed over the door of a family mausoleum or on

Fig. 5.18 Flanked
by Peter and Paul.
420–430. Santa Sabina
Basilica door panel,
Rome. Wiegand,
Altchristliche, pl. 18

a tombstone. Sometimes she is portrayed praying while standing by her-self. Sometimes she is portrayed with her son, both as an infant and as a grown man. Although, as in the catacombs, this featured woman is vir-tually never named, the families who buy the tombstones and tend the memory of their dead seem to know who she is—*Mary pray for us.*[102]

Mary is the sole woman who in the fourth century was identified by name when depicted arms-raised and paired with a shepherd—on the Novalje reliquary box. The pairing of mother and son, however, is seen in even older catacomb art, from the Adoration of the Magi to their pair-ing on sarcophagi. This pairing continued for centuries in art, includ-ing perhaps most prominently, on Eucharistic utensils. The Six Books explains why mother and son were vertically paired; this iconography represented the scene of her praying to her son in heaven, a scene associated with her own death and ascension, or Assumption, to heaven. But why were mother and son horizontally paired? Did their side-by-side pairing perhaps represent a scene from a long lost, or nearly lost, gospel?

CHAPTER 6

The *Life of the Virgin* and Its Antecedents

The scene that most clearly explains why Mary was depicted as a high priest, as well as being paired with her son on liturgical utensils, is preserved only in Tbilisi A-40, the oldest manuscript of the *Life of the Virgin*.[1] The *Life of the Virgin* is a biography compiled from much older texts, whose author detailed Mary's entire life—not only her birth and death as told in ancient recensions of the popular *Protevangelium* and Dormition narratives but also a nearly lost account of her activities during her son's ministry. This account is by far the longest, fullest, most detailed narrative about Mary and other women during the ministry of Jesus—and more than found in any other surviving Christian text, its author remembered a discipleship of equals, such as Elisabeth Schüssler Fiorenza hypothesized.[2]

This author elevated not only Mary, but also the other women and described a Second Temple Jewish community around Jerusalem where the impulse toward gender parity was strong.[3] For example, in stark contrast to theologians who emphasized a chain of male apostolic authority, the *Life of the Virgin*'s author also called women "apostle" and portrayed Mary Magdalene "as an apostle equal in rank to Peter."[4] In an echo of the Six Books, which described Mary giving women small books to take

This chapter in part is an update and expansion of Ally Kateusz, "'She Sacrificed Herself as the Priest': Early Christian Female and Male Co-Priests," *Journal of Feminist Studies in Religion* 33, no. 1 (Spring 2017): 45–67. *Feminae* Article of the Month, March 2018.

© The Author(s) 2019
A. Kateusz, *Mary and Early Christian Women*,
https://Doi.org/10.1007/978-3-030-11111-3_6

131

around the Mediterranean, this text describes Mary, after her son died, teaching the apostles, both male and female, closely supervising their preaching, and sending them forth to evangelize.[5]

Mary was inseparable from her son, this author repeatedly said, and she was present at all his healings and miracles, as were the women disciples.[6] This author called the women "disciples," seemingly unaware, despite repeatedly quoting scripture, that the gospels of Matthew, Mark, Luke, and John never call the women disciples "disciples."[7] Sometimes this author reported women disciples where the canonical gospels were silent about who was present, and sometimes even where the canonical author remembered only men. For example, Matthew and Luke are silent on who was present when Jesus healed Peter's mother-in-law, but Mark 1:29–31 depicts only male disciples present. By contrast, the *Life of the Virgin*'s author remembered only female disciples there: "When the Lord entered Peter's house and healed his mother-in-law, who was confined to her bed because of a fever, his all-holy and blessed mother, the Virgin Mary, was with him as well as the women who were disciples of the Lord."[8] This author's identification of women specifically as "disciples" affects how the term "disciples" is understood in the rest of the narrative. For example, when the *Life of the Virgin* says that the "disciples" baptized people, this does not mean that only male disciples baptized.[9] It means that women disciples were baptizing people also, just as the *Acts of Philip* described Mariamne baptizing, and just as the other long narratives about women apostles described those women baptizing people.[10]

According to this account, Mary and the women disciples were at the last supper along with the men. The institution of the Eucharist at the last supper has been used as an excuse to exclude women from officiating, because supposedly only men were at the meal, but the author of the *Life of the Virgin* described both men and women there, as if Jesus's first-century followers had participated in a gender-parallel meal similar to that of the first-century Therapeutae Jews of Judea.[11] The very oldest manuscript of the *Life of the Virgin*, the eleventh-century Tbilisi A-40, preserved yet one more scene of gender parity at this shared meal. During the meal, first Mary, and then her son, modeled a ritual of female and male co-priesthood. According to the text, Mary was the teacher of the women and, "for this reason," at the supper, "she sacrificed herself as the priest and she was sacrificed, she offered and she was offered."[12] Then, Jesus offered his body and blood:

She was always inseparable from the Lord and king her son, and as the Lord had authority over the twelve apostles and then the seventy, so the holy mother had over the other women who accompanied him, as the holy evangelist said, "There were there many women who followed Jesus from Galilee and who served him." The holy Theotokos was their leader and teacher. For this reason when the great mystery, the supper, took place, she sacrificed herself as the priest and she was sacrificed. She offered and she was offered. Then the Lord Jesus presided over the twelve apostles and those he wanted, and he delivered the sublime mysteries and signs of God's Passover, he gave them some of his precious body and blood as the bread and the drink.[13]

This supper scene would appear to explain why Mary was widely portrayed as a Eucharistic officiant, for example, wearing the episcopal pallium or holding the Eucharistic cloth, as well as why she and her son were paired on Eucharistic utensils. When was this supper scene originally conceived or composed? Was it derived from first-century memories of a ritual meal?

In analyzing this passage, it is important to know that leading scholars of first- and second-century Jesus followers are of nearly one accord that these groups met more or less exclusively in small reclining meal groups.[14] The leadership patterns of these groups were relatively informal, featuring a bevy of symposiarchs (presidents) who alternated every meeting,[15] and various hosts when the groups were able to meet in a home.[16] This was all in the context of great conviviality and informal rules for a long and festive gathering.[17] There is much evidence that women and men led such groups regularly.[18]

Almost certainly no one who was actually at Jesus's final meal wrote about it. Later memories, passed down through oral tradition until finally pen was put to papyrus, and then edited again, provide our clouded window onto the distant event itself. Even the canonical gospel writers did not agree what day the supper took place, or what events led up to it. The supper, especially as told in John, could easily encompass women as well as men being present. Here then the proposal for a strong relationship between the supper scene in the *Life of the Virgin* and the first-century "last supper" is textual in that the *Life of the Virgin*'s text has a strong content and literary connection to 1 Corinthians, Markan, Matthean, and Johannine first-century texts. It may also have a theological connection to Galatians 3:28, because

Epiphanius of Salamis (ca. 310–403) reported that some Jesus groups used that verse to justify female as well as male officiants: "They have women bishops, presbyters and the rest; they say that none of this makes any difference because 'In Christ Jesus there is neither male nor female.'"[19] This Pauline gender theology would appear to be consistent with Mary and Jesus officiating together at the meal ritual described in the *Life of the Virgin*.

The meal ritual in the *Life of the Virgin* also appears to have a strong content parallel with Philo's description of an early first-century Judean meal ritual among the Therapeutae, which is the most detailed first-century liturgy that has survived from any Jewish or Christian community. In addition to men and women being present at the ritual meal, Philo likewise described two leaders, a male, and a female. Among the Therapeutae, the male represented Moses and the female, Miriam. Other parallels include the names *Mariam* and *Miriam* and that both women were considered prophetesses.[20] Most revealing is that for both Mary and Miriam, her leadership of the other women was given as the reason for why she was paired with her son or brother during the meal ritual.[21] Although distant from Jerusalem, the liturgy of the Therapeutae signified the Temple, complete with raised arms, two choirs, bread as holy food, a time of libation, an altar table, and priests.[22] Joan E. Taylor says, "Ultimately, both men and women saw themselves not only as attendants or suppliants but as priests in this Temple."[23] Brooten's study of stone epigraphs that memorialized Jewish women with titles such as "Head of the Synagogue," "Mother of the Synagogue," "Elder," and "Priestess," suggests that the Therapeutae's gender-parallel ritual, or similar, may have continued in some synagogues in the Mediterranean diaspora.[24] Some Jesus groups, especially those about whom we know very little because their writings were later anathematized, potentially also may have had such rituals. For example, there were "ebionite" and other Jesus groups around Jerusalem, who were embedded in the culture of Israel and Judea.

A Judean meal ritual that signified the Temple liturgy evokes Mary's own association with the Jerusalem Temple, including the way that she sometimes was depicted as a Temple priest. Perhaps just as significant in interpreting this ritual meal, Lily Vuong has detailed how the *Protevangelium*'s author repeatedly described Mary as a Temple sacrifice.[25] Here, Mary appears to have arrived at the sacrifice foretold. She sacrifices herself as the priest and she is sacrificed.

In searching for the source of this narrative, the *Life of the Virgin*'s scribe left us a clue. This scribe claimed to have compiled the text from canonical gospels and patristic teachings, but also, "from apocryphal writings that were also true and without error and had been accepted and confirmed by the saintly fathers."[26] In this chapter and the next, I demonstrate that some of the literary antecedents behind the *Life of the Virgin*, including especially antecedents behind its scene of Jesus and Mary presiding together at the last supper, appear to have been writings from the earliest centuries of the Jesus movements.

The Oldest Text of the *Life of the Virgin*

Originally penned in Greek, the *Life of the Virgin* survives in an Old Georgian manuscript tradition that unanimously identifies its composer as Maximus the Confessor (580–662), although he probably was not its author.[27] Perhaps his name was later added to protect the text, for he was revered in Georgia. Shoemaker proposed that it was written not long after the seventh-century Avar siege of Constantinople, a time when Marian appreciation blossomed along with the legend that Mary had run along the city walls and killed the enemy herself, thereby ensuring victory and saving the city.[28] Recently, however, Phil Booth proposed that the *Life of the Virgin* was composed as late as the tenth or even eleventh century, a proposition Shoemaker attempted to rebut.[29]

My primary concern with Booth's argument for a tenth-century dating of the *Life of the Virgin*'s compilation is that Booth essentially argues that all the texts which the compiler of the *Life of the Virgin* used in this composition were available in the tenth century. Yet Booth overlooks some important early narrative elements found solely in books that by the tenth century had been lost or severely censored. For example, narrative elements found only in the fifth-century palimpsest text undergird the post-Passion Dormition narrative that concludes the *Life of the Virgin*—yet Booth asserts that there is "no evidence at all that the author of the text translated in the *Georgian Life* has before him a version of the *Six Books*, and … there are no narrative elements within the *Georgian Life* which are absent from the *Transitus* but present in the *Six Books*."[30] On this, Booth is incorrect. As an analysis of Booth's footnotes demonstrates, he unfortunately made his claim looking only at the shorter sixth-century Six Books; he did not cite the long fifth-century Six Books palimpsest.[31] As the chart in Fig. 2.9 illustrates, four important narrative elements, or motifs, are found in both the *Life of the Virgin* and the long fifth-century Six Books palimpsest—but not in the sixth-century Six Books nor in the later Six Books Greek homily (Booth's "*Transitus*"). These four narrative elements are Mary preaching, Mary teaching women, Mary sending evangelists out from Jerusalem, and Mary raising her hands in the context of blessing people besides the Twelve.[32] Across the eight manuscripts that I analyzed, the only ones to preserve all four of these narrative elements together are the fifth-century palimpsest and the Georgian *Life of the Virgin*. Furthermore, in most cases, the *Life of the Virgin* preserves the most detailed narrative associated with these four motifs, which, given the trajectory of redaction demonstrated in Chapter 2, strongly suggests that its compiler had access to an even longer and older narrative than preserved in the fifth-century palimpsest. It thus seems likely that the *Life of the Virgin* was compiled well before Booth proposes, because even the fifth-century Six Books text itself was concealed in the eighth century when a scribe scrubbed and wrote over it, making it into a palimpsest. Regardless, the particular century in which the *Life of the Virgin* was compiled is not of great importance to my argument; I am more focused on the ancient books—"apocryphal writings that were also true and without error and had been accepted and confirmed by the saintly fathers"[33]—upon which the compiler claimed to have relied when compiling it.

In 1986, Michel van Esbroeck, a Jesuit scholar who had already published an Old Georgian dictionary and over two dozen Georgian texts, published the critical edition and French translation of the oldest surviving manuscript of the *Life of the Virgin*, the eleventh-century Tbilisi A-40. He apparently anticipated questions about its supper scene with Mary sacrificing, because he analyzed the passage at length, both from within the text itself and also across variants in other manuscripts.[34] For example, van Esbroeck noted that later in the narrative, Mary was called "a second sacrifice," which tends to affirm the reading "she sacrificed herself as the priest."[35] Van Esbroeck also extensively compared Tbilisi A-40 to Jerusalem 108, a later manuscript of the *Life of the Virgin*, as well as to John Geometrician's tenth-century revision of the *Life of the Virgin*.[36] Both of their meal scenes omitted Mary's role as an officiant, but with different variants, and van Esbroeck therefore concluded that both variants were differently censored versions of the text preserved in Tbilisi A-40.[37]

In 2012, in his first published Georgian translation, Shoemaker presented what he purported was a new translation of the *Life of the Virgin*, which he said would correct what he called van Esbroeck's "mistakes," "unintelligibility," and "hyper-literalism."[38] Shoemaker, surprisingly, did not retranslate Tbilisi A-40. He instead relied upon three different manuscripts, the first being Jerusalem 108[39]—the same manuscript that van Esbroeck said contained a censored Last Supper. Shoemaker mentioned neither van Esbroeck's claim that Jerusalem 108 was censored, nor that it was dated thirteenth to sixteenth century, up to five hundred years later than Tbilisi A-40.[40]

Most directly relevant to the thesis of this chapter, Shoemaker's edition erased the scene of Mary sacrificing as the priest at the supper. Where van Esbroeck's translation read that Mary sacrificed herself, Shoemaker's was identical except for its gender; Shoemaker's reads "*he* sacrificed *himself*"[41]—the very same variant in Jerusalem 108 that van Esbroeck called censored.[42] Shoemaker briefly justifies his gender change in a footnote, primarily by citing one of his own articles.[43]

In that article, Shoemaker admitted that van Esbroeck's translation is plausible: "On a rhetorical level, then, it seems rather plausible that Mary should, in fact, be understood as this sentence's subject who somehow at the Last Supper offered herself as a reconciling sacrifice"—but, he added, a text that actually elevated Mary that far was, for him, "rather difficult to imagine."[44] Shoemaker then ended his discussion of the passage with the argument that van Esbroeck's translation was undermined by John Geometrician's variant[45]—yet he neglected to mention that van Esbroeck himself had at length argued the very opposite. Van Esbroeck, as mentioned above, argued that John Geometrician's complex variant, together with Jerusalem 108's simple variant—two variants, each of which eliminated Mary's priesthood, but in different ways—validated van Esbroeck conclusion that both later scribes had censored the original text preserved in Tbilisi A-40.[46]

Shoemaker's translation contains other changes to some of van Esbroeck's descriptions of female religious authority. Sometimes Shoemaker footnotes these changes. For example, where van Esbroeck called the women who evangelized with John "apostles," Shoemaker calls them "co-apostles"[47]—but footnotes a minor spelling correction, concluding, "Of course, the meaning is the same in either case."[48] In other instances, and despite that he footnotes dozens of small one-letter

changes to van Esbroeck's Georgian text, Shoemaker does not footnote some of the far more significant changes that his text makes to van
Esbroeck's edition, changes that in some cases erase ancient descriptions
of female authority preserved in Tbilisi A-40. Following are three of the
most important.

THE ANNUNCIATION TO MARY IN THE TEMPLE

The first important change that Shoemaker does not footnote is where
Tbilisi A-40's text describes an Annunciation scene that took place while
Mary was praying "between the doors of the altar."[49] A bright light lit
up the Temple and "from the altar" a bodiless voice said, "Mary, from
you my son will be born."[50] Mary's proximity to the altar in this scene
suggests her priesthood—but Shoemaker's edition removes her from the
altar area. His edition, instead, says Mary was praying "in front of the
doors of the sanctuary" and that the voice came "from the sanctuary."[51]

Indicating the plausibility of van Esbroeck's reading of Tbilisi A-40—
that the Annunciation took place while Mary was at the Temple altar—
the third-century *Gospel of Bartholomew*, sometimes called the *Questions
of Bartholomew*, preserves an Annunciation to Mary at the Temple
altar.[52] This gospel describes a great angel, who made the earth trem-
ble, partaking of bread and wine with Mary at the Temple altar. When
they finished their Eucharist ic meal, the angel announced: "Three years
more, and I shall send my word and you shall conceive my son."[53]

The antiquity of Tbilisi A-40's Annunciation scene is further
affirmed by the text of Papyrus Bodmer 5, the oldest manuscript of the
Protevangelium, the narrative about Mary's early life. Papyrus Bodmer
5 was penned during the third or fourth century and is one of the oldest Christian manuscripts, but according to its editor, Émile de Strycker,
its text already contained evidence of having been shortened as well as
the "corrections" of a second redactor.[54] George Zervos provided an
extensive analysis of Bodmer 5 and demonstrated that its oldest layer
described an Annunciation to Mary by a bodiless voice while she was
in the Temple[55]—much as in the Tbilisi A-40 narrative, where a bodiless voice spoke to Mary from the Temple altar. In the *Protevangelium*
narrative, the voice of the initial Annunciation to Mary is through a
bodiless voice, at which Mary, getting water, looks this way and that
for the source of the voice. Zervos identified the bodiless voice that
spoke to Mary as the voice of God in the Temple, which in rabbinic

tradition was known as the *Bath kol.*[56] According to Bodmer 5's text, after the Annunciation, Mary went and sat on the throne—*thronos.*[57] Zervos assessed that the "throne" upon which Mary sat originally must have been the throne of God in the Holy of Holies,[58] where the Protevangelium twice says Mary resided.[59] Zervos concluded that this Annunciation in the Temple "was one of the primary concerns of the ancient redactor."[60]

Building on Zervos's analysis of Bodmer 5, Michael Peppard recently argued that the Annunciation to Mary in the Temple by the *Bath kol* also appears to have been known to the artist who painted what is likely the oldest art of the Annunciation, a wall painting in the third-century Dura-Europos church baptistery. Peppard identified this wall painting as the Annunciation to Mary by the *Bath kol.*[61] The core iconography of this wall painting is almost identical to later iconographic analogues of the Annunciation to Mary at the well[62]—a woman looking over her shoulder in front of a water source[63]—and both Peppard and Zervos concluded that the water source may have represented the spring or laver in the Temple courtyard.[64] All later art of the Annunciation to Mary at a water source includes an angel, but this angel may have been added in order to harmonize the scene with the angel Gabriel who speaks in the Annunciation story of Luke 1:26–38. No angel is in the Dura-Europos painting, however, and a line drawing of the painting made in situ shows two rays pointing toward the woman's back; Peppard concludes that these rays perhaps visually represented the voice of God, the *Bath kol.*[65]

Tbilisi A-40 preserves an Annunciation to Mary by the *Bath kol* in the Temple as witnessed in Bodmer 5 and the Dura-Europos fresco. It also preserves that Mary was at the Temple altar, as witnessed in the *Gospel of Bartholomew.* Tbilisi A-40's Annunciation scene suggests that the compiler either had very early manuscripts of both texts and combined the Annunciation scenes, or, had access to an even earlier gospel, the gospel behind both the *Protevangelium* and *Gospel of Bartholomew.* This gospel source would appear also to be behind the Six Books palimpsest text, which says that after the Annunciation, Mary set out the censer of incense to God, which again invokes the Temple location of the Annunciation. While Shoemaker's edition preserves the Annunciation by the *Bath kol*, it omits that the voice came from the altar, and also, that Mary herself was at the altar. Only the text of Tbilisi A-40 preserves all these ancient narrative elements.

MARY AT THE BAPTISM OF HER SON

The second important way that van Esbroeck's edition differs from Shoemaker's is where the text of Tbilisi A-40 first suggests that Mary was at her son's baptism, and then subsequently affirms that she was there.[66] Mary's presence at her son's baptism, like her presence at his last meal, is a strong marker of her own ecclesial authority, including her right to baptize, such as seen in the palimpsest text, which described her sealing and sprinkling water on people in what appears to be an early baptismal ritual.[67] Luigi Gambero concluded that van Esbroeck's edition of Tbilisi A-40 depicted "Mary's presence at the baptism of her Son."[68] Shoemaker's edition subtly obscures this reading.

The canonical gospels are silent on whether Mary was at her son's baptism, but the *Life of the Virgin* places her there. First, the text internally places her there, because, as mentioned earlier, the text repeatedly states that she was inseparable from her son.[69] Second, additional passages further suggest she was there. One of these passages is in both van Esbroeck's and Shoemaker's edition. This passage states that before his baptism, Mary became "a disciple" of her son and never forgot anything he said or did.[70] This passage suggests that she was present with him in the next scene, the baptism. Shoemaker's edition has subtle differences that harmonize its account with the canonical baptismal account. For example, Shoemaker's edition states that Jesus taught his disciples "*after* his baptism."[71] Van Esbroek's edition of Tbilisi A-40, by contrast, states that Jesus taught the disciples "*with* his baptism"[72]—a phrasing that implies his disciples were at his baptism, disciples that included his mother since the narrator had just stated that she had become his disciple. Teaching his disciples *after* his baptism, per Shoemaker's text, suggests that they were not with him at his baptism. Teaching his disciples *with* his baptism, per Tbilisi A-40's text, strongly implies that they were there. Finally, when introducing Mary's role at Cana, Tbilisi A-40's text says that she "was there also"—*also*. This "also" signifies that she was with him at his baptism and in the desert—and *also* at Cana.[73] Shoemaker's edition omits the "also," and again does so without a footnote.[74]

Did ancient antecedents also portray Mary at her son's baptism? The only art of which I am aware that depicts Mary at her son's baptism is very old, the bottom right frame of the painted reliquary box from Palestine dated to the 500s (Fig. 4.3). Its artist portrayed Mary and a man standing behind John the Baptist, with angels holding Mary's black maphorion as if waiting to dry off Jesus. This art likely conserves a very old narrative scene, because two early Christian writings that have been lost, the Hebrew gospel and the *Preaching of Paul*, placed Mary at her son's baptism.

Like the estimated 85% of the writings known to have been written by Jesus followers in the first two centuries, but which did not survive,[75] no copy of either the Hebrew gospel or the *Preaching of Paul* survived. We know about them solely because some early Christian writers who quoted from them named them. For example, in the second to fourth centuries, a variety of patristic writers described, or quoted from, a gospel they usually called the *Gospel According to the Hebrews*, including Papias, Irenaeus, Pantaenus, Clement of Alexandria, Hegesippus, Hippolytus, Origen, Eusebius of Caesaria, Ephrem the Syrian, Didymus of Alexandria, Epiphanius of Salamis, John Chrysostom, and Jerome. Several said it was composed by Matthew in his native language.[76] Its earliest mention was probably by Papias, Bishop of Hierapolis (ca. 60–130), who reportedly said, "Matthew composed his history in the Hebrew dialect."[77] Irenaeus (ca. 130–203) similarly reported, "Matthew also issued a written Gospel among the Hebrews in their own dialect."[78] Some scholars propose that additional second-century writers, such as Ignatius, Polycarp, and Justin Martyr, may have been quoting from the Hebrew gospel when they quoted gospel sayings that are not in any of the canonical gospels.[79] The dating of the composition of the Hebrew gospel to either the first or the second century appears to largely depend on whether the scholar believes this gospel could be the lost source relied upon by the authors of both Matthew and Luke,[80] or not.[81]

By contrast, the *Preaching of Paul* was mentioned only once, in passing, by a third-century author known as pseudo-Cyprian. Most importantly in this context, according to pseudo-Cyprian, the *Preaching of Paul* contained an expanded scene of Jesus's baptism, a scene which included Mary telling her son what to do (much as she told him what to do at Cana). Pseudo-Cyprian complained that the scene in the *Preaching of Paul* included "both Christ confessing His own sin—although He alone did no sin at all—and almost compelled by his mother Mary unwillingly to receive John's baptism."[82]

The Hebrew gospel may have had three recensions used by different Christian communities around Jerusalem. At least, various writers referred to the gospel of the Hebrews, of the Nazareans, and of the

Ebionites. The gospel used by the Nazareans is relevant to the discussion of Mary at her son's baptism, because Jerome (347–420) recorded a passage from it which is similar to the passage in the *Preaching of Paul*. It describes Jesus's mother at his baptism as well as the remission of sins. According to Jerome, this gospel read, "Behold, the mother of the Lord and his brethren said to him: 'John the Baptist baptizes unto the remission of sins, let us go and be baptized by him.'"[83]

These two passages are the most explicit to suggest that Mary was at her son's baptism. Another well-known passage in the Hebrew gospel, however, merits consideration because it places Jesus's mother at his baptism, but in a different form. This passage was quoted twice by Origen (ca. 184–254), an influential theologian who lived in Alexandria and Palestine, and three times by Jerome.[84] For example, in his homily on the gospel of John, Origen referenced the *Gospel of the Hebrews* in a discussion of how John had "baptized with the Holy Spirit and with Fire," and then Origen quoted Jesus himself speaking of "My mother, the Holy Spirit."[85] Origen said: "There is nothing absurd in the Holy Spirit's being His mother."[86]

Worthy of a note here is that until the end of the fourth-century, "spirit" was grammatically feminine gendered in Syriac, a dialect of Aramaic. In Ancient Syria, scribes described Holy Spirit not only as female, but also as mother.[87] Evidence of this is preserved in the *Gospel of Thomas*,[88] the *Gospel of Philip*,[89] the *Gospel of the Egyptians*,[90] the *Odes of Solomon*,[91] the *Acts of Thomas*,[92] the *Acts of Philip*,[93] as well as other writings.[94] Even in the Latin West, the femaleness of Holy Spirit was apparently so important that some Latin Christians feminized the masculine-gendered *spiritus*—"spirit" in Latin—making it the feminine *spirita*. In any case, some Christian funeral epigraphs in Latin in the city of Rome and northern Africa, including one dated 291, use *spirita sancta* for Holy Spirit, instead of the grammatically correct masculine *spiritus sanctus*.[95] Around the end of the fourth century, however, scribes began to masculinize the gender of Holy Spirit, most notably in Ancient Syria, where "spirit" had always been grammatically feminine. Susan Ashbrook Harvey says when scribes began to change the gender from feminine to masculine, it "did violence to the fabric of the language."[96] Sebastian Brock adds that at the same time, "Syriac writers began to become wary about addressing Holy Spirit as Mother."[97] No one quite understands why scribes changed the gender of Holy Spirit, but perhaps it had something to do with the Council of Constantinople in 381, which added that the Holy Spirit "proceeds from the Father" to the Nicene Creed.[98] This creedal addition essentially defined the Holy Spirit as the same substance as the Father, that is, male.

It is with this understanding of Holy Spirit in Ancient Syria that we return to Origen, who lived in Caesaria on the coast of Palestine. In a second homily, Origen again quoted the same Gospel of the Hebrews passage, but this time he invoked Mary when explaining why the Holy Spirit was Jesus's mother:

> Is he not able to declare as women both soul and Mary? But if a person accepts these words: "My mother, the Holy Spirit, has recently taken me and carried me up to the great mount Tabor," and what follows, one is able to see his mother.[99]

Origen invoking Mary in this context of the Holy Spirit is reified in yet one more saying attributed to the Gospel of the Hebrews. This saying is in a homily on Mary, purportedly written by Cyril of Jerusalem (ca. 315–386), although quite possibly a later homilist wrote it under Cyril's name. This homilist described an encounter with a monk who was still using the Gospel of the Hebrews and recorded a saying that the monk quoted from it: "The 'power' came down into the world, and it was called Mary, and [Christ] was in her womb for seven months. Afterwards she gave birth to him."[100] Two additional statements in the homily, one earlier, and one later, help contextualize this saying. Earlier, apparently with this saying in mind, the homilist complained that some Christians believed, "She was a force (or, abstract power) of God which took the form of a woman, and came upon the earth, and was called 'Mary,' and this force gave birth to Emmanuel for us."[101] Although the homilist quoted Jesus's mother as a "power" who came down, and Origen quoted his mother as the Holy Spirit who descended, both were discussing Jesus's mother according to the Gospel of the Hebrews. Later, the homilist invoked Mary in the role of Holy Spirit in the baptismal ritual, and did so by using the same ritual formula, *in the name of Mary*, which both the liturgical manual embedded in the Six Books, as well as the "collyridian" women priests whom Epiphanius of Salamis described, used when sacrificing bread to Mary on the altar.[102] The homilist wrote that after he burned the monk's Gospel of the Hebrews, he baptized the monk *in the name of Mary*. He said, "I baptized him in the name of the Lady of us all, Saint Mary."[103]

What is most important at this juncture is that ancient sources, including repeatedly the Gospel of the Hebrews, in one form or another placed Jesus's mother at his baptism. Van Esbroeck's edition of the *Life of the Virgin* based on Tbilisi A-40 preserves the tradition that she was at her son's baptism. Shoemaker's, based on later manuscripts, does not.

THE WOMEN AT THE LORD'S SUPPER

Finally, the third important time that Shoemaker's edition, without any footnote, changes van Esbroeck's, is with respect to the women at Jesus's last meal. Shoemaker's edition replaces van Esbroeck's "twelve apostles" with "twelve disciples."[104] This substitution has the effect of obscuring the women's presence at the meal, despite that the scene is immediately preceded by statements that Mary was inseparable from her son and that she was the leader of the women who followed him from Galilee.

Shoemaker's change essentially harmonizes the *Life of the Virgin*'s supper scene with the gospels of Mark and Matthew, both of which present the Twelve—twelve men—as the sole disciples present, with the result that subsequent mentions "of disciples" appear to refer back to those twelve. By contrast, van Esbroeck's edition of Tbilisi A-40 presented the "twelve apostles" as a distinct subset of a much larger group of disciples at the meal, which were both men and women. Affirming that the text of Tbilisi A-40 was original to the *Life of the Virgin*'s narrative, John Geometrician's recension of the *Life of the Virgin* is explicit—in both the Greek and the Latin translation—that the "men disciples" and the "women disciples" were at the meal.[105]

Further affirming the antiquity of a Last Supper tradition where both men and women were present, as well as Mary and Jesus officiating, three texts—the *Gospel of Bartholomew*, the *Didascalia Apostolorum*, and the *Apostolic Church Order*—suggest that some Jesus followers were familiar with this tradition, or one like it. The following sections detail each of the three texts and how the author, or compiler, of each signaled that they were aware of an even older supper tradition, a tradition about a ritual meal much like the one preserved in Tbilisi A-40.

Partaking at the Temple Altar
in the *Gospel of Bartholomew*

The author of the *Gospel of Bartholomew* described a male and female pair partaking at the Temple altar, a pairing which suggests the ritual meal with Mary and Jesus officiating. This author depicted Mary and the great angel standing together at the Temple altar, sharing a loaf of bread and a cup of wine. They are envisioned side by side, because just prior, the angel wipes dew off Mary's robe. At the altar, first the angel eats, and then gives to Mary to eat; the angel drinks wine, then gives the cup to Mary to drink.[106] Chronologically, the pairing of Mary and the great angel at a ritual meal on the Temple altar, which takes place before her son is born, foretells the pairing of Mary and her son at a ritual meal before her son dies.

Gender Parallelism in the Liturgy
in the *Didascalia Apostolorum*

The order of the liturgy in a second text, the third- or fourth-century Syriac *Didascalia Apostolorum*, again appears to preserve the cultural memory of Jesus and Mary co-officiating at a ritual meal. This compiler—a compiler because the *Didascalia* also was compiled from even older sources—described a liturgical pair, a male deacon, who stood in for Jesus, and a female deacon, who stood in for the Holy Spirit. As discussed above, Mary herself sometimes appears to have been regarded as a manifestation of the Holy Spirit. Thus the woman deacon potentially was seen as standing in for Mary, but in any case, standing in for a holy female. Originally composed in Greek, the *Didascalia* was widely translated.[107] Some of its elements belong to the early era, but the *Didascalia* subsequently underwent revisions so that its oldest surviving redaction is probably from the early third century, although perhaps later.[108]

A relatively large number of scholars have proposed that a fundamental concern of *Didascalia*'s final redactor was to make changes to the text in an effort to increase the perception of the bishop's power, and also, to decrease the perception of the power of women clergy who previously had been described sharing power more equitably.[109] One kernel that survived the final redactor preserves a stunning example of its original gender parity—a liturgical pair, a male deacon and a female deacon:

> The bishop is the high priest ... The deacon, however, is present as a type of Christ, and is therefore to be loved by you. And the deaconess is to be honoured by you as a type of the Holy Spirit. The presbyters are also to be reckoned by you as a type of the apostles... Therefore you should make your offerings to the high priest, doing so yourself or through the deacons.[110]

Notably here, the male and female deacons are described with more authority than the presbyters, who are merely the type of the apostles. According to the text, at the offering table the male deacon stood in for "Christ" and the woman stood in for "the Holy Spirit," whom in Ancient Syria was considered female and mother. This practice suggests that the community may have followed a liturgical tradition such as seen in the *Life of the Virgin*.

THE RITUAL OF BODY AND BLOOD ACCORDING TO THE *APOSTOLIC CHURCH ORDER*

A third text, the *Apostolic Church Order*, preserves an explicit memory of both men and women at Jesus's last meal, and an implicit memory of Jesus authorizing the women there like the men, as ministers of his body and blood. This is preserved in a passage compiled sometime between the early third and early fourth centuries.[111] Its scribe, or compiler, accepted without debate that the women disciples had attended Jesus's last meal. The memory that the women were also at the meal appears to have been strong in his community, for the scribe repeated it and did not question it. What he contradicted was not that women were at the meal, but the ancillary tradition that Jesus gave the women who were there ministerial authority like he gave the men. Furthermore, consistent with this scribe knowing a tradition that said Mary was the role model for the women at the meal—a tradition consistent with the *Life of the Virgin*—this scribe attempted to discredit the women's liturgical authority by discrediting Mary's. Jesus did not give a ministerial role to women, this scribe claimed, because Mary laughed.[112]

Regarding this passage, Alistair Stewart-Sykes, its most recent editor, concludes, "The whole point of the discussion is to subordinate women's participation in the celebration of the eucharist."[113] Allie Ernst notes that the scribe gave four distinct reasons to exclude women from ministering at the offering of the Body and the Blood: (1) John said Jesus did not permit the women to stand with the men, (2) Martha said it was because Jesus saw Mary smiling, (3) Mary admitted she laughed, but claimed Jesus had taught that women are weak, and (4) Cephas said it was because women should pray seated on the ground, not upright. This is an exceedingly large number of reasons, especially considering that the same scribe usually gave only one reason for an injunction.[114] Ernst argues that such over-wording points to women's Eucharistic authority as a site of ideological conflict in the culture.[115] Here is the scene:

> John said: You are forgetting, brothers, that when the teacher requested the bread and the cup and blessed them saying: This is my Body and Blood, he did not permit the women to stand alongside us.
> Martha said: It was on account of Mary because he saw her smiling.
> Mary said: I did not laugh at this. Previously he said to us, when he was teaching, that the weak would be saved through the strong.
> Kephas said: Some things should be remembered: that women should not pray upright but seated on the ground.[116]

Since Martha is mentioned, the Mary in this passage might be thought to refer to Mary of Bethany. Alternatively, François Bovon argued that scribes sometimes added "Martha" to a passage in order to diminish the authority of an important Mary.[117] Elizabeth Schrader recently argued the same—that the scribal addition of "Martha" diminished the authority of the important original Mary.[118] In the case of the *Apostolic Church Order*, the scribe unquestionably used "Martha" as a literary device to delegitimize Mary. The scribe's accusation, via "Martha," that Mary smiled/laughed during the ritual is a particularly complex accusation, because not only did the scribe give this as the reason why Jesus did not ordain the women like the men, but also the claim itself seriously undermines Mary's credibility as a minister. Unquestionably, a minister smiling or laughing during a sacred ritual would be inappropriate. Furthermore, this scribe made Mary corroborate Martha's accusation that she had smiled—by having Mary correct Martha and say that she had in fact *laughed*—an even greater transgression in a minister—and then this scribe put in Mary's mouth a Jesus saying about women that Jesus never said. Thus, in order to bolster the position that women could not be ministers like men, this scribe first undermined Mary's religious authority—and then turned around and used her authority to validate a fictional Jesus saying that is not in any gospel: "The weak [women] would be saved through the strong [men]."[119] These words appear to have been put in Mary's mouth to signify, as Jane Schaberg suggests, that it was "unnecessary for women (the weak) to take part in the Eucharist performed by men (the strong)."[120]

This scribe's focus on repeatedly undermining Mary's authority suggests that the scribe considered Mary herself a threat. The text itself belies a raging ideological conflict over the role of women officiants. One faction was using Mary to justify women officiants, and the other faction, represented by this scribe, was going to great lengths to try to undermine Mary's authority. This scribe, thus, was not only aware of a pre-existing tradition that said women had been present at the last supper, and that Jesus had authorized them as ministers there—he also knew that the communities who followed this tradition considered Mary herself the model for these women clergy.

Some scholars have argued that the scribe of the *Apostolic Church Order* was probably familiar with a now lost extracanonical gospel.[121] Given the similarity between Mary's role at the last supper in the *Apostolic Church Order*'s adverse report, and Mary's role in the *Life of the Virgin*'s positive report, it seems probable that both compilers had the same lost gospel in mind.

Van Esbroeck's edition of Tbilisi A-40 preserved that both men and women were at the last supper, including that it was because Mary was the leader of the women that she sacrificed. The *Life of the Virgin*, thus, preserves the clear implication that Mary performed this ritual as a role model for women. The scribe of the *Apostolic Church Order*, through his fanciful edits, inadvertently preserved that he, too, was aware that Mary provided both the model and the justification for women to officiate at the Body and Blood. That was why, in four different ways, he undermined Mary's authority.

These three ancient texts, the *Gospel of Bartholomew*, the *Didascalia apostolorum*, and the *Apostolic Church Order*, each appear to have preserved a tradition about Mary as a co-officiant at a ritual meal. The *Gospel of Bartholomew* portrayed her at the Temple altar with a Great Angel at a Eucharistic meal. The *Didascalia* preserved two officiants, a male deacon and a female deacon, the male standing in for Jesus and the female for Holy Spirit, who in Ancient Syria was envisioned as female and mother, and, according to Origen, like Mary. The scribe of the *Apostolic Church Order* takes for granted that women were at the last supper, and, by focusing his attack on Mary's authority, demonstrates that he considered Mary the crucial justification in the competing tradition, a tradition which taught that the women who were at the last supper were made ministers, an alternate view of the institution of the Eucharist.

These three texts together provide significant validation of the antiquity of the last supper tradition preserved in the *Life of the Virgin*, which says that the women were there, and also, that Mary, their teacher and role model, presided with her son at the ritual meal. Shoemaker's edition, based on later manuscripts, preserves neither the women at the supper nor Mary officiating with Jesus. Van Esbroeck's edition of Tbilisi A-40 preserves both, as well as the equally ancient traditions of the Annunciation inside the Jerusalem Temple and Mary at her son's baptism.

CHAPTER 7

Women and Men
at the Last Supper: Reception

Gender parallel officiants at the ritual meal, as witnessed by the *Life of the Virgin*'s last supper scene, comports with actual reported Christian practice into the sixth century, and occasionally beyond. Both positive and adverse reports evince that some communities of Jesus followers around the Mediterranean followed a tradition of men and women presiding together at the ritual meal. This meal was called by many names depending in part upon the community: the agape, the blessing, the offering, the Eucharist, the sacrifice, the Body, and Blood. Similarly, the officiants of the ritual were variously known as presidents, ministers, deacons, priests, presbyters, bishops, and other titles.

FEMALE AND MALE CHRISTIAN PRESIDERS
FROM THE SECOND CENTURY ONWARDS

The oldest datable account of female and male co-officiants was written in Gaul by Irenaeus of Lyon (ca. 155–205). Like the scribe behind the *Apostolic Church Order*, Irenaeus opposed a competing community of Christ followers where men and women presided together. Irenaeus

---

This chapter is in part an update and expansion of Ally Kateusz, "'She Sacrificed Herself as the Priest': Early Christian Female and Male Co-Priests," *Journal of Feminist Studies in Religion* 33, no. 1 (Spring 2017): 45–67. *Feminae* Article of the Month, March 2018.

© The Author(s) 2019
A. Kateusz, *Mary and Early Christian Women*,
https://doi.org/10.1007/978-3-030-11111-3_7

used the transitive verb *eucharistein* when referring to the woman's consecration of the ritual wine, and this community's practice almost certainly was archaic, not innovative.[1] Furthermore, just as the scribe of the
Acts of Philip described opponents sexually slandering male and female
priests and other clergy in that community, Irenaeus sexually slandered
the women officiants in this community.[2] Embedded in his complaints,
however slanted, Irenaeus unwittingly left a record of this community's
Eucharistic ritual:

> Handing mixed cups to the women, he bids them consecrate these in his
> presence. When this has been done, he himself produces another cup of
> much larger size than that which the deluded woman has consecrated, and
> pouring from the smaller one consecrated by the woman into that which
> has been brought forward by himself.[3]

Irenaeus was merely the first of many writers in this region to record
female officiants. Apparently, the early tradition was strong, because it
persisted for centuries. For example, two centuries later, just south of
Lyon, at the Council of Nîmes (ca. 394), some bishops were still complaining about women ordained into Levitical ministry.[4] A century later,
Pope Gelasius (r. 492–496) likewise complained that in southern Italy
"women are encouraged to serve [minister] at the sacred altars (*minis-
trare sacris altaribus*) and to perform all the other tasks (*cunctaque*) that
are assigned only to the service of men."[5] The term *cuncta* here signified
all related things and thus appears to have included all liturgical, juridical, and magisterial work of the ordained ministry.[6]

In similar fashion in 511, bishops north of Lyon chastised priests
in Brittany for officiating masses with women "employed in the divine
sacrifice; so that, while you are distributing the Eucharist, they hold
the chalices and presume to administer the blood of Christ to the people."[7] As late as 829, bishops in this region are on record complaining
about women performing this sacrament. "We have attempted in every
way possible," they wrote Louis the Pious, "to prevent women from
approaching the altar ... and—more monstrous, improper, and inappropriate than all else—giv[ing] the people the Body and Blood of the
Lord."[8] These adverse reports indicate that the Council of Laodicea's
late fourth-century admonition against women approaching the altar had
little impact, at least in some communities.

WRITINGS THAT PAIRED MALE
AND FEMALE CLERICAL TITLES

Various writers paired male and female clergy. Bishop Epiphanius of Salamis, writing around 370 in the Eastern Mediterranean, reported in the present tense regarding New Prophecy churches: "They ordain [*kathistantai*] women to the episcopate and presbyterate."[9] The *Martyrdom of Matthew* likewise described men and women who were ordained as both priests and deacons. Composed in Greek, the dating of this martyrdom has not been well studied and is uncertain, but the fourth century would probably be conservative.[10] While Epiphanius of Salamis complained about the practice of ordaining women priests and bishops, this author positively paralleled their ordination, as well as the church titles for men and women, including *presbuteros* and *presbutis*, which different modern translators have translated as priest and priestess, or presbyter (m.) and presbyter (f.). According to the *Martyrdom of Matthew*, Matthew ordained/appointed King Bulphamnus a "priest", Queen Ziphagia a "priestess," their son a deacon, and his wife a deaconess.[11] Here, different Greek scribes used *echeirotonēsen* (ordain) or *katestēsan* (appoint), and in the Latin translation, *ordinavit* (ordain).[12]

Passages in manuscript *Xenophontos* 32, which preserves the longest text of the *Acts of Philip*, describe similar gender parallelism in the clergy. For example, one passage, in Act 14, reads, "Philip was baptizing the men and Mariamne the women."[13] This gendered division of responsibility is also specified in the Syriac *Didascalia Apostolorum*, which pairs the male and female deacons standing in for Christ and the Holy Spirit (f.) at the offering table, and with other duties of these deacons, including baptism, the *Didascalia* says: "A woman should be devoted to ministry among women, and a male deacon to ministry among men."[14] Most likely this gender division of clerical duties was limited to situations where both male and female clergy were present, such as in established churches, or in scenarios such as that of the *Acts of Philip*, which specifies that Mariamne and Philip evangelized together. By contrast, the long narratives about Thecla, Irene and Nino specify that they evangelized alone, and that they baptized both men and women.

Act 1 in *Xenophontos* 32's text of the *Acts of Philip* again lists gender-parallel church titles. In one instance, these titles are listed in a scene that describes blasphemers being tortured in hell, and the archangel

Michael explains that these people were in hell because, when they were alive, they had "blasphemed against male and female priests, eunuchs, deacons, deaconesses, and virgins with lies about debauchery and adultery."[15] In this list of church titles, which parallels male priest and female priest, Bovon translated the Greek *presbuterous* and *presbutidas* with gender equivalence, as male and female priests.[16] He gave considerable thought as to why he did so, and a significant piece of evidence that he cited in support of his translation was the similar passage in the *Martyrdom of Matthew*, where that author also paralleled masculine and feminine church titles. Bovon concluded that when there is a list of gender-parallel church titles, then the titles for both men and women must be translated with parallel meaning.[17]

WOMEN OVERSEERS OR BISHOPS

Almost all the house churches named in the New Testament are identified by the name of the women who apparently oversaw them: Chloe, Nympha, Apphia, Priscilla, Lydia, Mary the mother of Mark, as well as an unnamed woman.[18] Additional evidence suggests that women continued for several centuries in the role of overseer, or bishop, of churches in various communities around the Mediterranean. For example, as mentioned above, in the late fourth century in the East, Epiphanius of Salamis reported that some Christians ordained women bishops.

Some communities in the West also appear to have had women clergy with the title of bishop—not the masculine *episcopus*, but the feminine *episcopa*. For example, a funerary inscription from near the city of Rome, most likely dated to the late fourth/early fifth century, gave a woman the title of *episcopa*.[19] As with the other clergy, we sometimes find the *episcopa* paired with the *episcopus*, for example, Canon 14 of the second Council of Tours (567) instructed, "A bishop (male) who has no bishop (female) may have no women in his entourage"—*Episcopum episcop(i)am non habentem nulla sequatur turba mulierum.*[20] Canon 14 seems to signify that the *episcopus* was the overseer of the men and the *episcopa* the overseer of the women. If so, their responsibilities would be similar to the gender parallel responsibilities that the *Didascalia* ascribed for male and female deacons, as well as the way that the *Acts of Philip* says Philip baptized the men and Mariamne the women.

It seems likely that in some cases the *episcopa* might be the spouse of a male bishop, but the meaning of the term *episcopa* did not necessarily mean that she was a wife. For example, Canon 13 of the Council of Tours, which immediately preceded the abovementioned Canon 14, specifically addressed the bishop's wife, and called her *coniux*, not *episcopa*.[21] Other Latin writers likewise did not call a bishop's wife an *episcopa*. For example, Gregory of Tours, who wrote about the wives of various bishops, referred to each as *coniux*, as in Canon 13 of the Council of Tours, not an *episcopa* as in Canon 14.[22] The understanding that an *episcopa* was not necessarily married to an *episcopus* is consistent with the way Epiphanius of Salamis described women who were ordained bishops. Epiphanius complained that women bishops were *not* under the authority of their husbands.[23]

A fascinating inscription on a nave pier near the Chapel of San Zeno inside the Church of Santa Prassede in Rome pairs the *episcopus* of Rome at that time, Pope Paschal I (r. 817–824), with his mother, the *episcopa* Theodora.[24] Notably, this is the same pope who commissioned the apse mosaic of Mary holding the Eucharistic cloth, by then called the maniple, in Santa Maria in Dominica (Fig. 4.15). Paschal also commissioned a full-length mosaic portrait of his mother in the Chapel of San Zeno inside Santa Prassede, with her title *EPISCOPA* written in black tesserae horizontally above her head and her name *THEODORA* vertically beside it. Theodora could have been portrayed wearing the episcopal pallium in her portrait, just as Mary was portrayed wearing it 150 years earlier in the San Venantius apse, but we can never know for sure because sometime after 1630 the lower wall, with the mosaic of Theodora's body, was removed to make a doorway. Perhaps that was when the last two letters of her name were destroyed and replaced with gold tesserae instead of the black letters *RA*.[25] This rendered her name into an otherwise unattested masculine name, *THEODO*, as if to suggest that the *EPISCOPA* was somehow masculine gendered. Ute E. Eisen provides detailed research regarding *Theodora episcopa* and points out that the *Liber Pontificalis* named Paschal's father, Bonosus, without any official title, so he was not a bishop. Paschal's mother Theodora therefore was not titled *episcopa* because of her husband.[26] There appears to be no good reason to assume that a woman was called an *episcopa* because of her marital relationship. More likely, just as with a male bishop, her title had to do with merit and responsibility.

CERULA AND BITALIA, ORDAINED BISHOPS

Given the trajectory of redaction with respect to markers of female litur-gical leadership, it seems likely that other epigraphs and evidence of ordained women bishops may have been defaced or destroyed. The late fifth- or early sixth-century grave portraits of two women church lead-ers, Cerula and Bitalia, probably survived only because they were under-ground, in the San Gennaro Catacomb in Naples. Various scholars have suggested that one or both may have been a deacon, a priest, or some other kind of clergy in the Naples church.[27] Their portraits suggest they were ordained bishops.

Cerula's portrait was doubly hidden. A marble slab concealed her arcosolium, a rare phenomenon in the Naples catacombs, according to Antonio Ciavolino, who discovered it in 1977.[28] The catacomb's local management, the Societá Cooperativa La Paranza—Catacombe di Napoli, took over management of the catacombs in 2009 and in 2011 oversaw the restoration of the fresco. For Cerula's portrait, see Fig. 7.1.

Fig. 7.1   Cerula and the open gospel books. Fresco dated late 400s/early 500s. San Gennaro Catacomb, Naples. © Societá Cooperativa La Paranza - Catacombe di Napoli

Cerula's portrait is inside an arcosolium that was cut into the center of the main wall of an underground gallery, a gallery down a corridor from the underground basilica. When viewers enter this long room, Cerula's portrait is immediately visible as it and its decoration take up virtually the entire wall at other end, with the arcosolium the focal point. The top of the wall has a *tabula,* or banner, today blank, but it originally may have had an inscription. That Cerula's role was religious is unmistakably suggested by the large amount of Christian symbolism. Both the *alpha omega* and the *chi rho* cross were delicately painted in red above her head. Two open codices, with the names of the four evangelists written on their pages, were painted floating on either side of her head. Her arms are raised. *CERULA* and *IN PACE*, meaning "Cerula, rest in peace," was at the base of her portrait. The intrada, the inside arch, is painted with five large green wreathes that encircle more alpha-omegas and chi rho crosses.[29] Finally, wall frescos of Paul, seen gesturing toward Cerula as if blessing or acclaiming her, and probably also a fresco of either Peter or some other saint (which has not survived) originally flanked her arcosolium.[30]

The portrait of Bitalia was painted in a smaller niche, nearby on the long side wall of the same chapel. Bitalia's portrait was painted with less detail, but in a similar composition to Cerula's—her arms are raised, open gospel books flank her head, and a red *chi rho* cross is above her head.[31] The symbols used in both of their grave portraits were consistently Christian and highly auspicious. For comparison, neither the *chi rho* nor the *alpha omega* symbols are seen with the men in the nearby so-called crypt of the bishops, but both symbols are inside the halo of Saint Gennaro, the important martyr bishop for whom these catacombs were named, who himself is painted nearby, and with his arms raised, like the women.[32]

Neither Cerula nor Bitalia were depicted wearing any sort of jewelry, providing an austere contrast, for example, to the portrait of a young girl painted wearing pendant earrings, a small crown of pearls, a jeweled collar, and a huge jewel on her belt in the nearby arcosolium of Theotecnus.[33] Both Cerula and Bitalia were portrayed wearing an overgarment, a *pænula* which Mary M. Schaefer likens to a short chasuble.[34] Indeed, this vestment is almost identical in style to Pope Clement's ornately embroidered blue and white chasuble (Fig. 4.8), which he is depicted wearing while performing the Eucharist, his arms also raised. It is also similar to the vestment worn by the women processing to the altar on the sixth-century ivory pyx, three of whom were arms-raised, and each of whom wore the Eucharistic cloth (Figs. 2.8a, b and 4.18). Cerula and Bitalia's portraits were bust portraits and do not show any insignia below, but they also resemble Mary, who a century or so later was depicted arms-raised and wearing the archiepiscopal pallium hanging from below her *maphorion* in her mosaic portrait in the Lateran baptistery in Rome (Fig. 4.11a, b). Bitalia's chasuble is a plain deep red, but Cerula's, like Clement's, has an ornate design. After the recent restoration, a Greek cross is visible inside one of the circles in its red-on-white pattern, and originally other crosses may have been inside other circles.[35] The design itself suggests a joyful procession of people, some arms-raised like Cerula, such as the procession of women approaching the Anastasis altar on the ivory pyx. Another similar procession may have been in the lost second register of mosaics of the Parousia of Christ in the fourth- or fifth-century Rotunda Church in Thessaloniki, where the outline of Christ is inside a circle at the apex of the dome, and the procession of "dancing" celebrants[36]—only their feet remain today—encircled the dome below him.[37] A joyful procession, whether in memory of Christ's resurrection or in anticipation of his return, would be an appropriate design for the chasuble of a woman bishop in a catacomb setting, for the motif would remind the viewer of Christ's promise that the beloved dead would be raised again.

The rarest and most unusual element of Cerula and Bitalia's portraits is a symbol that signifies they were bishops. This symbol is the books, which were painted on either side of their heads. These books are clearly identified as gospel books, for Mark, John, Luke, and Matthew are written in Latin on the open pages. This composition of open gospel books flanking the deceased person's head is extremely unusual, and to my knowledge, no other such compositions have survived besides theirs.[38]

In Christian art of this era, books were typically associated with bishops. The association between bishops and books is so powerful that in another room in this same catacomb, Vatican specialists identify portraits of unnamed men depicted holding a closed book as bishops. These men are identified as bishops despite that their portraits typically do not include a name, a title, or any episcopal or Christian insignia—not even a *chi rho* or *alpha omega* to identify them as a Christian instead of a philosopher or magistrate—only the book.[39] Artists in Rome around the time that Cerula and Bitalia's portraits were painted associated open books with bishops. For example, in the

Maria Maggiore Basilica dated 432–440, Peter and Paul are depicted holding open books on either side of the empty bishop's throne in the center of the triumphal arch mosaics, as if waiting to ordain the new bishop of Rome, Pope Sixtus III, after Pope Celestine died. As previously mentioned with respect to Fig. 4.16, ten years earlier, in the basilica of Santa Sabina dated 420–430, two women were portrayed holding open books, with the woman holding the book with Greek letters also holding the Eucharistic cloth like Pope Clement several centuries later (Fig. 4.8). Even earlier, in an apse mosaic in Saint Pudianza Church in Rome dated ca. 400, Jesus himself was portrayed holding a large open book. Earliest of all, in a fourth-century fresco in the Domitilla catacomb, an open book was painted floating in the air adjacent two women. Originally, a second book may have been painted on the other side of them to balance the composition, but today that half of the fresco is destroyed. One of the women is titled "Veneranda"—which some scholars have suggested may have referenced the title of a woman bishop.[40] The other woman is titled "Petronella," and a century ago, the famous Vatican art historian Josef Wilpert argued that Petronella was painted wearing the oldest example of the episcopal pallium, *il pallio sacro*.[41] In this geographical area, thus, the open books, such as associated with Cerula and Bitalia, appear to have symbolized high ecclesial authority, including women's.

The way the artist painted the gospel books—open on either side of their heads—further associates Cerula and Bitalia with the episcopacy. Bishops—*and bishops only*—were, and still are, ordained with the open gospel book held over their head.[42] This ordination ritual appears to be what Peter and Paul are waiting to perform while holding open books on either side of the empty episcopal throne, as seen in the Maria Maggiore triumphal apse mosaic.[43] The open gospel books on either side of Cerula's and Bitalia's heads appear to signify that they had undergone the same episcopal ordination ritual. If they were men, no doubt they already would have been identified as bishops.

Twenty years ago before Cerula's portrait was restored, Catharine Kroeger inspected Bitalia's portrait and identified her as a priest, although she also mused whether the dark red color of Bitalia's chasuble signified that she also had been a bishop. Kroeger regarded the red pendants around the books in Bitalia's portrait as "bookmarks placed in special readings" for Bitalia's preaching, so that she could "minister the word of God."[44]

These red pendants could signify bookmarks, or even book ties or straps—especially if there were not such an excessive number of them—but based on the images in J. A. Szirmai's *Archeology of Medieval Bookbinding*, as well as depictions of codices from this era, books sometimes had long wrapping straps, triangular flaps, toggles or other clasps, and/or bookmarkers, but none survived with this excessive number of pendants. More pendants are seen emanating from these books than on any other codice, or representation of a codice, from this era. In addition, the shape of these wavy red tendrils is rather uniform, as well as specific, and does not mirror any combination of straps, flaps, ties, markers, or toggles reconstructed in Szirmai's study. The portrait painter's skill suggests that something specific was intended to be represented. The closest in iconography, as well as in time and place, are the smaller number of rather uniform red tendrils that descend from each of the two open books that Peter and Paul hold while waiting on either side of the vacant episcopal throne in Maria Maggiore, and from the two open books that the two women titled "Church" hold while flanking the inscription to Celestine as the foremost bishop of the world in Santa Sabina (Fig. 4.16). Worthy of consideration is that the red tendrils may have represented tongues of fire descending from the open books.[45] According to the popular preacher and bishop, Severian of Gabala (ca. 380–425), the reason the gospels were held over the episcopal ordinand's head during the ordination rite was so that, as in the upper room at Pentecost, the Holy Spirit's tongues of fire would *descend* from the book and ordain the new bishop and inspire their preaching.[46] The wavy red tendrils emanating from the sides and bottom of the two open books on either side of Cerula and Bitalia's heads even more clearly suggest flames or tongues of fire. The absence of flames *rising* in similar fashion from the top of the books is explained by Severian's description that the tongues of fire *descended*. Additionally, Severian said that during this part of the ritual, a flame would be visible above the episcopal ordinand's head[47]—and the delicate red *alpha omega* and *chi rho* painted above Cerula and Bitalia's heads resemble, in shape and color, the delicate flames of the Holy Spirit painted above the heads of Mary and the male apostles in the Rabbula Gospels illumination of Pentecost.[48]

Cerula and Bitalia's grave portraits were painted at the end of the fifth century or the beginning of the sixth century. They therefore may have been contemporaneous with Pope Gelasius' letter, detailed above, wherein he complained that in southern Italy women were ministering at the sacred altars and performing all associated liturgical, magisterial, and juridical tasks—that is, performing the duties of bishop. Cerula and Bitalia's portraits appear to identify two of these women. Whoever commissioned Cerula and Bitalia's portraits, quite likely their own church community, may have specified that flaming open gospel books be painted next to their heads to proclaim that Cerula and Bitalia were *ordained* bishops—and that their community rejected Gelasius's view.

What did the liturgy look like when women and men had parallel church titles and authority? The two very oldest surviving iconographic artifacts to depict people at an altar table inside a real church portray men and women in parallel. Both artifacts are usually dated within decades of the year 430. Signifying that this gender parallel liturgy was vibrant and widespread, to my knowledge, zero iconographic artifacts have survived from the fifth century or earlier that depict a Christian man alone at an altar table in a church, that is, without a woman also there.[49]

These two iconographic artifacts depict a gender parallel liturgy at the altar table in the consecrated sanctuaries of two of the most important orthodox basilicas in the Roman Empire. One portrays the sanctuary of the second Hagia Sophia in Constantinople. The other portrays the sanctuary of Old Saint Peter's Basilica in Rome

HISTORICITY OF PULCHERIA INSIDE THE HOLY OF HOLIES OF THE SECOND HAGIA SOPHIA

The first of the two artifacts that depict a gender parallel liturgy at the altar table was carved on the massive stone front of a sarcophagus. It was discovered in 1988 in an underground hypogeum adjacent the Theodosian walls in Istanbul. The stone panel's large size—approximately 3½ feet by 6½ feet—as well as the dress of the people carved on it, signified that the sculptor's patron or patroness was of high rank[50] (see Fig. 7.2).

The sculptor carved a man and a woman flanking the altar table with its cross and curtains beneath the canopy of the ciborium. Next to the woman, a boy, not yet a man, stands closest to the altar, sculpted holding an open book, presumably the gospels, and lifting his right hand in the gesture of speech, as if he were the bishop.[51] Significantly, the woman and man have almost mirror symmetrical poses—raised arms, solemn gazes, the curve of their torsos, and even the pointing of their feet.

Art historian Johannes Deckers and archeologist Ümit Serdaroğlu published this find in 1993, pointing out that the column capitals carved on this sarcophagus panel were the same as those of the nearby second Hagia Sophia, completed in 415. The second Hagia Sophia burned

Fig. 7.2   Liturgical scene in the second Hagia Sophia. Constantinople, ca. 430.
Courtesy Author and Archeological Museum of Istanbul

during the Nika riots under Justinian, who built the third Hagia Sophia, which still stands. Based on the hypogeum's site, the early Christian cross, and the style of the man's clothing and bulb clasp, they dated the sarcophagus front tightly to the end of the first third of the fifth century, that is, just prior to the year 434.[52]

Deckers and Serdaroğlu's dating makes this carving almost precisely contemporary with a reported conflict in 428 at the door to the Holy of Holies in the second Hagia Sophia—a conflict between the virgin Augusta Pulcheria (399–453) and Nestorius, the new patriarch of Constantinople. At the age of fifteen, Pulcheria had become regent for her seven-year-old younger brother, Theodosius II, and, according to the church historian Sozomen, not long after, with a rich new altar table in the newly consecrated second Hagia Sophia, Pulcheria consecrated herself as a virgin in a spectacular ceremony before all the priests and people.[53]

According to two adverse reports, the Augusta Pulcheria's portrait was above the altar table in the second Hagia Sophia. Her portrait may have been much like that of the Augusta Theodora, who a century later was depicted above the altar table holding the Eucharistic chalice (Fig. 4.17). Signaling an impending conflict in Constantinople, both sources say Nestorius removed Pulcheria's portrait.[54]

The most violent conflict between the princess and the patriarch was preserved in only one source, an adverse report in the *Letter to Cosmas*. The historicity of this letter has sometimes been challenged,[55] but to date no one previously has considered it in context with the liturgical scene on the sarcophagus front, which has a strong correspondence to the liturgical traditions described in the letter. The author of the *Letter to Cosmas* said that Pulcheria was accustomed to taking communion inside the Holy of Holies with her younger brother.[56] The sculptor of the massive sarcophagus front carved a liturgical scene in the second Hagia Sophia that comports with what the *Letter to Cosmas* said was Pulcheria's custom: a young woman standing next to a boy who had a very important role at the altar table in the second Hagia Sophia. Certainly Roman emperors had traditionally taken the title of *pontifex maximus*, or chief priest, but acceptance of the title is usually thought to have ended at least with Gratian (r. 375–383),[57] although Canon 69 of the Council of Quinisext in 692 explicitly affirmed the emperor's right to enter the Holy of Holies and later sources continued to describe Byzantine emperors taking communion with their own hands at the altar "as the priest."[58] The *Letter to Cosmas* did not specify what the Eucharistic ritual looked like, only that when the previous patriarch Sisinnius was alive, Pulcheria took communion in the Holy of Holies with her brother. But the letter also said that the new patriarch Nestorius disagreed with Pulcheria's practice and attempted to end it. Just before the Easter service in 428, Nestorius heard about Pulcheria's custom. He ran to the door of the Holy of Holies to physically stop her and her women from entering.

> Pulcheria ordered, "Let me enter as is my custom."
> He answered, "Only priests can walk in this place."
> She asked him, "Why have I not given birth to God?"
> He said, "You, you have given birth to Satan," and he drove her away from the Holy of Holies.[59]

Scholars debate why Pulcheria claimed to have given birth to God, essentially invoking Mary the Theotokos, the God-bearer, to justify her own entry as a priest into the Holy of Holies.[60] One explanation is that influential theologians taught that virgins gave birth to Christ like Mary.[61] For example, an earlier patriarch of Constantinople, Gregory of Nazianzus (329–390), preached: "Practice virginity, women, in order to become mothers of Christ!"[62] This teaching for virgins explains the virgin Pulcheria's question, "Why have I not given birth to God?" Another explanation might be that Pulcheria was familiar with the *Gospel of Bartholomew*, where the apostles themselves told Mary that because she gave birth to the Lord she had more right than they to lead the prayer.[63] Pulcheria, asking Nestorius this particular question as she demanded entry to the Holy of Holies, suggests that she was accustomed to following Mary's example—in the Holy of Holies, at the altar table, and as the liturgical leader of the male apostles through whom Nestorius claimed his own authority.

One thing is certain. We may assume that Pulcheria soon resumed her custom, because not long after the conflict, the Council of Ephesus exiled Nestorius. In this Nestorius followed the humiliating trajectory of an earlier patriarch of Constantinople, John Chrysostom (ca. 349–407), who also opposed women in the priesthood.[64] After Chrysostom became patriarch, he came into conflict with Pulcheria's mother, the empress Aelia Eudoxia—and he too was expelled from Constantinople.[65] The sacral basileía of these imperial women appears to have been considerably greater than that of the patriarchs.

Regarding the design of the mosaics installed in the huge Maria Maggiore basilica after the Council of Ephesus, the reason the papal patron—whether Sixtus or the future Pope Leo—demoted Mary's motherhood may have been fear of Mary's liturgical authority as a role model for women, including fear of the Augustas. Is there evidence that during this period some women in the city of Rome were entering the Holy of Holies as priests like Pulcheria did in Constantinople?

FEMALE AND MALE CLERGY AT THE ALTAR TABLE IN OLD SAINT PETER'S BASILICA

A delicate carving on an ivory reliquary box known as the Pola Ivory is the second of the two oldest iconographic artifacts to illustrate Christians at the altar table in a liturgical scene inside a real church. Subsequent excavations beneath the high altar of the modern basilica of Saint Peter's proved that this carving depicted the liturgy inside the sanctuary of Old Saint Peter's Basilica in Rome. As such, it provides substantial evidence that, like their sisters in Constantinople, women in the city of Rome had parallel roles in the liturgy.

This reliquary box most often dated to the second quarter of the fifth century[66]—essentially contemporary with the sarcophagus front, as well as Pulcheria, who lived until 453. Due to its quality and as well as a papal motif, some art historians have hypothesized that it was a papal commission, perhaps for an imperial patron.[67] Like the sarcophagus front, this ivory box was also dug up in the twentieth century, discovered in 1906 buried beneath the altar area of a church near Pola, Croatia. Nonetheless, the ivory box was carved elsewhere, with the most common suggestions Rome or Milan[68] (see Fig. 7.3).

Anton Gnirs, the first scholar to publish an article about the exquisite ivory box, described this as a liturgical scene inside a church presbytery. The sculptor carved two men and two women, their arms raised, standing on either side of the ciborium, the beautiful columned structure around the altar. Inside the sacred space beneath the ciborium, the

Fig. 7.3 Liturgical scene in Old Saint Peter's Basilica, Rome. Ivory reliquary box, ca. 425–450. Discovered near Pola, Croatia. Museo Archeologico, Venice. © Alinari Archives-Alinari Archive, Florence

sculptor carved a man and a woman facing each other across the altar. Gnirs assumed that the man and woman at the altar must have represented spouses at a marriage liturgy, although, as he pointed out, where was the third party, the priest?[69] The three women were sculpted with veils, and there is virtually no controversy that they are women.[70] Cerula and Bitalia, also portrayed arms-raised as well as dressed like these arms-raised women, could have performed in a liturgy like this one inside Old Saint Peter's sanctuary. They even may have traveled to Rome and performed in the liturgy in Old Saint Peter's itself.

In a significant resonance with the liturgy of the first-century Therapeutae, a close-up of this liturgical scene on the Pola Ivory shows that the arms-raised men and women outside the ciborium were sculpted with open mouths, as if singing. The closest documented parallel to these two gender-divided choirs is the Therapeutae's divided choirs of men and women. Philo said that during their sacred all-night festival these two choirs sang like the Israelites, with "Moses the prophet leading the men, and Miriam the prophetess leading the women." They sang all night, and "when they saw the sun rising, *they raised their hands to heaven*."[71] For the arms-raised women singing, see Fig. 7.4.

Fig. 7.4 Arms-raised women singing. © Alinari Archives-Alinari Archive, Florence

THE CIBORIUM IN OLD SAINT PETER'S BASILICA

The six spiral columns carved on the ivory panel closely resembled the six famous columns that Constantine reputedly originally donated to Old Saint Peter's. These six spiral columns still exist and were reused in the modern Saint Peter's galleries. In 1939, the well-known early Christian art historian Henri Leclercq pointed to the spiral columns and proposed that the ivory scene depicted a liturgy in Old Saint Peter's. Leclercq, like virtually all previous scholars, identified both a man and women at the altar. Instead of a marriage ceremony, Leclercq wondered if possibly they were venerating the True Cross—but then pointed out that no relic of the True Cross had been reported in Old Saint Peter's. He described the scene as whimsical and unexplainable.[72]

The very next year, ignoring the outbreak of World War II, the Vatican began excavations beneath the high altar in the modern basilica of Saint Peter's. These excavations were purportedly to discover Peter's tomb, despite that this entailed breaking the Vatican's own rule that such holy places were inviolable. Due to pilgrim traffic in the Confessio (the large marble pit in front of the altar), excavators were not permitted to dig there, so they excavated behind the altar, through the underground Clementine chapel.[73] Beneath the modern altar, they discovered a stack of medieval altars. At the bottom of the stack, they found the approximately eight-foot by eight-foot wall of a second-century Roman *aedicule*, or shrine. Embedded in the shrine wall was a horizontal travertine slab with long stone legs holding up each outside corner[74]—a stone *mensa*, or table, where since the second century followers of Jesus may have made offerings.[75]

As seen on the Pola Ivory, a rounded wall niche behind the stone tabletop, still present in the ruins, once held a cross. On each side of the stone tabletop the sculptor carved what has been suggested as steps, steps that would have permitted even the shortest woman access to the four-foot high tabletop.[76] Below the stone tabletop, excavators found the remains of an underground grave structure, which they speculated had at one time contained Peter's bones.[77] The ivory sculptor had illustrated two doors beneath the stone tabletop, doors that had opened to provide access to the underground tomb structure, such as Gregory of Tours (538–594) had described.[78]

Gregory of Tours, whose deacon, Agiulf, had lived in Rome for ten years, was one of two well-known ancient witnesses who had reported that the old basilica's altar had been over Peter's tomb. Gregory reported, "The tomb is located beneath the altar"—*sub altare*.[79] Even earlier, at the end of the fourth century, Jerome, who himself was from Rome, said that the bishop of Rome offered sacrifices over Peter's bones and that Peter's tomb was worthy of being that altar.[80] When excavators found a grave structure under a stone table in Old Saint Peter's, they seemed to have confirmed a long Catholic tradition that Old Saint Peter's altar was above Peter's tomb, a tradition detailed in the 1907 *Catholic Encyclopedia*.[81]

According to Jocelyn Toynbee and John Ward Perkins, the excavators discovered that construction for Pope Gregory the Great's (r. 590–604) raised presbytery had resulted in "obliterating all trace of the Constantinian shrine except for the small central edifice."[82] The second-century shrine was all that remained. Fortunately, the ivory sculptor had accurately reproduced the second-century shrine, so much so that Vatican excavator Engelbert Kirschbaum conceded the ivory was "so striking even in its details as to confirm conclusively its interpretation as the Constantinian apse in Saint Peter's." He added, "This ancient representation is therefore our authority for the interpretation and reconstruction of the missing portions."[83]

The excavators' most important "missing portion" to be reconstructed from the ivory was the ciborium that had been above the second-century shrine and its mensa. Today, virtually every ciborium is square, but during the fourth century, some were not. For example, the famous monument over Christ's tomb inside the Anastasis rotunda in Jerusalem was multi-sided, perhaps hexagonal. Various types of souvenirs that pilgrims brought back from Jerusalem depicted the front of the monument with four staggered front columns, or three triangular roof panels, which is how the front columns and roof panels would look if it were a hexagon. This shape is seen on the ampoules shown in Figs. 2.6 and 2.7, as well as the top left frame painted on the reliquary box in Fig. 4.3, and also on six-sided glass vessels for holy oil that imitated the shape of the shrine.[84] Many artifacts, including the ampoule and ivory pyx seen in Figs. 2.6 and 2.8, identified spiral columns on the monument over Christ's tomb.[85] The altar areas of these two famous fourth-century churches are in fact so strong that the curators of the Metropolitan Museum of Art point out the similarity in their description of the Anastasis altar area sculpted on the ivory pyx: "The iconography of the altar area is familiar from the fifth-century Pola Ivory (Museo Archeologico, Venice), a representation of the sanctuary area of Old Saint Peter's in Rome."[86]

Galit Noga-Banai has demonstrated how the visual motif of Jerusalem was employed during the Christianization of Rome.[87] The ciborium in Old Saint Peter's, which visually imitates the monument over Christ's tomb inside the Anastasis, may be an example of this. The eight-foot high wall of the second-century shrine may have been too tall to aesthetically accommodate a hexagon around it, because, as seen on the ivory, the ciborium instead was constructed as a half-hexagon. The two extra columns were placed on the sides of the apse. The second-century shrine is on the half-hexagon's longer back face, demarked by columns. Two more columns formed the shorter front face and framed the shrine behind. Worshippers in the nave saw a hexagon profile with spiral columns over Peter's tomb, beneath the half dome of the apse—a vision that evoked the famous multi-sided monument with spiral columns over Christ's tomb beneath the rotunda dome of the Anastasis.[88]

THE ALTAR IN OLD SAINT PETER'S BASILICA

The Vatican excavators took nearly a decade to write their final report, yet still neglected to mention that prior scholars had repeatedly concluded that the fifth-century sculptor had portrayed a man and a woman at a church altar. When published, the Vatican report contained two new drawings, both of which illustrated the ciborium as a square. Like the ivory sculptor, the Vatican illustrators drew the second-century shrine with its stone table in the middle of the back face of the ciborium—but instead of drawing the ciborium as a half-hexagon, they incorrectly drew it as a 20' × 20' *square*.[89]

What was the point of the square ciborium? A few years later, Vatican excavator Kirschbaum clearly explained the point in his 1957 book on the excavations. The overhead ribs of a square ciborium, he said, intersect in the middle. The big lamp, he said, would have hung from that midpoint, i.e., over vacant floor, ten feet in front of the shrine. The altar, Kirschbaum added, would have been under the lamp's light. He concluded, "We have to suppose a *portable* altar table."[90]

For a side-by-side comparison of the two ciboria, see Fig. 7.5a, b. Figure 7.5a is taken from the ivory. Figure 7.5b is taken from one of the Vatican drawings.[91]

As seen in Fig. 7.5a, the ivory sculptor carved a half-hexagon ciborium that is beautifully proportionate to the apse and wonderfully lights it. This half-hexagon ciborium's rear face was wider than its front

(a)   **(b)**

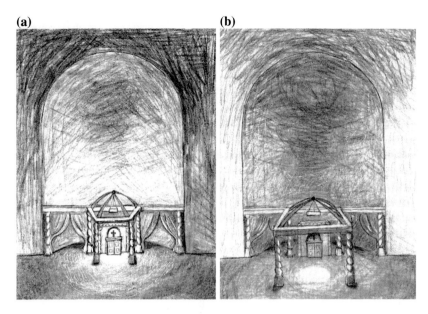

Fig. 7.5 **a** Half-hexagon ciborium per ivory sculptor (*left*). **b** Hypothetical square ciborium per Vatican (*right*). © Author

face—so the sculptor carved the side beams angling *in* toward the front. Finally, the sculptor carved the overhead ribs intersecting in the middle of the back face, which was on the chord of the apse, and sculpted the big lamp hanging over the second-century shrine—exactly where one would expect the light to be focused when the shrine had been "the architectural focus of the whole building."[92]

In comparison, as seen in Fig. 7.5b, the Vatican illustrator's hypothetical square ciborium would have jutted awkwardly out into the transept. Artistic perspective meant that the Vatican illustrator drew this square ciborium's front face wider than its rear face—and so turned the side beams angling *out*. The illustrator drew the overhead ribs intersecting in the middle of the square, where the big hanging lamp would have lit up vacant floor—ten feet in front of the shrine.

Some prominent scholars contradicted the Vatican report and said that the stone table above Peter's tomb had been the basilica's altar, just as Jerome and Gregory of Tours had reported. André Grabar made that case.[93] So did the Vatican Apostolic Library scholar José Ruysschaert, who in 1954 rebutted each tortured reason the excavation team gave for why the stone table could not be the altar, such as that it was too tall, or too small.[94]

The Vatican proposal that the second-century shrine's stone mensa had not been the basilica's altar table, however, became reified after 1957, when Kirschbaum collaborated with Toynbee and Perkins to publish two books, both oriented to wider audiences. Two examples serve to demonstrate their extraordinary collaboration. First, in circular fashion, these scholars cited each other for the portable altar theory. Toynbee and Perkins credited Kirschbaum for the portable altar theory, and Kirschbaum credited them for it.[95] Second, they divided and conquered the two ancient witnesses. In this, their censorship of the two ancient witnesses is almost humorous once one realizes what was at stake. Kirschbaum purported to quote the relevant passage from Gregory of Tours—but started his quote one sentence *after* Gregory said the tomb was below the altar.[96] Kirschbaum then paraphrased Jerome, saying that the sacrifice was "at" (instead of "over") Peter's tomb, and then, in an astonishing feat of defensiveness, in his footnote for his paraphrase, Kirschbaum referred the reader to a *second* footnote, where, at the very bottom of a long excursis, he finally quoted Jerome—in Latin.[97] Toynbee and Perkins did the opposite. They ignored Jerome. His name is not even in their book's Index. They quoted Gregory—in English until the key phrase which said the tomb was below the altar, at which point they inserted the Latin, *sub altare*.[98]

While Toynbee moved onto other projects, Perkins appears to have remained deeply invested in debate about the location of the altar in Old Saint Peter's. For example, during the Anglican infighting prior to the 1968 Lambeth Conference over female ordination, Perkins, an Anglican, vigorously argued that Old Saint Peter's altar could have been anywhere—except where Jerome and Gregory of Tours had said it was. His final shot was in his opening address for the Seventh International Congress of Christian Archeology in 1965, which was published in the 1966 *Journal of Theological Studies*. Without giving any hint as to why the location of the basilica's altar mattered, he stated: "Wherever the altar may have been (presumably in the nave and very possibly of a portable nature) it was certainly not over the grave of the Apostle."[99]

Twenty-two years later, in 1988, the huge stone sarcophagus front that depicts a gender parallel liturgy at the altar was discovered in

Istanbul. This artifact debunks the underlying false premise of the portable altar theory, that is, that the altar could not have been where the ancient authorities said it was because that would mean both a man and a woman were at the altar. A man and a woman flank the altar on this carving, too. Unfortunately, the sarcophagus front remains relatively obscure in the Archeological Museum of Istanbul, where it did not even have a plaque when I saw it a few years ago.

Some scholars, without much fanfare, have continued to assert the obvious, just as Grabar and Ruysschaert did. Peter Brown in his *Cult of the Saints*, for example, quoted Jerome, then bluntly stated, "Tomb and altar were joined."[100] Likewise, in 2000, John Crook quoted Jerome and then described "the tomb beneath the altar."[101] Most recently, experts in early Christian sacred space have identified the altar on the Pola Ivory as the altar, just as scholars from Gnirs onwards identified it as the altar until the Vatican intervened. Jelena Bogdanović, an expert on the earliest ciboria, or canopies, over altars, in her 2017 *The Framing of Sacred Space*, details the ivory. She mentions the portable altar theory, but then describes the two people under the ciborium as "leaning towards the altar."[102] Similarly, Noga-Banai describes the man and woman standing under the ciborium and then mentions the "altar between them."[103] For scholars who study ancient iconography, the altar in Old Saint Peter's looks like other altars. Clearly, it is high time to re-engage with the Vatican excavators' "reconstruction" of Old Saint Peter's sanctuary.

POSSIBLE IDENTIFICATION OF THE MALE AND FEMALE OFFICIANTS AT THE ALTAR TABLE

Quite arguably neither the Vatican's excavations nor the subsequent defensive scholarship would have occurred had the ivory sculptor carved the liturgical scene in Old Saint Peter's with two men at the altar instead of a man and a woman. Somewhat humorously, on the rare occasion when the sex of the woman goes unnoticed, the assumption is that both are priests.[104] Almost all art historians, however, identify the veiled woman on the right-hand side as a woman[105]—sometimes without further comment,[106] often as the spouse of the man opposite, but sometimes as the empress in an imperial pair, usually a mother and son.[107] For detail of the scene under the ciborium, see Fig. 7.6.

Fig. 7.6 Man (*left*) and woman (*right*) flank the altar. Old Saint Peter's Basilica. © Alinari Archives-Alinari Archive, Florence

Who was this woman? Margherita Guarducci in her 1978 book on the box proposed that this couple was Emperor Constantine and his mother, the Empress Helena. According to the book of popes, the *Liber Pontificalis*, Constantine and Helena donated a massive gold cross engraved with their names for the basilica's altar—perhaps the very cross shown in the niche just above the altar. Guarducci suggested that they could have been depicted at the mass that consecrated the basilica, most likely in 326, the last time they were in Rome together.[108] Nonetheless, more recent research demonstrates that the first section of the *Liber Pontificalis*, which includes the erection of Old Saint Peter's, was probably compiled around 535[109]—and it is remarkably unreliable regarding Old Saint Peter's construction. For example, its claim that Constantine completed the basilica may be a false later attribution intended to retroactively burnish Constantine's reputation.[110]

Davide Longhi, in his 2006 book about the ivory box, alternatively proposed that the woman was the western Augusta Galla Placidia (392–450) and that the man on the opposite side of the altar was her son, Valentinian III, the Augustus.[111] These Augusti lived during the period that the box was carved. Perhaps, like her niece Pulcheria, Galla Placidia modeled herself after Mary, because Bishop Ambrose himself instructed her as a child that empress mothers should follow Mary's example.[112] Supporting Longhi's identification of this woman as Galla Placidia, both Longhi and Guarducci identified Galla Placidia and Valentinian in one of the scenes on the other sides of the ivory box.[113] Another connection to Galla Placidia is that she built several churches in Ravenna, which is the box's most probable original destination.[114] A century later, Bishop Maximianus of Ravenna (499–556), who had been a deacon in Pola, is the best candidate to have re-donated the ivory reliquary box to the church near Pola, where it was then buried beneath the altar. Most importantly, both Augusti are known to have attended the annual all-night masses commemorating Peter in Old Saint Peter's.[115] And, after one of those rituals, Galla Placidia herself wrote in a letter that she and Valentinian had been "at the martyr's very altar."[116]

Various art historians have noticed that this woman was sculpted lifting some kind of container with both hands.[117] This container is sometimes hypothesized a pyxide holding a *brandea* or cloth strip, such as Gregory the Great described a hundred and fifty years later.[118] Bogdanović suggested that the container lifted was a *patera*, a bowl of liquid.[119] Indeed, if the sculptor had carved this woman as a man, then almost certainly from the beginning other scholars also would have identified her as the priest, the stone table as the altar in Old Saint Peter's, and the bowl she lifted with both hands the bowl of Eucharistic wine—a bowl like the jeweled bowl of the chalice that a century later the Augusta Theodora is seen lifting with both hands inside the Holy of Holies of San Vitale. The sculptor of this beautiful ivory box, therefore, potentially carved an imperial mother and son reprising the scene of Mary and her son at the Last Supper.

THEODORA AND JUSTINIAN IN SAN VITALE:
MODELING MARY AND JESUS AT THE LAST SUPPER

A century later, around the year 547, huge mosaic portraits of the Augusti Justinian and Theodora were installed flanking the altar inside the Holy of Holies of the orthodox Basilica of San Vitale in Ravenna, at that time the Western Empire's capital.[120] These mosaics suggest that Pulcheria's custom of participating at the communion in the Holy of Holies continued for at least a hundred years in Constantinople. The designer of these mosaics portrayed the Augusti, Theodora and Justinian, holding the chalice and paten on either side of the altar, apparently modeling the gender-parallel liturgy in the Hagia Sophia that they built, which still exists today. See the San Vitale apse in Fig. 7.7.

Almost all the art of this era has been lost in the East due to successive iconoclasms there, but here in the Western capital, on the left side of the altar, Justinian (483–564) was shown holding a large gold paten for the bread. He is flanked (if tops of heads are counted) by twelve men, including Bishop Maximianus (see Fig. 7.8). On the right side of the altar, Theodora (500–548) was shown lifting the large jeweled bowl of a Eucharistic chalice with both hands.[121] She is flanked by seven women, and also, two eunuchs, not quite men. They stand next to a curtained doorway, which may have meant that Theodora waited in the church vestibule to enter the altar area after Justinian, since she is also depicted inside the Holy of Holies with him.[122] See Theodora and her entourage in Fig. 7.9.

In addition to the chalice and platen, another motif of liturgical gender parallelism between these two mosaics is the way Justinian and Theodora are portrayed as the leaders of men and women clergy on each side. Most art historians note that to Justinian's left is Bishop Maximianus, who holds a large gold cross and whose name is written above his head. He has the episcopal pallium over his shoulder, one of the oldest representations in art of a man wearing the pallium, made in the same decade as the mosaics of Mary and Elizabeth wearing the episcopal pallium in the altar apse of the Euphrasiana Basilica (Figs. 4.9a, b and 4.10). Next to Maximianus is a second member of the male clergy, who holds a jeweled book, and finally, a deacon who carries a censer of incense.

Far less noticed is that to Theodora's left, three women have Eucharistic cloths, two with the white fringed strip of cloth hanging from the girdles at their waist, and a third carrying it in her hand.[123] Alexei Lidov cautions against a secular interpretation of this cloth just

Fig. 7.7 Apse mosaics flank the altar. Justinian and his entourage (*left*). Theodora and her entourage (*right*). San Vitale Basilica, Ravenna, ca. 547. © RCS/Alinari Archives Management, Florence

because women have it here: "Let me remind those who are convinced of the lay provenance of the handkerchief that Theodora with her retinue, as well as Justinian, are presented in San Vitale in a liturgical procession in the sanctuary, both holding liturgical vessels."[124] It appears, thus, that three male clergy were depicted to Justinian's left and three female clergy to Theodora's left.

Worthy of mention here is that although Procopius in his *Secret History* repeatedly identified Theodora as a prostitute, this may have been

Fig. 7.8   Justinian holds paten for the bread. San Vitale Basilica, Ravenna, ca. 547. Wilpert, *Römischen Mosaiken*, pl. 109

Fig. 7.9   Theodora holds chalice. Wilpert, *Römischen Mosaiken*, pl. 110

another example of sexual slander against a woman religious authority. Susan Ashbrook Harvey has identified a competing Syriac tradition about Theodora, a tradition which said Theodora was the righteous daughter of a Syriac priest.[125] A priestly lineage would be consistent with Theodora's pairing with Justinian at the ritual meal, as seen in these mosaics.

Byzantine historian Mischa Meier has detailed Justinian's extraordinary devotion to Mary, and also how Justinian interchanged imperial images with the divine image to create inescapable two-way visual analogies.[126] Justinian was not always portrayed with a halo, but here, both he and Theodora have large gold halos, the aura of divinity.[127] Thus, Justinian flanked by twelve men could have been seen as an analogy to Jesus with the Twelve. Theodora accompanied by seven women might have reminded viewers of Mary and the seven Hebrew virgins who accompanied her to the Temple, according to the popular *Protevangelium*.[128] Another clue that Theodora was to be viewed as interchangeable with Mary may be provided by an unusual scene of Epiphany on the hem of Theodora's *chlamys*—here three magi hold up their large gold platters toward Theodora with her halo.

The clergy and laity who approached the altar in San Vitale would have seen Theodora and Justinian flanking the altar with their clergy. Theodora offered the chalice and Justinian the paten in a liturgical ritual that paralleled that of the Eucharist taking place below. Together, the empress and emperor modeled a scene analogous to Mary and Jesus at the last supper sacrifice in the *Life of the Virgin*.

THIRD-CENTURY EVIDENCE OF GENDER PARITY AT THE OFFERING TABLE

Irenaeus's second-century complaint about a man and woman performing a Eucharistic ritual together in Gaul is affirmed by the above art that subsequently depicted similar gender parallelism at the altars of fifth- and sixth-century churches. Even earlier evidence of this gender parallel liturgy is suggested by third-century archeological artifacts, both from Palestine and from the Christian catacombs of Rome.

Third-century floor mosaics that flanked the offering table in the so-called Megiddo Church in Palestine provide very early evidence that men and women stood on opposite sides of the offering table. This small church building, in a Roman military compound, is dated ca. 230 and was abandoned ca. 305. Two stones in the floor are all that remain of the offering table, but on one side of these stones a floor mosaic commemorates two men, and on the other side, two mosaics commemorate five women, including Akeptous, who donated the table. This building was next to the bakery, which Joan E. Taylor suggests may indicate that meals of shared bread were a key function of the space.[129] The placement of these gendered mosaics on opposite sides of the offering table may identify where a man and a woman customarily stood during the offering. Given the depictions of gender parallelism at the altar in fifth- and sixth-century churches, these floor mosaics appear to provide concrete evidence of the same ritual practice.

Pre-Constantinian frescos of meal scenes in the Christian catacombs of Rome suggest a similar pairing, and also, female leadership in some cases. Numerous pre-Constantinian catacomb meal scenes with people around a tripod mensa laden with fish and bread, like this one, resemble later iconography of the Last Supper, such as seen in the sixth-century Last Supper mosaic in Sant'Apollinare Nuovo in Ravenna.[130] Catacomb meal scenes, however, often include women at the table.[131] These catacomb meal scenes may have represented funeral meals, and if so, may have been Eucharistic, because the Latin *Didascalia apostolorum* instructed that the Eucharist be performed in cemeteries.[132] Most unexpected is that artists typically depicted women raising the cup as the leaders of this meal. According to Janet Tulloch, "female figures dominate the cup action."[133] This female leadership is the opposite of what artists depicted in funeral scenes in Roman religion, which almost invariably portrayed men, not women, lifting the cup.[134] Tulloch noticed that several of these meal scenes portrayed pairs, a man and a woman, each holding a cup—but the woman standing and raising the cup as the leader.[135]

A slightly different scene of a gender parallel leadership at an offering table is found in a third-century fresco in the so-called Cubiculum of the Sacraments in the Callistus Catacomb in the city of Rome.[136] No cup is present, but the veiled woman stands with raised arms. She and a young man flank a tripod table laden with fish and bread.[137] The young man gestures with his right hand toward the fish and bread on the table; the woman stands slightly forward of the man[138] (see Fig. 7.10 for this fresco).

As suggested by the fact that its cubiculum was called the Cubiculum of the Sacraments, the fresco with the arms-raised woman and young man has often been described as Eucharistic, although today there is no agreement.[139] On the one hand, Paul Corbey Finney says, "No one (myself included) has the foggiest idea."[140] On the other hand, Karen Jo

Fig. 7.10 Gender parity at the offering table. Third-century fresco, Callistus Catacomb, Rome. Wilpert, *Malereien*, pl. 41.1

Torjesen calls the offering table a "Eucharistic altar."[141] To my knowledge, no one has suggested that the male and female pair in this fresco could represent Jesus and his mother presiding at the Last Supper, but a fresco depicting a meal scene with seven diners is adjacent.[142] In addition, an arms-raised woman and a young man is how early Christian artists paired Mary and her son on Eucharistic utensils.

The very oldest surviving Christian inscription that can be dated with any certainty tends to support the potential identification of the arms-raised woman as Mary. The fish and bread on the tripod table are common in catacomb meal scenes, and the fish itself was associated with a sacred meal in Judaism, as well as in some Jesus communities.[143] An epitaph written around the year 180 by Bishop Abercius of Phrygia, who called himself "a disciple of a holy shepherd," explains the symbolic importance of this fish as a communion, served along with bread and Christ wine.[144] This inscription, the very oldest, also preserves a clue about the identity of the arms-raised woman at the tripod table. Abercius had traveled widely, and he wrote that from the city of Rome to Ancient Syria, he was served "fish from a fountain, utterly huge and pure, which a holy virgin grasped and she freely distributed this to friends to eat at all times, having good wine/Christ-wine, giving it mixed, with bread."[145] The "holy virgin" that Abercius describes distributing the fish, bread, and wine seems likely to have represented the arguably best known of holy virgins, Jesus's mother. With Abercius's inscription, the tripod table laden with fish and bread now suggests a Eucharistic altar table, as Torjesen identifies it. In addition, it is fair to consider whether the artist intended the arms-raised woman to represent the holy virgin named Mary. In any case, the woman is on the right side of the offering table and the young man is on the left, the same as the woman and man at the altar that we see aboveground two centuries later inside Old Saint Peters Basilica.

Philo's report of the Therapeutae's gender parallel liturgy in Judea and the floor mosaics that flanked the offering table in the Megiddo army church in Palestine suggest that the tradition of male and female officiants at the offering table may have originated around Jerusalem. Whether the gender-parallel meal tradition among the Jesus followers originated in a Jewish meal ritual such as the one that Philo described, or not, both advocates and opponents described a gender-parallel clergy in some Jesus communities. We have many pieces of evidence, both text and art, which document the spread of this liturgy around the Mediterranean, from Palestine to Gaul, from East to West, from the backwaters of the empire to the most important orthodox basilicas in its imperial capitals of Rome, Constantinople, and Ravenna.

The *Life of the Virgin's* scribe said that the narrative was compiled from extracanonical writings that were "true and without error."[146] Given all the evidence, a now lost gospel, perhaps even the Hebrew gospel, may have been the source of its Last Supper scene. Although no copies of this lost gospel have survived, its tradition of gender parity in the liturgy must have been powerful, because it is witnessed in both literary and archeological remains, including in the two oldest iconographic artifacts to depict real people at the altar of a real church. I suggest that for early Jesus followers, catacomb meal scenes with both men and women at the table may have symbolized the Last Supper in this narrative tradition.

The gender theology behind Mary and Jesus co-officiating at the last supper is likely related to ancient concepts of pairs such as *koinonos* (Jewish and Christian), *syzygoi, conhospitae*, spiritual brothers and sisters, and double monasteries. Almost certainly this gender theology was based on scripture such as Genesis 1:27 and Galatians 3:28—both male and female in the divine image. What is certain is that for centuries, gender parallelism persisted in the Christian liturgy, the most symbolic place where the divine gender order is modeled.

Acknowledgements Special thanks to Luca Badini Confalonieri, Research Director of the Wijngaards Institute of Catholic Research, who initiated my research on Cerula and Bitalia, and contributed to it.

CHAPTER 8

Modes of Silencing the Past

The pendulum of cultural change always swings—perhaps not as far as where it started, but never still. Cultural change takes place under competing forces. Its graph is not a straight line. It is a series of waves. No pope, emperor, theologian, or church council is ever so influential as to immediately change deeply embedded gender roles.

Pope Gelasius himself died after only four years. And by no means did all subsequent popes appear to agree with him. The pendulum swung. A hundred and fifty years later, Pope John IV commissioned the mosaic in San Venantius chapel in the Lateran Baptistery, where *Maria archiepisocopa* stands arms-raised above the altar, wearing the episcopal pallium. John IV was from Zadar, the same city where today the archeological museum holds the reliquary box that portrays an arms-raised woman titled MARIA paired with a shepherd titled PASTOR, and a day's sail from the Euphrasiana Basilica, where the apse mosaics portray both Mary and Elizabeth wearing the episcopal pallium. Two hundred years after John IV, Pope Paschal twice commemorated his mother as *Theodora episcopa* in Santa Prassede. Paschal also commissioned the apse mosaic in Santa Maria in Domnica, which portrays Mary holding the Eucharistic cloth above the altar.

The transformation of gender roles in Christianity was slow, a series of undulations over time and geographical areas. Not only popes, but also communities and churches opposed the cultural change. For example,

© The Author(s) 2019
A. Kateusz, *Mary and Early Christian Women*,
https://doi.org/10.1007/978-3-030-11111-3_8

the churches of Cerula and Bitalia publicized their support for the ordination of women bishops. The mere fact that Gelasius complained provides historical evidence, not only that some women were Eucharistic officiants, but also, of the conflict.

MODES OF SILENCING THE PAST

Over many centuries, the redaction of markers of female authority, from both art and early Christian narratives, slowly continued. This effort has been largely successful in silencing some of the oldest memories of biblical and apostolic women who held central ritual and community leadership roles. The silencing extends to memories of the women named in the canonical gospels. What do we really know, for example, about the apostle Junia? Or Prisca? Or Mary Magdalene? Or Martha?

Christoph Markschies estimates that 85% of the early Christian texts *that we know about* from the first two centuries did not survive.[1] Who knows how many more were lost that we do not know about because the silencing of them was complete and no mention of them has survived? Consider, for example, the *Gospel of Mary*. The scribal silence around the *Gospel of Mary* was so thorough that until 1896, when the first fragment was purchased in Egypt, no one had any clue that a gospel by this name had ever existed. Yet since 1896, fragments of two more manuscripts of the *Gospel of Mary* have been discovered, one Coptic and another Greek.[2] Three fragments in two languages suggest that at one time the *Gospel of Mary* was widely read. Yet the ancient silence around this gospel was profound. Not a word. Not a whisper. Crickets.

Harriet I. Flower says with respect to Roman political culture: "Choosing what to remember must entail also the choice of what to forget, what to pass over in silence, and what to obscure."[3] In the fourth century, Athanasius came up with the first list of books in a canon, and in the same letter that he listed these, he instructed that the other books be rejected *and silence be maintained about them*—"Let us command ourselves not to proclaim anything in them nor to speak anything in them."[4] Book burning decrees, such as the Gelasian Decree, chose what was to be silenced, and the list of books to be burned was long. In the case of some books, such decrees likely influenced scribes to redact their sacred texts. If these scribes, or their masters, wanted to keep at least a skeleton of the story that traditionally had been read in church in order to preserve the memory of a beloved heroine such as Mary or Thecla or

Mariamne—whose narratives the Gelasian Decree anathematized[5]—they had to choose what in her story to silence.

Most scribes were silent about their silencing. The Gelasian Decree, however, survived. Cyril of Jerusalem recounted burning the Gospel of the Hebrews. Some Dormition homilists—John of Thessalonica and pseudo-Melito—tried to defend their censorship of the longer narrative, and thereby left a record of their shortening. Nonetheless, the vast majority of scribes were silent about what they had done—but by comparing multiple manuscripts of a text we can identify some of what they excised. Most texts, as Markschies calculates, did not survive since 85% of the texts we know about did not. We can only suppose, from our sample of one, the *Gospel of Mary*, that the level of silencing that took place with respect to other gospels that featured important women—Junia, Chloe, Nympha, Apphia, Lydia, Phoebe, Tryphaena, Tryphosa, Mary the mother of Mark, Rufus's mother, Nereus's sister, Prisca, Priscilla, Maximilla, Quintilla, Philip's prophetess daughters—was equally profound.

These scribes' silence about their silencing followed the various cultural practices of erasing memory, from the formal *damnatio memoriae* of the Roman Senate, to the Jewish and Christian tradition of *anathema*. As Flower says, these types of sanctions "are deliberately designed strategies that aim to change the picture of the past, whether through erasure or redefinition, or both."[6] Charles W. Hedrick Jr. explains why the Roman silence about their silencing was so important: "It is integral to the process of forgetting that it pretend not to be a repression at all, that it dissimulate itself."[7]

The scribal activity associated with the redaction of the markers of female religious authority functioned as a form of *damnatio memoriae*, but instead of obliterating a single powerful political foe or family from the written record, it attempted to erase the memory of powerful historical women who had exercised religious authority. Perhaps as time passed some scribes came to consider these early women leaders as enemies; in any case, scribes' selective pruning of markers of female liturgical authority indicates that *female* liturgical authority, not male, was their concern. Did scribes redact memories of men? Without doubt, yes, as the Gelasian Decree's list of anathematized books demonstrates, books about men and written by men were also condemned when the men or their books were later called "heretical"—including, remarkably, even the "Works of Tertullian," after he himself proved the awesome spiritual power of New

Prophecy prophetesses by joining them.[8] Yet relative to narratives about women with religious authority, more long narratives about male apostles have survived. The same silencing appears to be the case for the writings authored by men versus those by women. For example, despite all their books condemned to the fires in the Gelasian Decree, large numbers of books by Tertullian and Clement of Alexandria have nonetheless survived, yet not one page has survived of the many books written by the New Prophecy prophetesses Priscilla and Maximilla.[9]

BREAKING THE BOX OF OUR FALSE IMAGINATION OF THE PAST

The scribal custom of silently excising depictions of female authority, while leaving male authority intact, cannot be attributed to serendipity. Given what was redacted—Mary's liturgical authority, the title of "apostle" for Thecla, Mariamne, Irene, and Nino—this mode of domination reimagined the Christian past with an exclusively all-male apostolate. The scribes, including modern translators, who changed the apostle Junia's name to the masculine *Junius* in Paul's letter to the Romans—"a sex-change by translation"[10]—performed the same type of silencing with the same type of motive, that is, the motive of defending the false proposition that only men had been apostles, because that false proposition supported the claim that only men had the right to leadership roles in the church.[11]

In ways both subtle and heavy-handed, scribes—ancient, medieval, and modern—buttressed, and continue to buttress, the myth of an all-male clergy. Shoemaker's *Life of the Virgin* is by no means the only modern English edition of an important text that did not footnote redactions of the markers of female religious authority that were in the original text. A prominent case in point is Douglas M. Parrott's translation of *The Sophia of Jesus Christ* in Nag Hammadi Codex III, which was published in the widely relied upon *The Nag Hammadi Library in English* edited by James M. Robinson. Without any explanation or footnote, Parrott translated the Coptic word for "disciples"—from the Greek loan word μαθητής—as "disciples" when in the masculine, but as "women" when in the feminine. Thus Parrott's translation reads: "After he rose from the dead, his twelve *disciples* and seven *women* continued to be his followers."[12] The correct translation of the Coptic is: "After he rose from the dead, his twelve male *disciples* and seven female *disciples* continued to be his followers." Without explanation or footnote, Parrott did not translate the word literally and thereby obscured the original meaning to all but Coptic scholars. Imagine how often this has been done over the centuries if scholars are still doing it, and seemingly without consequence.

Perhaps some modern scholars' lack of imagination about ancient gender roles led them to innocently redact or translate a text so that it better matched what they believed *must* have been the original. Or, perhaps they did so acceding to the demands of their dissertation supervisor, or editor, or publisher. Or, perhaps, they deliberately redacted the text in order to support a desired status quo in their church's gender politics. The result is the same: the continuing cultivation of a myth.

Unlike the doubt that can be entertained regarding the naïve motives of some scholars, a rather clear-cut example of deliberate institutional self-interest would appear to be the Vatican excavation report with its two incorrect drawings of the ancient ciborium as square. Contriving how to successfully censor the ivory image of the woman at the altar inside Old Saint Peter's Basilica—inside the heart of the Vatican's symbolic power—probably consumed most of the ten years that the Vatican excavators took to write their report. One can only imagine how much they began to sweat when they realized that their own excavations had proven that the ivory scene was in Old Saint Peter's. Not surprisingly, their report passes over in silence the fact that previous art experts identified a woman at the altar in the ivory scene.[13] This case is particularly annoying to me because it consumed literally months of my time as I tried to reconcile my own imagination of the truthfulness of Vatican specialists—yes, I assumed they were honest—against what I was actually seeing on the ivory scene that everyone agreed depicted the liturgy in Old Saint Peter's sanctuary.

This is how the Vatican excavators used my own imagination against me. Their final report sandwiched the photo of the ivory scene between two drawings that they purported were reconstructions of Old Saint Peter's ciborium, both of which drew the ciborium as a square. The first drawing was a floor plan of the supposed excavations, and it illustrated a square ciborium. Later when I more carefully studied the floor plan, I realized that the lines demarking the square ciborium were dotted, signaling that this area actually had *not* been excavated—but the dots were faint and easy to overlook. The next page was a photo of the ivory with its scene of the liturgy in Old Saint Peter's sanctuary—yet when I turned the page and saw the photo, I was still visualizing the dotted lines of the hypothetical square ciborium from the previous page. The following page had yet another drawing of the reconstruction, this time a full-page three-dimensional drawing of a square ciborium—presented as real, no longer hypothetical—*and it reinforced my imagination of a square ciborium*. Whenever I looked at the photo of the ivory, I flipped back and forth between it and the two drawings. I could see that the ciborium on the ivory was *not* a square—but I imagined it *was* a square because that was what the Vatican drawings showed. This tactic of sandwiching the photo of the ivory between two drawings of a "reconstructed" square ciborium confounded me for months. I tried to imagine why such a talented ivory sculptor had been unable to execute basic artistic perspective and represent a square. The ciborium didn't look square, but it was square. I blamed the artist. When I think back now I realize how absurd it was that I could not see the truth in front of me—my imagination had been skillfully manipulated. Over several months, I repeatedly pulled out the two drawings of the square ciborium, then looked at the ivory scene, with the effect that the two drawings continued to exert control over my imagination!

It was only when I *finally* translated the excavators' Italian beneath the photo of the ivory that the mystery suddenly solved itself. The Italian said the ciborium on the ivory had the very same function and similar form as the famous monument over Christ's tomb inside the Church of the Anastasis in Jerusalem—"*ha esattamente la medesima funzione e forma simile al monumento eretto da Costantino nella* Anastasis *sulla tomba del Salvatore.*"[14] I knew that the famous monument over Christ's tomb had *not* been square. It had fit inside the Rotunda, and was round shaped, quite likely hexagonal. Suddenly, I saw that the ivory sculptor's artistic perspective was perfect. The ivory ciborium was not sculpted as a square. It was sculpted as a trapezoid, a half-hexagon. The Vatican excavators had hidden a woman at the altar in plain sight—and for months my own imagination of the fictional square ciborium prevented me from seeing the obvious.

Censorship appears to have been intense in some periods during the first millennium. For example, according to Paul Bradshaw almost no liturgical manuscripts have survived from the first seven centuries, neither Christian nor Jewish.[15] We would expect the liturgy in at least some of these manuscripts to have paralleled the liturgy seen on the ivory, but almost no liturgical manuscripts have survived. In the eighth century, however, large numbers of liturgical manuscripts suddenly filled the void, all looking the same, or, as F. L. Cross says, they have "a specious similarity. They are written in similar scripts and on similar writing materials ... their intent was *not* to make an accurate reproduction of an existing model."[16] It may have been during this same period that art depicting both men and women at the altar was destroyed. In any case, the only such art to survive was by then buried underground—the ivory box under the altar of the church near Pola and the sarcophagus front inside a hypogeum near the Theodosian walls in Istanbul.

Censorship is seldom complete. Draw together all the perceived outliers in the data. What pattern do they create? In the current study, the outliers, both literary and iconographic, speak of Mary and her son paired in liturgical authority. They speak of women apostles and women leaders in the assembly, including women overseers or bishops—they speak of men and women together at the offering table. Whether today they are called pastors, priests, presbyters, presidents, ministers, deacons, bishops, or archbishops, the pattern reveals men and women presiding at the offering together, male and female standing in for God, *elohim*, the divine image, both male and female, in accordance with Genesis 1:27 and Galatians 3:28.

The Therapeutae in Judea had a gender parallel liturgy. Quite likely, given Bernadette J. Brooten's epigraphs of gender parallel synagogue titles, this liturgy continued to be performed around the Mediterranean in some synagogues. At the same time, it was performed in army churches in Palestine, as witnessed by the Megiddo army church. In Gaul and Asia Minor, Jesus communities followed the same liturgical pattern, which was painted in the catacombs of the city of Rome, where, aboveground, two hundred years later, women and men flanked the altar in Old Saint Peter's Basilica. In Constantinople, this liturgy was modeled in the second Hagia Sophia, and, as portrayed in the San Vitale mosaics, it continued to be modeled in the next Hagia Sophia, which still stands.

Further suggesting the importance of women in the liturgy during the early Christian era, women, and only women, were depicted in the liturgical procession to the altar table at the most holy site in Christendom, the Anastasis Church built over Jesus's empty sepulcher in Jerusalem. By comparison, through the end of Theodora and Justinian's reign in 565, to my knowledge, no art has survived that depicts a Christian man without a woman at an altar table in any church.[17] Instead, iconographic and textual evidence supports the claim that from the beginning of the Christian era, women—both alone and with men—stood at the table and officiated the blessing, the agape, the offering, the Eucharist, the sacrifice, the Body and Blood, whatever their community called it.

These women church leaders formed a continuous line from the first recorded church mothers, the leaders of the New Testament house assemblies, almost all of which were attributed to women—the houses of Chloe, Nympha, Apphia, Priscilla, Lydia, and Mary the mother of Mark. These women church leaders also followed in the footsteps of Phoebe, Prisca, Mary, Tryphaena, Tryphosa, Julia, Euodia, Syntyche, Dorcas, Damarias, Rufus's mother, Nereus's sister, the apostle named Junia, and other women apostles. Their Jewish foremothers were their models: Mary the mother of Jesus, Elizabeth the mother of John the Baptist, Mary Magdalene, Mary of Bethany, Anna the prophet, Martha, Joanna, Susanna, Salome, and many more women leaders in Judea, Israel, and the diaspora.

The overarching goal of this study was to demonstrate how our false imagination of the past impedes our interpretation of ancient artifacts that depicted Christian women as ministerial and Eucharistic leaders. The past is political. Therein lies its power. Therein lies why it has been censored. When such evidence exists, no church can exclude women from its leadership and remain true to its origins.

*   *   *

"Be submissive like the Virgin." What a horrible lie to tell a girl. How many times has it been told to how many little girls? How many little boys have heard the same aberrant teaching about how a girl should behave?

Would my friend's submission to a violent man have happened if her priest had taught the girls about the early Christian Mary? Would the abuse have happened if she had grown up seeing both a woman and a man celebrating the Eucharist? It was for little girls that I did this research.

Notes, Abbreviations, and References

Notes Chapter 1

1. For example, Warner, *Alone of All Her Sex*, 333–39; Kristeva, "Stabat Mater," 160–86; Haskins, *Mary Magdalen*, 386–94.
2. Schüssler Fiorenza, *Memory of Her*, 97–241, quote from 97.
3. See Brock, *Mary Magdalene*; Schaberg, *Resurrecting Mary*; de Boer, *Mary Magdalene Cover-Up*; Jansen, *Making of the Magdalen*.
4. Most interesting, they do not clearly identify her at the cross or tomb. Perhaps in these scenes for some reason they called her by the name of her less important son, as *Mary of James*, as it reads in the Greek, but according to Richard Bauckham, the identification of a woman by the name of her son without also the word "mother"—μήτηρ—was unattested in Palestine; see Bauckham, *Gospel Women*, 206.
5. Weitzmann, *Frescoes of the Dura Synagogue*; for discussion, see Pearce, *Image and Its Prohibition*; for examples, see Levine, *Visual Judaism in Late Antiquity*; Fine, *Art and Judaism in the Greco-Roman World*; and Fine, *Sacred Realm*.
6. Cohen, *Beginnings of Jewishness*, 263ff.
7. Bernstein, "Women and Children in Legal and Liturgical Texts from Qumran," 204–9.
8. Philo of Alexandria, *On the Contemplative Life*, 1–90, esp. 68–69. For the leadership of women in this sect, as is suggested by the text, see Taylor, *Jewish Women Philosophers*, 309–43; that these women were not actually virgins, because Philo simply called high-status women *parthenos*, see Tervanotko, *Denying Her Voice*, 231–33, and for Tervanotko's

© The Editor(s) (if applicable) and The Author(s) 2019
A. Kateusz, *Mary and Early Christian Women*,
https://doi.org/10.1007/978-3-030-11111-3

parsing together varied traditions about Miriam's leadership more on a par with Moses' leadership, see the rest of *Denying Her Voice*.

9. Brooten, *Women Leaders in the Ancient Synagogue*, 5–99.

10. For diversity of opinion among rabbis regarding women, see Ilan, *Integrating Women into Second Temple History*, 1–8, 43–81; and Sassoon, *Status of Women in Jewish Tradition*.

11. Ilan, *Integrating Women into Second Temple History*, 253–62; and Ilan, "Notes and Observations on a Newly Published Divorce Bill," 195–202.

12. Kearns, *Virgin Mary, Monotheism, and Sacrifice*, 88–108, 137–65.

13. Kearns, *Virgin Mary, Monotheism, and Sacrifice*, 97.

14. For example, recensions of the Dormition narrative, about the death of Mary, survive in Syriac, Greek, Latin, Georgian, Coptic, Armenian, Ethiopic, and Gaelic; see van Esbroeck, "Textes littéraires sur l'Assomption," 265–68. The *Protevangelium* was even more widely translated.

15. Schüssler Fiorenza, *Jesus: Miriam's Child*, 182; Zervos, "Dating the Protevangelium," 415–34; Zervos, "Early Non-Canonical Annunciation Story," 686–88; Cartlidge, *Art and the Christian Apocrypha*, 23; Elliott, *New Testament Apocrypha*, 50. Also see Lowe, "IOYΔAIOI of the Apocrypha," 56–71.

16. Lowe, "IOYΔAIOI of the Apocrypha," 56–71. For more regarding issues of Jewish and Christian identity, and the fluid boundaries between the two until Late Antiquity, see Boyarin, *Borderlines*.

17. See especially, Horner, "Jewish Aspects of the *Protevangelium of James*," 313–35; and Smid, *Protevangelium Jacobi*, 9–12. For Mary in the Temple, see Nutzman, *Protevangelium of James*, 551–78; and Vuong, "Let Us Bring Her Up to the Temple," 418–32.

18. Peppard, *World's Oldest Church*, 155–201, Fig. 5.1. For more discussion substantiating Peppard's identification, see Chapter 6.

19. Kateusz, "Ascenson of Chris or Ascension of Mary," esp. 298–302, Fig. 12. For more evidence, see Chapters 4 and 5.

20. Cartlidge, *Art and the Christian Apocrypha*, 17–18.

21. For the donkey, see *Protevangelium*, 17.2–18.1, and for the ox-manger, see *Protevangelium*, 22.2 (Cullmann, "Protevangelium of James," 433, 436). For more of the earliest art of the nativity, see Cartlidge, *Art and the Christian Apocrypha*, Figs. 1.2 and 1.3, and Chapter 5.

22. *Protevangelium*, 13.2, 15.2 (Schneemelcher, *New Testament Apocrypha*, 1:431, 432); in one passage, Joseph reminds Mary that she was raised in the Holy of Holies, and in the second passage as Temple priest reminds her of the same. Note that Vuong asserts that Mary was depicted in the Temple to emphasize her purity, but Vuong does not specifically address why Mary also was depicted in the Holy of Holies;

see Vuong, *Gender and Purity*, esp. 173–76. See also, Hollman, "Temple Virgin and Virgin Temple," 110–28, yet Hollman also does not specifically address the Holy of Holies references.

23. *Gospel of Bartholomew*, 2.15–21 (Schneemelcher, *New Testament Apocrypha*, 1:544–45).

24. Regarding the non-controversial third-century dating, see Schneemelcher, *New Testament Apocrypha*, 1:540; and Shoemaker, "Mary the Apostle," 217. For the archaic elements, see *Gospel of Bartholomew*, 1.7 and 1.9 [Jesus vanished from the cross]; 2.15–20 [a Being came down as a great angel]; 3.17 and 4.61 [Mary gave birth without pain]. For detailed discussion on its archaic elements (some likely second century) and dating (difficult), see Kaestli, *Évangile de Barthélemy*, 45–94.

25. *Gospel of Bartholomew*, 2.6–13 (Schneemelcher, *New Testament Apocrypha*, 1:543–44). For the description of Mary in this scene as essentially their liturgical leader, see Shoemaker, "Mary the Apostle," 217.

26. *Gospel of Bartholomew*, 2.6–7 (Schneemelcher, *New Testament Apocrypha*, 1:543).

27. For a debate between Peter and Paul, which Peter wins, see Ethiopic *Liber Requiei*, 46–49 (Shoemaker, *Ancient Traditions*, 317–18). Also see Chapter 4, which demonstrates how later scribes replaced Mary with Peter, including as the leader of her prayer scene.

28. *Gospel of Bartholomew*, 2.7 (Schneemelcher, *New Testament Apocrypha*, 1:543).

29. *Gospel of Bartholomew*, 2.7 (Schneemelcher, *New Testament Apocrypha*, 1:544). The author used a version of 1 Corinthians 11:3 here.

30. *Gospel of Bartholomew*, 2.8 (Schneemelcher, *New Testament Apocrypha*, 1:544). Emphasis mine.

31. For more discussion about this scene, see Kateusz, "Two Women Leaders"; Brock, *Mary Magdalene*, 139–40; also Shoemaker, *Mary in Early Christian Faith*, 93–95.

32. *Gospel of Bartholomew*, 2.13 (Schneemelcher, *New Testament Apocrypha*, 1:544).

33. *Gospel of Bartholomew*, 4.1–5, quote from 4.5 (Schneemelcher, *New Testament Apocrypha*, 1:545–46, esp. 46). Emphasis mine.

34. Demetrius of Antioch, *Discourse on the Birth of Our Lord*, 35b (Budge, *Miscellaneous Coptic Texts*, 664). Emphasis mine.

35. Ephrem, *Hymn on Mary, no. 2*, 10 (Brock, *Bride of Light*, 36). Emphasis mine.

36. Epiphanius of Salamis, *Panarion*, 78 23.3–4 and 79 1.7 (Frank, *Panarion*, 618, 621). Some recensions of Epiphanius's letter *Ancoratus*

do not specify it was women who offered bread, but in the text of *Ancoratus* that Epiphanius inserted at the end of his Book 78 in the *Panarion*, which immediately precedes Book 79 on the "collyridian" women priests, he specifies that *women officiants* were offering this sacrifice in Mary's name, which is consistent with what he also reports in Book 79.

37. For the detailed Six Books liturgy where bread was offered to Mary on the altar of the church, see Wright, "Departure of My Lady Mary," 152–53, as this folio is missing from the fifth-century palimpsest text, although the palimpsest text several times mentions this liturgy.
38. Kateusz, "Collyridian Déjà vu," 86–89; and Shoemaker, *Mary in Early Christian Faith*, 157–63.
39. Haines-Eitzen, *Gendered Palimpsest*, 77.
40. Kateusz, "Collyridian Déjà vu," 84–85.
41. Kateusz, "Collyridian Déjà vu," 79–84; for more detail on Mary performing these activities, see Chapter 2.
42. Fairclough, *Language and Power*, 73.
43. Fairclough, *Discourse and Social Change*, 137–99.
44. See, for example, Brown, *World of Late Antiquity*; Brown, *Power and Persuasion*; and Brown, *Authority and the Sacred*.
45. See the following chapters, especially Chapter 7.
46. Foucault, *History of Sexuality*, 139–44.
47. Fig. 1.2, MARIA on catacomb gold glass is from Perret, *Catacombes*, vol. 4, pl. 32, Fig. 101. Figure 1.3 is Mary in an apse painting in Maria in Pallara, Rome, from Wilpert, *Römischen Mosaiken*, pl. 224. Figure 1.4 is an oil painting by Antonio Solario (1465–1530), today in the National Gallery of Denmark, Open Access.
48. Thompson, "Vatican II and Beyond," 409–19.

NOTES CHAPTER 2

1. See 1 Corinthians 1:11 for Chloe's house; Colossians 4:15 for Nympha's; Philemon 1:2 for Apphia's; Romans 16:3 for Priscilla listed first, and 1 Cor 16:19 for the church in her house; Acts 16:40 for Lydia's; Acts 12:12 for Mary the mother of Mark's; and 2 John 1:1 for the unnamed lady.
2. See Romans 16. Regarding the use of *prostatis* for women such as Phoebe, see Montevecchim, "Donna 'prostatis,'" 103–15.
3. I follow Eldon Epp regarding that later scribes redacted the gender of Junia's name, remaking it into the male gendered name, *Junius*, and thereby eliminating a female apostle; see Epp, *Junia*. See Chapter 3 for more women titled "apostle," thereby further validating Paul's use of this title for Junia.

4. Especially given the pairing of Junia and Andronicus, our earliest evidence for the apostolate, see Taylor, "Two by Two." Bauckham suggests that Junia may have been Joanna, known from Luke 8:3 and 24:10; Bauckham, *Gospel Women*, 109–202.

5. Pliny the Younger, *Epistle*, 10.96.

6. Celsus, *On the True Doctrine*, 6:111–18.

7. Clark, "Holy Women," 413.

8. Clark, "Holy Women," 415.

9. See, for example, the narratives about the male apostles Andrew, John, Paul, Peter, Thomas, and others in Schneemelcher, *New Testament Apocrypha*.

10. Clark, "Holy Women," 416.

11. Clark, "Holy Women," 413–16; and Delehaye, *Legends of the Saints*.

12. Knust, *To Cast the First Stone*, 115–16.

13. Hurtado, "Pericope of the Adulteress," 152.

14. Goodacre, *Thomas and the Gospels*, 109–27. Compare, however, to Matthew D. C. Larsen in *Gospels before the Book*, where he comes to essentially the opposite conclusion from the shorter verses and text of Mark, and argues that the longer version of Matthew is a later elaboration of Mark; notably, Larsen does not significantly engage with recent scholarship related to the validity of *lectio brevior potior*.

15. Epp, *Studies in the Theory and Method*, 14. Emphasis added.

16. Metzger, *Text of the New Testament*, 120. Emphasis added.

17. Butts, "Manuscript Transmission as Reception History," 281.

18. Bauckham, *Fate of the Dead*, 347.

19. Bovon, "Introduction to the *Acts of Philip*," 7–8. Emphasis added.

20. Bovon, "Byzantine Witnesses," 11.

21. Slater, "Relationship Between Community and Text," 286.

22. Shoemaker, "Mary the Apostle," 212–13.

23. Van Esbroeck, "Textes littéraires sur l'Assomption," 265–68; Nubian Coptic manuscripts can now be added to van Esbroeck's list; see Hubai, *Koptische apokryphen aus Nubien*.

24. Shoemaker, *Ancient Traditions*, 238–45; Shoemaker, "Jesus' Gnostic Mom," 162; Shoemaker, "New Syriac Dormition Fragments," 266; and also see 259n1 where Shoemaker notes additional scholars who concur with his dating.

25. Ethiopic *Liber Requiei*, 1; Shoemaker, *Ancient Traditions*, 6–7, 32–46, 232–56. For more discussion of the Great Angel, see Frend, "Gnostic Origins of the Assumption Legend"; Shoemaker, "New Syriac Dormition Fragments," 259–78; and Sellew, "Early Coptic Witness," 37–69.

26. Bagatti, "La verginità di Maria negli apocrifi del II–III secolo," 281–92; Bagatti, *New Discoveries at the Tomb of the Virgin Mary*, 14, 57–58.

For rabbinic Midrash influence, see Manns, "Mort de Marie," 507–15; see also Norelli, "Letteratura apocrifa sul transito di Maria," 121–65; and Cothenet, "Traditions bibliques et apocalyptiques," 155–75.

27. This manuscript, usually dated fifth century, is detailed below. A fifth-century fragment called the "Obsequies," edited by William Wright, is probably not Six Books, but it is difficult to tell because what remains of the narrative begins after Mary's death; all other folios are lost.

28. Van Esbroeck, "Textes littéraires," 265–85; van Esbroeck calls it the "Bethlehem and incensings" text tradition because its text also says Mary went to Bethlehem. For censers and incense, also see Kateusz, "Dormition Urtext."

29. Baldi, "Assunzione di Maria," 121–25; and Cothenet, "Marie dans les Apocryphes," 118–30, 143. Also Kateusz, "Collyridian déjà vu," 92, regarding the possibility of first-century oral traditions about Mary behind the text.

30. Smith Lewis, "Transitus Mariae," 39–43. Note that a second, apparently later, passage, which has nothing to do with Mary and which Shoemaker describes as "awkwardly joined," contains a story about the burial of the cross and is appended to the end of this passage in some manuscripts, including the palimpsest; it likely reflects fourth-century concerns about validating the story of the Empress Helena's discovery of the cross; see Shoemaker, "Peculiar Version of the *Inventio Crucis*," 75–81, 79.

31. For more discussion on the gradual parting of the ways, see Boyarin, *Border Lines*; and essays in Becker, *Ways That Never Parted*.

32. Bauckham, *Fate of the Dead*, 358–60, quotations on 358 and 359.

33. Förster, *Transitus Mariae*, 225–29; and Kateusz, "Collyridian Déjà vu," 77–78, 92.

34. Kateusz, "Collyridian Déjà vu," 79–84.

35. Schneemelcher, *New Testament Apocrypha*, 1:395, 423.

36. Smith Lewis, "Transitus Mariae," 12–69. Today the Six Books manuscript is in the Agnes Smith Lewis collection at Westminster Theological College at Cambridge, apparently still uncatalogued and unnumbered, per Mimouni, *Dormition et Assomption de Marie*, 101n90.

37. Smith Lewis, *Old Syriac Gospels*; Smith Lewis, *Light on the Four Gospels*; and Smith Lewis, *Translation of the Four Gospels*.

38. Smith Lewis, "Transitus Mariae," x; Shoemaker usually refers to it as fifth century; Shoemaker, *Ancient Traditions*, 33, 46–48, esp. 48; and Shoemaker, "New Syriac Dormition Fragments," 259–78, esp. 264.

39. Tertullian, *On Prescription Against Heretics*, 41 (*ANF* 3:263).

40. McGowan, *Ancient Christian Worship*, 153–54.

41. Smith Lewis, "Transitus Mariae," 34. Also see Kateusz, "Collyridian Déjà vu," 79–85. For sealing as an early form of baptism, see more discussion in Chapter 3 with respect to Thecla; also McGowan, *Ancient Christian Worship*, 153–54; and Ferguson, *Baptism in the Early Church*, 218–20. If not for the water, sealing here could possibly refer to the redemption by oil that Irenaeus of Lyon knew (*Against Heresies*, 1.21.4); alternatively, it could potentially signify the bishop's signing the forehead of the newly baptized after the bishop's hand laying ceremony, or a chrism or chrismation. All of these would have signified that Mary was a bishop, since these were sacraments performed by or controlled by a bishop; see McGowan, *Ancient Christian Worship*, 154, 174; Johnson, *Rites of Christian Initiation*, 90–91; and Mitchell, *Baptismal Anointing*, 85.

42. For detailed comparisons of scribal redactions of female religious authority between the texts of these three manuscripts, see Kateusz, "Collyridian Déjà vu," 79–85.

43. Wright, "Departure of My Lady Mary," 129–60. For its dating, see Wright, *Contributions to the Apocryphal Literature*, 8. This manuscript is in the British Library, catalogued as BL, syr. Add. 14 484, f. 16r.–45r.

44. Shoemaker, *Ancient Traditions*, 142–67 for discussion, 375–96 for the text; also Chaine, *Apocrypha de beata Maria Virgine*, 17–42; this manuscript is Paris BN éthiop. 53, per Mimouni, *Dormition*, 242n13. Another Ethiopic manuscript contains a *very* similar narrative; see Budge, "History of the Holy and Pure Mary," 168–201.

45. Smith Lewis, "Transitus Mariae," 34–35; Wright, "Departure of My Lady Mary from This World," 141–42; *Ethiopic Six Books*, 35–36 (Shoemaker, *Ancient Traditions*, 385).

46. For the passage in the palimpsest text, see Smith Lewis, "Transitus Mariae," 34, but also see the same complete passage in Budge, "History of the Blessed Virgin Mary," 136; and Gonzalez Casado, "Relaciones lingüísticas entre el siríaco y el árabe," 572.

47. Jensen, *God's Self-Confident Daughters*, 6–8.

48. For Sozomen, *Ecclesiastical History*, 2.7 (*N&P-NF* Series, 2.2, 263); for Rufinus, see Lerner, *Wellspring of Georgian Historiography*, 38.

49. See Wardrop, *Life of Saint Nino*; and Lerner, *Wellspring of Georgian Historiography*.

50. Jensen, *God's Self-Confident Daughters*, 8. Emphasis mine. Cornelia Horn documents that some Eastern Orthodox critics even tried to declare Nino was a man; Horn, "St. Nino and the Christianization of Pagan Georgia," 258.

51. Van Esbroeck, "Textes littéraires," 265–85; van Esbroeck calls it the "Bethlehem and incensings" text tradition because its text also says Mary went to Bethlehem.

52. Smith Lewis, "Transitus Mariae," 24–25, 46–47; Wright, "Departure of My Lady Mary from This World," 135–36, 146; and *Ethiopic Six Books*, 26–27, 40 (Shoemaker, *Ancient Traditions*, 378–79, 389).

53. For an excellent study on the early use of incense in Christianity, see Harvey, *Scenting Salvation*, esp. 11–98. Note that Harvey wondered whether the dating of Six Books manuscripts was correct, because that dating means that over time mentions of incense decreased rather than increased, which goes against the grain of what is assumed to have been the trajectory of use of incense in the Christian liturgy. The evidence I present here indicates that the use of incense by *women* decreased over time, and that decrease is reflected in scribal excisions. At the same time as the scribal excisions, men apparently increasingly took over the role.

54. Smith Lewis, "Transitae Mariae," 20.

55. *Ethiopic Six Books*, 24 (Shoemaker, *Ancient Traditions*, 376).

56. Wright, "Departure of My Lady Mary," 133.

57. Smith Lewis, "Transitus Mariae," 47–48.

58. Wright, "Transitus Beate Virginis," 33–34; see more about this fragment, called "S-2," below.

59. Wright, "Departure of My Lady Mary," 146–47.

60. *Ethiopic Six Books*, 40 (Shoemaker, *Ancient Traditions*, 389).

61. Lewis, "Transitus Mariae," 24–25; *Ethiopic Six Books*, 26–27 (Shoemaker, *Ancient Traditions*, 378–79, quotation on 379). See also Wright, "Departure of My Lady Mary," 136.

62. A fresco of Mary on a bed painted in the Fortuna Temple in the city of Rome around the end of the ninth century could potentially be as old as the Deir al-Surian painting, but it depicts only Jesus popping his head into the scene, no other people are with Mary; see Lafontaine, *Peintures Médiévales*, pl. 8. Some of the paintings are missing, but three provide additional unusual scenes from the Dormition narrative; one depicts Mary with a crowd of women going to Bethlehem; one depicts John greeting Peter at the door to Mary's house; and one depicts three apostles carried by angels (many Dormition narratives describe only three apostles, not twelve); see plates 6, 9, and 10.

63. For more about this painting, see Innemée, "Virgins with Censers," 69–85; and Kateusz, "Ascension of Christ or Ascension of Mary," 295–97. Chiasm could explain why the artist painted only six women, three on both sides of Mary, indicating Mary's holiness as the seventh number. The *Protevangelium*, for example, specified that seven Hebrew virgins accompanied Mary to the Temple.

64. For the dating of the wall painting, see Innemée and Youssef, "Virgins and Censers," 69–70.

65. For an image of this token, see Rahmani, "Eulogia Tokens from Byzantine Bet She'an," 113–15, Fig. 10. This small token is marked with the symbol for the *Theotokos* and appears to depict Mary on her bed with three veiled women at her head. The token was broken at the foot of her bed and only one figure remains, but given that three women are at the foot of Mary's bed in the wall painting, it seems highly likely that originally the token depicted three there also. For more discussion, see Kateusz, "Ascension of Christ or Ascension of Mary," 295, 295n73. Rahmani posited that the faces were bearded, but he was unaware of the Deir al-Surian painting, which was discovered over a decade after he published; the painting clearly depicts women wearing head coverings—an explanation more consistent with both the iconography of the token and Rahmani's sketch of it; notably, a miniature painted in the Benedictional of St. Æthelwold, which is usually dated to the second half of the tenth century—very early for a Dormition scene—depicts Mary on her deathbed also accompanied by three women who are oriented near her head. Prescott, *Benedictional of St. Æthelwold*, folios 102v–103.

66. For dating of later examples of the iconography of the Dormition of Mary, see Myslivec, "Tod Mariens," col. 333–38. For examples of the later Dormition iconography, see Cutler, "Mother of God in Ivory," 170, 173, Fig. 112; Evangelatou, "Symbolism of the Censer," Figs. 10.1, 10.3–10.5, 10.9; and Miner, *Early Christian and Byzantine Art*, pl. 26, Fig. 142, pl. 28 Fig. 141, and pl. 29, Fig. 140. Some Dormition art retained the women in the background behind the twelve apostles, or in a few Byzantine examples, in the foreground. For a Western example dated 950–1000 that preserved women around Mary's bed, see Prescott, *Benedictional of St. Æthelwold*, folios 102v–103.

67. Innemée, "Dayr al-Suryan," 1.

68. Shoemaker, "Gender at the Virgin's Funeral," 552–58.

69. Smith Lewis, "Transitae Mariae," 20.

70. For discussion, see Ernst, *Martha at the Margins*, 152–58; and Karras, "Liturgical Functions of Consecrated Women," 109–15. For the text of the *typikon*, see Papadoupolos-Kerameus, *Analekta*, 179–99. See also the correspondences between the Anastasis liturgy in Egeria and in the Armenian lectionary, per Bertonière, *Historical Development*, 72–105, esp. 88.

71. For an example when an artist clearly depicted Mary the mother as one of the two Marys at the tomb, see the Sancta Sanctorum reliquary box

in Fig. 4.3; Mary the mother of Jesus was typically identified as one of the two Marys in these scenes, and this was due to a tradition in Eastern Christianity that identified Jesus's mother as one of the women at the empty tomb, a tradition that comported with John 19:25, which listed Jesus's mother first among the women at the foot of the cross, which suggests her leadership of the women listed. For more details, see Kateusz, "Two Women Leaders"; Murray, *Symbols of Church*, 148, 329–35; Gianelli, "Témoingnes Patristiques Grecs," 106–19; Bellet, "Testimonios Coptos," 199–205; and Breckenridge, "Et Prima Vidit," 9–32.

72. Grabar, *Ampoules*, 20–23, 34–36, 39–40, plates 9, 11–13, 16, 18, 26, 28, and 47; Biddle, *Tomb of Christ*, Figs. 17–19, and 26; St. Clair, "Visit to the Tomb," Figs. 1 and 4.

73. *Diary of Egeria*, 24.10 (Wilkinson, *Egeria's Travels*, 144).

74. Martimort, *Deaconesses*, 35–58; Eisen, *Women Officeholders*, 158–62, esp. 160.

75. Syriac, *Didascalia apostolorum*, 9 (Stewart-Sykes, *Didascalia*, 150–51).

76. For Holy Spirit imaged as female and mother, and the frightened scribes at the end of the fourth century who began to change the Holy Spirit's feminine gender to masculine, see Brock, *Holy Spirit in the Syrian Baptismal Tradition*, 19–26; Harvey, "Feminine Imagery for the Divine," 111–22; and Murray, *Symbols of Church*, 312–20. Prior to this change, the feminine gender for Holy Spirit was widespread. Even in the West, the femaleness of Holy Spirit was apparently so important to some Latin Christians that in the third century they changed the masculine gendered *spiritus* to the feminine gendered *spirita* with the effect that some Christian tombstones in the city of Rome and northern Africa were inscribed with *spirita sancta* instead of the grammatically correct *spiritus sanctus*; for one dated 291, see Snyder, *Ante Pacem*, 126; for two more, see Cabrol, *Dictionnaire d'Archéologie Chrétienne*, vol. 3, part 1, 1335, and vol. 7, part 1, 1006.

77. Syriac, *Didascalia apostolorum*, 9 (Stewart-Sykes, *Didascalia*, 150–51).

78. Karras, "Female Deacons in the Byzantine Church," 280.

79. Förster, "Sich des Gebrauchs der Frauen enthalten," 584–91.

80. For its identification as an altar, see St. Clair, "Visit to the Tomb," 130; Weitzman, *Age of Spirituality*, 581; Goldschmidt, "Mittelstüke fünfteiliger Elfenbeintafeln," 32.

81. For discussion, see St. Clair, "Visit to the Tomb," 129–31, Figs. 7 and 8. Goldschmidt argued this altar was that of the Anastasis, which the sixth-century Piacenza pilgrim wrote was made of the stone that sealed the cave; Goldschmidt, "Mittelstüke fünfteiliger Elfenbeintafeln," 33. Frazer, "Holy Sites Representations," 581, argues that the altar on this pyx more likely represented the altar in a Palestinian church rather than

the Anastasis (which nonetheless most likely would have been taken from the Anastasis model), yet on page 580, Wietzman identifies the altar with the gospel *men* flanking it as the Anastasis altar—and its altar area looks almost identical to that populated by the women with censers, that is, both altar areas have three steps up to the altar, a stone altar on three spiral legs, what appears to be a book on the altar, a diamond-shaped lamp hanging above it, four spiral columns, arches, and curtains on the sides.

82. Goldschmidt, "Mittelstüke fünfteiliger Elfenbeintafeln," 32, concludes it is a scene at the Anastasis depicting the altar instead of the grave. St. Clair, "Visit to the Tomb," 130–31 details various arguments on what the pyx represents, from the Anastasis rotunda altar to a liturgical interpretation. Frazer, "Holy Sites Representations," 581, suggests that it alternatively may have represented the altar of an unknown Syrian church that shared liturgical traditions with the Anastasis; regardless, the conclusion would be essentially the same, i.e., that women with censers performed in at least some liturgies. This pyx may provide the earliest evidence of an altar placed over the tomb of Jesus, which is consistent with the Christian practice in an era when saints' relics and tombs were often below altars.

83. See Princeton's Index of Christian Art; also a color image: http://www.livius.org/pictures/libya/qasr-libya-theodorias/qasr-libya-mosaic-1.01.b-kosmesis/ (accessed November 8, 2017).

84. I base this on a search of the Princeton Index of Christian Art. For the mid-sixth-century mosaic of a cleric in San Vitale Basilica in Ravenna, see von Simson, *Sacred Fortress*, plate 2; also see donor Theodor with a censer in a sixth-century floor mosaic in Jerash, Jordan, in Hamarneh, "Cosmas and Damian," 79; and a pilgrim token of Simeon Stylites the Younger (521–562) carrying one in the Royale Ontario Museum, inventory no. 986.181.78.

85. See St. Clair, "Visit to the Tomb," 131–33, Fig. 9.

86. For the ampoules, see Grabar, *Ampoules*, pl. 9, 11, 14, 34, and 35. For the hexagonal glass pilgrim vessels from Jerusalem that Barag argues represented the architecture of the Anastasis shrine, see Barag, "Glass Pilgrim Vessels from Jerusalem, Parts 2 and 3," 51–63. For the painted box and mosaics, see Biddle, *Tomb of Christ*, Figs. 17 (painted), 22 and 23 (mosaics); also see Figs. 18 and 19, which are representative of ampoules that depicted the women approaching what appears to be an ornate gate; the full composition—the gate, the hexagonal shrine, and the rotunda above—is only on one artifact, the painted reliquary box shown in Fig. 19, my Fig. 4.3; note also that four frontal columns on an artifact may represent the four frontal columns visible on a hexagon,

which are most clearly signified by a staggered placement as seen in Figs. 18, 23, and 24, as well as in Grabar, *Ampoules*, 9, 14, 22, 13, 34, 35, 36, and 45.

87. For additional examples, see Biddle, *Tomb of Christ*, Figs. 17, 22, and 23; Grabar, *Ampoules*, plates 9, 11, and 14.

88. Grabar, *Ampoules*, plates 9, 11, 14, 22, 24, 26, 28, 34, 35–38, 45; Barag, "Glass Pilgrim Vessels from Jerusalem, Part 1," Figs. 1, 2A–2F, 8, and Fig. A I–VIII; Barag, "Glass Pilgrim Vessels from Jerusalem, Parts 2 and 3," 51–63; St. Clair, "Visit to the Tomb," Figs. 1 and 9; and Biddle, *Tomb of Christ*, Fig. 18. Note also that many artifacts depicted the shrine with arches between the columns as does the pyx, for example, the painted panel (Biddle's Fig. 17, which is the top left panel of my Fig. 4.3) and a mosaic (Biddle's Fig. 23), as well as many of the ampoules in Grabar's study.

89. St. Clair, "Visit to the Tomb," 131, Fig. 1 is a pyx with a similar scene of two women with censers approaching a similar ciborium with spiral columns, but with what is usually identified as Christ's tomb beneath it, no altar.

90. McEnerney, *St. Cyril of Alexandria*, 1:107.

91. Eusebius, *Ecclesiastical History*, 10 4.68.

92. Tertullian, *Apology*, 42 (*ANF* 3:49).

93. Wright, "History of the Virgin Mary," 18–24; and Wright, "Transitus Beate Virginis," 24–41.

94. Wright, *Contributions to the Apocryphal Literature*, 8, 10. Both fragments are in the British Library, with the first catalogued as syr Add. 14 484, f. 7v.–9r., and the second as syr Add. 12 174, fol. 449r.–452r.

95. Van Esbroeck, "Textes littéraires," 266; Mimouni, *Dormition*, 87–91, 683.

96. Wright, "History of the Virgin Mary," 31–34.

97. Wright, "Transitus Beate Virginis," 31–34, quote on 31.

98. Budge, "History of the Blessed Virgin Mary," 97–168. This manuscript is in the British Library, syr Add. 12 174.

99. Budge, "History of the Blessed Virgin Mary," 136.

100. Gonzalez Casado, "Relaciones lingüísticas entre el siríaco y el árabe," 559–92. This is Ms. Vat. Ar. 698, currently in the Vatican Library.

101. Gonzalez Casado, "Relaciones lingüísticas entre el siríaco y el árabe," 572.

102. Walker, "Book of John Concerning the Falling Asleep of Mary," 587–91, 587n1; see 587n1 that sometimes this text was attributed to John of Thessalonica, but this homily in the Six Books tradition is different from the one usually attributed to John of Thessalonica, which is in the *Liber Requiei* or "Palm" tradition; for that homily, see Daley, *On the Dormition of Mary*, 12–13, and for its text, 47–70.

103. See Walker's summary in *ANF* 8, 359–60.
104. See van Esbroeck, *Vie de la vierge*; and Shoemaker, *Life of the Virgin*; they used different manuscripts for their respective editions, and in Chapter 6, I demonstrate why van Esbroeck's edition of the oldest manuscript of the *Life of the Virgin*, Tbilisi A-40, is to be preferred.
105. Van Esbroeck, *Vie*, vol. I, xv; Shoemaker, "Georgian Life," 320–26; and Shoemaker, *Life of the Virgin*, 16–17. Based on my analysis in Chapter 6, I would not argue the *Life of the Virgin*'s dependence on the Six Books, but instead that both authors probably relied upon an even older source.
106. Compare to Booth, "On the *Life of the Virgin*," 165–69; see my discussion of Booth's argument in Chapter 6.
107. Smith Lewis, "Transitus Mariae," 24; *Life of the Virgin*, 107–8.
108. Smith Lewis, "Transitus Mariae," 24, 34; *Life of the Virgin*, 74 (Mary was the women's leader and teacher); 99 (Mary taught the apostles, which included women in 98); 107 (she blessed and taught a crowd of people, including the women at her deathbed in 105).
109. Smith Lewis, "Transitus Mariae," 34; *Life of the Virgin*, 96 (Mary sent out disciples to preach, and women were called disciples in 69–71, plus women were called "apostles" in 98).
110. Smith Lewis, "Transitus Mariae," 47–48; *Life of the Virgin*, 97.
111. For more detail of the redaction of these narrative elements across the three main manuscripts, see Kateusz, "Collyridian déjà vu."
112. The text of the palimpsest preserves the apostles setting out the censer of incense after Mary prayed, but unlike later recensions, omits her instructing them to set it out; Smith Lewis, "Transitus Mariae," 32.
113. For more on this, see Kateusz, "Dormition Urtext?"
114. See, for example, the homilies in Daley, *On the Dormition of Mary*.
115. Wright, "Departure of My Lady Mary," 152–53.
116. John of Thessalonica, *On the Dormition* (Daley, *On the Dormition of Mary*, 48).
117. Pseudo-Melito, *Assumption of the Virgin*, 1 (Elliott, *Apocryphal New Testament*, 708).
118. See Macy, *Hidden History of Women's Ordination*; Wijngaards, *Ordained Women Deacons of the Chruch's First Millenium*; and the essays in Kienzle and Walker, eds., *Women Preachers and Prophets Through Two Millennia of Christianity*.
119. Ethiopic *Liber Requiei*, 1 (Shoemaker, *Ancient Traditions*, 290).
120. Smith Lewis, "Transitus Mariae," 34.
121. Gonzalez Casado, "Relaciones lingüísticas entre el siríaco y el árabe," 572.
122. *Life of the Virgin*, 96–99.

NOTES CHAPTER 3

1. For dating, see Bovon, "Women Priestesses," 247; and Bovon, *Acts of Philip*, 8–9 (Bovon lists other opinions on dating and asks if the text may be related to New Prophecy, a.k.a. Montanism), 26 (a lost collection of Jesus sayings may be embedded), and 29–30 (a fourth century compilation is most likely).

2. Bovon, "Editing the Apocryphal Acts," 16.

3. Bovon, *Acts of Philip*, 16–30.

4. Other texts that are unspecific about which Mary was meant include the *Gospel of Mary*, *Gospel of Thomas*, *Gospel of Philip*, *Dialogue of the Savior*, *Pistis Sophia*, and *Sophia of Jesus Christ*. For more discussion on this topic, see Beavis, "Mary of Bethany and the Hermeneutics of Remembrance"; Shoemaker, *Mary in Early Christian Faith*, 87–95; essays in Beavis, *Maria, Mariamne, Miriam*; and the essays in Jones, *Which Mary*.

5. *Acts of Philip*, 8.2; Beavis, "Mary of Bethany and the Hermeneutics of Remembrance," 750–51; and Beavis, "Reconsidering Mary of Bethany," 281–97.

6. Schrader, "Was Martha Added to the Fourth Gospel," 360–92; and Bovon, *New Testament Traditions and Apocryphal Narratives*, 150.

7. Bovon, "Mary Magdalene in the *Acts of Philip*," 78–80 and 88. See also Bovon, "From Vermont to Cyprus," regarding an icon depicting scenes from the *Acts of Philip*, esp. plates 15 and 16, where a thirteenth-century artist conflated Mariamne with both Mary the mother of Jesus and Mary Magdalene by giving her the same dark blue *maphorion* with stars on her head and shoulders traditionally associated with Jesus's mother in Eastern iconography, yet also giving her the red skirt most often associated with the Magdalene.

8. Brock, *Mary Magdalene*, 124–28. With respect to scribes replacing the figure of the Magdalene with Peter, note that in Chapter 4, I provide two examples where scribes used the figure of Peter to replace a Mary who was clearly identified as the mother.

9. *Acts Phil.*, 8.21 and 9.1 (Bovon, *Acts of Philip*, 74). These two examples clearly include Mariamne, and there are additional places in the text where Mariamne appears to be considered as one of the group of "apostles."

10. *Acts Phil.*, 8.2–3 (Bovon, *Acts of Philip*, 74); for the Greek text, see Bovon, *Acta Philippi*.

11. *Acts Phil.*, 9.1, 3–4 (Bovon, *Acts of Philip*, 81).

12. *Acts Phil.*, 15.3, 9 (Bovon, *Acts of Philip*, 95–96).

13. Bovon, "Women Priestesses," 256.

14. *Acts Phil.*, 14.9 (Bovon, *Acts of Philip*, 91).

15. *Acts Phil.*, 1.12 (Bovon, *Acts of Philip*, 36).

16. Bovon, "Women Priestess," 250–54; Bonnet edited the *Martyrdom of Matthew*, which said that the apostle Matthew made the king a priest, the queen a priestess, their son a deacon, and his wife a deaconess. See also Bonnet, "Martyrium Matthaei," 1.2:259; James also translated this passage as "priest" and "priestess" in James, *Apocryphal New Testament*, 462.

17. Jennifer Knust's *Abandoned to Lust* is perhaps the most thorough analysis of sexual slander in ancient Christianity to date, but she does not address the *Acts of Phlip*.

18. *Acts Phil.*, 1.12 (Bovon, *Acts of Philip*, 36).

19. Justin Martyr, *First Apology*, 26 (*ANF* 1:172).

20. Justin Martyr, *First Apology*, 26.

21. Jerome, *Letter 133*, 4. Jerome here listed many women who evangelized with men or otherwise supported them.

22. Tertullian, *On Prescription Against Heretics*, 41.

23. Epiphanius of Salamis, *Panarion*, 49.2.5 and 3.2 (Williams, *Panarion*, 2:22).

24. Bovon, *Acts of Philip*, 9–11.

25. Augustine, *Heresies*, 26–27 (Rotelle, *Arianism*, 38). Capitalization of Eucharist mine, for consistency.

26. Justin Martyr, *First Apology*, 26 (*ANF* 1:172).

27. *Acts Phil.*, 1.12 (Bovon, *Acts of Philip*, 36).

28. Bovon, *Acts of Philip*, 9–11.

29. Bovon, "Editing the Apocryphal Acts," 10–13.

30. Smith Lewis, *Select Narratives of Holy Women*, No. X for the translation and No. IX for the Syriac. She did not translate the narrative about Thecla.

31. Smith Lewis, "Eugenia," 1–35; book of Thecla on 2–3, cross-dressing on 4, became abbot on 13–14, and healings, exorcisms, and teaching on 15–16; for Eugenia leading a group of women see the rest.

32. Smith Lewis, "Irene," 94–148.

33. "The Holy Great-Martyress Irene," translated by Stephen Janos: http://www.holytrinityorthodox.com/calendar/los/May/05-01. htm (accessed January 26, 2014); Janos says his text is "a translation from the *Mesyatseslov* of Saints Lives from the 1978–1979 Volumes 2–3 of the Moscow Patriarchate texts, the 'NaStol'naya Kniga dlya Svyaschennoslushiteli' ('Reference Book for Clergy-Servers')."

34. See, for example, narratives about Andrew, John, Paul, Peter, Thomas, and others in Schneemelcher, *New Testament Apocrypha*.

35. Smith Lewis, "Irene," 94–97.

36. Smith Lewis, *Select Narratives*, 2–3, 37, 47, 60–61.
37. Smith Lewis, "Irene," 101–2.
38. Smith Lewis, "Irene," 102–5.
39. Smith Lewis, "Irene," 102, 106–7.
40. Smith Lewis, "Irene," 111–12.
41. Smith Lewis, "Irene," 113.
42. Smith Lewis, "Irene," 131.
43. Lerner, *Wellspring of Georgian Historiography*, 38.
44. Lerner, "Conversion of K'art'li," 139–93. See also an earlier translation of *The Life of Nino* in Wardrop, *Life of Saint Nino*, 7–66.
45. *Conversion of K'art'li* II.2 (Lerner, *Wellspring of Georgian Historiography*, 161).
46. *Conversion of K'art'li* II.12 (Lerner, *Wellspring of Georgian Historiography*, 139–93, 190). See also von Lilienfeld, "Amt und geistliche Vollmacht der heiligen Nino," 224–49.
47. For Nino baptizing specific tribes, see *Conversion of K'art'li* I.2; for Queen Soji and many with her receiving baptism "from the hands of Nino," see *Conversion of K'art'li* I.5 (Lerner, *Wellspring of Georgian Historiography*, 151); for a Jewish priest receiving baptism "from the hands of Nino," see *Conversion of K'art'li* II.9.1 (Lerner, *Wellspring of Georgian Historiography*, 180); for Nino baptizing Riphsime plus forty other women, *Conversion of K'art'li* II.2.
48. *Conversion of K'art'li* I.5 (Lerner, *Wellspring of Georgian Historiography*, 181).
49. For the Armenian translation, see Wardrop, *Life of Saint Nino*, 71–88; for details on the omissions, see 13n5, 42n1, 67–70, esp. 70.
50. Smith Lewis, "Irene," 122–26, quotation on 126.
51. Smith Lewis, "Irene," 139.
52. Smith Lewis, "Irene," 143.
53. Smith Lewis, "Irene," 145. When compared to some of the male apostles' acts, this number of people reportedly baptized is not particularly extravagant.
54. Smith Lewis, "Irene," 124.
55. Smith Lewis, "Irene," 119.
56. Smith Lewis, "Irene," 126–28.
57. Smith Lewis, "Irene," 115, 137.
58. Smith Lewis, "Irene," 115.
59. For discussion on sealing, see McGowan, *Ancient Christian Worship*, 153–57, 174; Johnson, *Rites of Christian Initiation*, 90–91; and Mitchell, *Baptismal Anointing*, 85. Also Irenaeus, *Against Heresies*, 1.21.4.

60. Smith Lewis, "Irene," 145.
61. For the *Acts of Thecla*, see the *Acts of Paul and Thecla* (Schneemelcher, "Acts of Paul and Thecla," 2:239–46).
62. Taussig, "Brief Technical History of Thecla," 3–5.
63. For the text, both Greek and French, see Dagron, *Vie*, 167–283.
64. Dagron, *Vie*, 141–47.
65. Monika Pesthy curiously claims that the *Life* "adds no new material" in Pesthy, "Thecla Among the Fathers," 169; Susan Hylen recognizes that the *Life* depicts Thecla baptizing other people, but accepts the view that somehow a fifth-century author would have anachronistically embellished a second-century narrative so that Thecla would be seen as a baptizer; Hylen, *Modest Apostle*, 109–13.
66. *Life of Thecla*, 1.2, 9.79–80, 13.55, 26.60–65, 28.36 (Dagron, *Vie*, 168 [Gr.], 69 [Fr.]; 206 [Gr.], 207 [Fr.]; 224 [Gr.], 225 [Fr.]; 274 [Gr.], 275 [Fr.]; 280 [Gr.], 281 [Fr.]).
67. *Life of Thecla*, 24.27–31 (Dagron, *Vie*, 266 [Gr.], 267 [Fr.]).
68. McGowan, *Ancient Christian Worship*, 153–54.
69. Dagron, *Vie et miracles*, 42; Hylen, "'Domestication' of Saint Thecla," 11.
70. Tertullian, *On Baptism*, 8.
71. *Acts of Paul and Thecla*, 3.41 (Schneemelcher, "Acts of Paul and Thecla," 246).
72. *Life of Thecla*, 26.59–67 (Dagron, *Vie*, 274–75). Emphasis added.
73. *Life of Thecla*, 28.1–7 (Dagron, *Vie*, 278–81). Hylen points out that the "many" here is masculine plural, indicating that Thecla was understood to have baptized both men and women; Hylen, "'Domestication' of Saint Thecla," 11.
74. *Acts of Paul and Thecla*, 3.43 (Schneemelcher, "Acts of Paul and Thecla," 246).
75. Talbot, *Miracle Tales*, 197.
76. Tertullian, *On Baptism*, 17 (Thelwall, "On Baptism," 677).
77. Dagron, *Vie*, 17–19; and Johnson, *Life and Miracles of Thekla*, 5n18.
78. For discussion, see Johnson, *Life and Miracles of Thekla*, 33–35, 62, 222.
79. Koester, *History and Literature*, 18.
80. Schaberg, *Father, the Son and the Holy Spirit*, 27.
81. *Life of Thecla*, 1.12–23.
82. *Life of Thecla*, 1.1–4 (Dagron, *Vie*, 168–69).
83. Turner, *Truthfulness, Realism, Historicity*, 1–22, quotation on 16.
84. Tertullian, *On Baptism*, 17 (*ANF* 3:677).

85. Davies, "Women, Tertullian and the Acts of Paul," 141. Emphasis added. (This is Steven Davies, not Stephen Davis who wrote *The Cult of St Thecla*.)

86. Davies, "Women, Tertullian and the Acts of Paul," 142–43.

87. Hilhorst, "Tertullian on the Acts of Paul," 162.

88. Johnson, *Life and Miracles of Thekla*, 6.

89. Taussig, "Brief Technical History of Thecla," 3.

90. Schneemelcher, *New Testament Apocrypha*, 1:38–40. Note that the Dormition narrative is listed as "Book which is called The Home-going of the Holy Mary." In addition, the composer of this list prioritized Thecla over Paul: "Book which is called the Acts of Thecla and of Paul."

91. Smith Lewis, "Transitus Mariae," 34.

92. McGowan, *Ancient Christian Worship*, 153–54. For more ways to possibly interpret this passage, see the above description of sealing with respect to Irene sealing.

93. Tertullian, *On Baptismi*, 17, *On Prescription Against Heretics*, 41, and *On the Veiling of Virgins*, 9.

NOTES CHAPTER 4

1. Smith Lewis, "Irene," 129.

2. Smith Lewis, "Irene," 111, 115, and 123 (teaching the king and his army).

3. Smith Lewis, "Transitus Mariae," 32. Worthy of mention here is that Shoemaker says the title "my Lady Mary" is better translated as "my master Mary"; and Shoemaker, *Ancient Traditions*, 370n3.

4. Smith Lewis, "Transitus Mariae," 24; *Ethiopic Six Books*, 27 (Shoemaker, *Ancient Traditions*, 378); Wright, "History of the Virgin Mary," 21; González Casado, *Relcaciones Lingüísticas*, 572; *Life of the Virgin*, 106–7.

5. Shoemaker notes that in the Old Syriac as well as the Ethiopic translation, the best translation of Mary's feminine gendered title is not "Lady," but "master." Shoemaker, *Ancient Traditions*, 370n3, 375n2.

6. *Ethiopic Six Books*, 27 (Shoemaker, *Ancient Traditions*, 378).

7. After Shoemaker, who thusly describes a virtually identical prayer scene in the *Gospel (Questions) of Bartholomew*; Shoemaker, "Mary the Apostle," 217.

8. Wright, "Departure of My Lady Mary," 140.

9. *Ethiopic Six Books*, 33 (Shoemaker, *Ancient Traditions*, 383).

10. See their homilies in Daley, *On the Dormition of Mary*.

11. St. John the Theologian, *Dormition of the All-Holy Theotokos*, 24, 30–32 (Shoemaker, *Ancient Traditions*, 361, 363–64). Apparently

because it mentions the great angel, Shoemaker calls it "the oldest Greek Dormition narrative," Shoemaker, *Ancient Traditions*, 351.

12. Donahue, *Testament of Mary*, 10.
13. Talbot, *Miracle Tales*, 191.
14. Brock, *Mary Magdalene*, 124–28, quotation from 128. See also Kateusz, "Two Women Leaders."
15. Lidov, "Priesthood of the Virgin Mary," 10.
16. Chrysostom, *Homily on Psalm 140*; translation by Lidov, "Priesthood of the Virgin Mary," 10.
17. Bradshaw, *Search for the Origins*, 3–4.
18. Borella, *Rito Ambrosiano*, 187–88; interestingly, the subsequent page lists the saints that were well-known in the history of the Milanese church, and two-thirds were women.
19. For a full analysis of the history of this iconography, see Kateusz, "Ascension of Christ or Ascension of Mary," 275–92.
20. Recent scholarship has determined that the Rabbula gospel illuminations were made separately and subsequently trimmed and bound in front of the gospel text; see Bernabò, *Tetravangelo di Rabbula*. Regardless of when bound, the model used for these illuminations was a very old iconography; this art closely reflects the Six Books iconography which was so popular in Ancient Syria and closely follows the text of fifth- and sixth-century Six Books Dormition manuscripts. For more detail on this close correspondence, see below, and also, Kateusz, "Ascension of Christ or Ascension of Mary," 274–77.
21. Wright, "Departure," 140–41; see also Smith Lewis, "Transitus," 32–33; *Ethiopic Six Books*, 33 (Shoemaker, *Ancient Traditions*, 383).
22. Wright, "Departure," 156–57; the Smith Lewis manuscript has a gap at the end.
23. For a high definition photo on the flaming wheels, see the full-page plate in Spier, *Picturing the Bible*, 140.
24. Smith Lewis, "Transitus Mariae," 55.
25. Smith Lewis, "Transitus Mariae," 28, 31.
26. Cartlidge and Elliott, *Art and the Apocrypha*, 134–71, including Figs. 5.4 and 5.17 for Junius Bassus sarcophagus portraits; and Jensen, *Face to Face*, 186–91, Figs. 93, 94, and 97.
27. See also Jensen, *Face to Face*, 186, Fig. 93.
28. Spier, *Picturing the Bible*, 276–82; Figs. 82B (Ascension), 82C (Nativity), 82F (Pentecost), 82D (foot of the cross, at the empty tomb, with the risen Christ).
29. Kateusz, "Ascension of Christ or Ascension of Mary?" 275–78, Fig. 2. For a color photo, see Lowden, *Christian Iconography*, 211, Fig. 118. Or google "Sancta Sanctorum reliquary box."
30. Lowden, *Christian Iconography*, 211, Fig. 118.

31. *Gospel of Bartholomew* 2.6–7 (Schneemelcher, *New Testament Apocrypha*, 1:543).

32. For this early tradition, see Murray, *Symbols of Church*, 148, 329–35; Gianelli, "Témoingnes Patristiques Grecs," 106–19; Bellet, "Testimonios Coptos," 199–205; and Breckenridge, "'Et Prima Vidit,'" 9–32. Also see, Kateusz, "Two Women Leaders."

33. See also Kateusz, "Ascension of Christ or Ascension of Mary?" 275–78, Fig. 2.

34. Miner, *Early Christian and Byzantine Art*, 106, pl. 68; Herrmann, "Two Men in White," Fig. 11.

35. D'Onofrio, *Romei & giubilei*, 327.

36. Grabar, *Christian Iconography*, 134, Figs. 323, 325; and Kateusz, "Ascension of Christ," 298–99, Fig. 11.

37. Grabar, *Ampoules de terre sainte*, pl. 3, 5, 7, 17, 19, 21, 27, 29, 30, 44, 50, 53.

38. Wolf, "Icons and Sites," 39–41, Figs. 3.9 and 3.10.

39. Grabar, *Ampoules de terre sainte*, pl. 3, 5, 7, 17, 19, 21, 44 (ampoule 13), and 53 depict her with erect posture; pl. 27, 29, 30, 44 (ampoule 14), and 50 depict her side-profile as the *Madonna advocata*.

40. For Mary praying orante at her son's tomb, see Cyril of Alexandria homily *Kitâb mayâmîr* (AB 2) and Six Books Ms. Vat. Ar. 698 (AB 9) in González Casado, *Relcaciones Lingüísticas*, 454, 564; on the Mount of Olives, *Life of the Virgin*, 104; while offering incense, Budge, *History of the Blessed Virgin Mary*, 102.

41. Dennison, *Studies in East Christian and Roman Art*, 68–75, Fig. 29. See also discussion of Fig. 4.13.

42. Mackie, "San Venanzio Chapel," 4.

43. The ampoule is in the Museo dell'abbazia di S. Colombano, Bobbio; Grabar, *Ampoules de terre sainte*, 43–44, Fig. 53; Kateusz, "Ascension of Christ," 279–81, Fig. 5.

44. Kateusz, "Ascension of Christ," 287–92, Fig. 7.

45. Marchiori, "Medieval Wall Painting," 250.

46. Marchiori, "Medieval Wall Painting," 242–43, 250, Fig. 6, pl. 1.

47. I argue this in Kateusz, "Ascension of Christ," 298–302, Fig. 12. See more discussion on this fresco and its composition below at the end of Chapter Five, Fig. 5.17.

48. Marchiori, "Medieval Wall Painting," 227.

49. Wilpert, *Sarcofagi*, plate 125.

50. Fixot, *Crypte de Saint-Maximin*, 32–33. Fixot adds that the possibility cannot be excluded that the plaques originally decorated a baptistery constructed around the year 500, and were later moved into the hypogeum. In my view, however, absent any evidence of this move,

there is no reason to assume it happened when the hypogeum where the plaques reside is late fourth century. Further substantiating the fourth-century dating, a parallel plaque of Daniel depicts him naked between the lions, and his nudity was a feature of third and fourth-century iconography of this scene, per Jensen, *Understanding Early Christian Art*, 174. As I discuss in Chapter 5, a circular dating methodology based on a false premise has led to incorrectly dating Marian artifacts later.

51. *Protevangelium* 4.1, 7.1–8.1 [Temple]; 13.2, 15.2. [Holy of Holies].
52. Lidov, "Priesthood of the Virgin Mary," 10.
53. Chrysostom, *Homily on Psalm 140*; translation by Lidov, "Priesthood of the Virgin Mary," 10.
54. Borella, *Rito Ambrosiano*, 187–88; interestingly, the subsequent page lists the saints that were well-known in the history of the Milanese church, and two-thirds were women.
55. Boyle, *Short Guide to St. Clement's*, 55–57.
56. For detail on the maniple, its origin and its comparable in the East, see Lidov, "Priesthood of the Virgin Mary," 17–23; and Braun, "Maniple," 9:601–2.
57. Murray, *Oxford Dictionary of Christian Art*, 399; also see Klausner, "Pallium," cols. 7–9.
58. Martyn, *Letters of Gregory the Great*, 79.
59. Terry, *Dynamic Splendor*, 1:59–69. For Justinian and Theodora's church building, see Procopius, *Buildings* I.3, plus many mentions throughout.
60. Deliyannis, *Ravenna*, 68–69, Fig. VIIa. See also Chapter 7, Fig. 7.8.
61. Deliyannis, *Ravenna*, 68–69, Fig. VIIIb.
62. Terry, *Dynamic Splendor*, 1:68–69, Figs. 2:3 and 2:4 (Mary in apse), Figs. 2:126–132 (Mary and Elizabeth).
63. Terry, *Dynamic Splendor*, 1:4–5, 68.
64. Terry, *Dynamic Splendor*, 2:2–31, pl. 1–43.
65. Terry, *Dynamic Splendor*, 2:3, Fig. 2, and 2:45–59, pl. 70, 71, 84, 85, 88–92.
66. See discussion regarding Mary as a guarantor for women clergy in Foletti, "Des femmes à l'autel," 51, 90–91, Fig. 2.
67. Terry, *Dynamic Splendor*, 2:80–84, pl. 126–133.
68. Robbins, "Priestly Discourse," 20–27, quotation on 25; and Robbins, "Bodies and Politics," 44–48.
69. Terry and Maguire dispute that this is a pallium; Terry, *Dynamic Splendor*, 1:103–104, but their most critical argument, that (supposedly) secular women in Theodora's entourage in the San Vitale mosaic wear a somewhat similar sash, is undermined by Lidov who argues that these women's

sashes were the Eucharistic cloth or handkerchief, itself a symbol of a priest or bishop, in Lidov, "Priesthood of the Virgin Mary," 17.

70. Schaefer, *Women in Pastoral Office*, 232, Figs. 4.11 and 4.12.

71. Lidov, "Priesthood of the Virgin Mary," 9–10, Fig. 2.

72. Foletti, "Des femmes à l'autel," 90–91, Fig. 2.

73. John of Ephesus, *Lives of Eastern Saints*, 15 (Brooks, "John of Ephesus, Lives of the Eastern Saints," 220–28, esp. 226–27).

74. Mackie, "San Venanzio Chapel," 4.

75. De Rossi's 1899 painting of this mosaic shows a red cross on Mary's pallium, but today the red tesserae are almost entirely are replaced with white.

76. Schaefer, *Women in Pastoral Office*, 229–30, Fig. 4.9.

77. See Kateusz, "Two Marys, Two Traditions." http://allykateusz.com/art-as-text-powerpoints/two-marys-two-traditions/ (accessed October 19, 2018).

78. Kearns, *Virgin Mary*, 283. For an old photo of the apse without the altarpiece, see Mackie, "San Venanzio Chapel," Fig. 3.

79. For a photo of the mosaic taken from the side of the altarpiece, see Foletti, "Des femmes à l'autel," Fig. 1.

80. A good recap of this iconography is in Dewald, "Iconography of the Ascension."

81. For the identification of Mary in this mosaic cycle, see Cormack, "Mosaic Decoration of S. Demetrios," 32–37; for the late fifth-century dating argument, pages 42–52; for W. S. George's watercolors, plates 3 and 4.

82. Kondakov, *Iconografia della Madre di Dio*, vol. 1, plate 7.

83. Kondakov, *Iconografia della Madre di Dio*, vol. 1, plate 6.

84. Evans, *Byzantium and Islam*, Cat. no. 45A, 74, Fig. 45A.

85. Miner, *Early Christian and Byzantine Art*, 50, pl. 21; Breck, "Two Early Christian Ivories of the Ascension," 242–44.

86. Lidov, "Priesthood of the Virgin Mary," 9, Fig. 1.

87. See examples in Lidov, "Priesthood of the Virgin Mary," as well as the Web site womenpriests.org: http://www.womenpriests.org/mrpriest/gallery1.asp (accessed March 9, 2018).

88. Lidov, "Priesthood of the Virgin Mary," 17–23.

89. Braun, "Maniple," 9:601–2. For an ivory plaque of the emperor Anastasis raising the cloth, see Volbach, *Early Christian Art*, Fig. 22; for the fifth-century consul Boethius, see Weitzmann, *Age of Spirituality*, 6, Fig. 5; for another dated 506, see Gaborit-Chopin, *Ivoires Médiévaux*, 45–47, Fig. 7.

90. Gaborit-Chopin, *Ivoires Médiévaux*, 41–42, Figs. 5A and 5B.

91. Volbach, *Early Christian Art*, 40, Figs. 226, 228 and 229.

92. For more documentation, see St. Clair, "Visit to the Tomb," 130n41.

93. Volbach, *Early Christian Art*, Fig. 233. This use appears similar to the concept of a *dominicale*, a cloth described at the diocesan synod of seven abbots and thirty-four priests who were called together by Bishop Annacharius in Auxerre in 578. They said women were to use the dominicale at the communion, but arguably the bulk of the evidence suggests that this practice had its origins in the clergy; it is quite difficult to assume that they meant something else.

94. Lidov, "Priesthood of the Virgin Mary," 20.

95. Braun, "Maniple," 9:601–2.

96. Lidov, "Priesthood of the Virgin Mary," 20, Figs. 13–15, 20, 25.

97. Wilpert, *Römischen Mosaiken*, 660–64, pl. 134; also Beckwith, *Early Christian and Byzantine Art*, 94.

98. For a good color photo, see Braconi, "Arcosolio di Cerula," Fig. 14.

99. Clédat, *Monastère et la nécropole de Baouît*, pl. 40 and 41; and Grabar, *Christian Iconography*, 134, pl. 323.

100. Maguire, "Fertile Crescent," 434–36, Figs. 1–3.

101. Maguire, "Fertile Crescent," 437.

102. Megaw, "Fragmentary Mosaic," 363–65, photo C; and Cormack, "Mother of God in Apse Mosaics," 101, Fig. 55.

103. Cormack, "Mother of God in Apse Mosaics," 97, Fig. 50.

104. Cormack, "Mother of God in Apse Mosaics," 94, and Fig. 3.

105. Cormack, "Mother of God in the Mosaics," 108–13, pl. 62.

106. Cormack, "Mother of God in the Mosaics," 97–99, pl. 98; and Webb, *Churches and Catacombs*, 99–100.

107. Lidov, "Priesthood of the Virgin Mary," 17; and Braun, "Maniple," 601–2.

108. For discussion, see Milliner, "Virgin of the Passion," 106–31.

109. Gaborit-Chopin, *Ivoires Médiévaux*, 41–42, Fig. 5A and 5B.

110. For detail on previous interpretations of these mosaics, see Thunø, "Looking at Letters," 19–41, and for the mosaics see Figs. 1–5.

111. Thunø, "Looking at Letters," 21–23, Fig. 5; Schaefer, *Women in Pastoral Office*, 203; and Schlatter, "Mosaic of Santa Pudenziana," Fig. 2.

112. Thunø, "Looking at Letters," 21–22.

113. Lidov, "Priesthood of the Virgin Mary," 17, Fig. 16.

114. Bradshaw, *Ordination Rites of the Ancient Churches*, 39–43.

115. *Apostolic Constitutions*, 8.4 (*ANF* 7:482). Also see Bradshaw, *Rites of Ordination*, 69–72, esp. 69.

116. Bradshaw, *Rites of Ordination*, 69–72; and Bradshaw, *Ordination Rites of the Ancient Churches*, 40.

117. Thunø, "Looking at Letters," Fig. 12.

118. For other interpretations related to the empty throne itself, see Ivan Foletti, "Cicut in caelo et in terra."

119. Krautheimer, "Publications on S. Maria Maggiore," 373–74.

120. Thunø, "Looking at Letters," 22, Fig. 5.

121. Clement of Alexandria, *Paedagogus*, 1.6

122. See Fig. 5.11.

123. For detailed discussion of this mosaic and the apse, see Chapter 7, including Figs. 7.7, 7.8, and 7.9.

124. Lidov, "Priesthood of the Virgin Mary," 17, Fig. 18.

125. For women as clergy, see Eisen, *Women Officeholders*, 116–42; Madigan, *Ordained Women*, 163–202; and Ramelli, "Colleagues of Apostles." See also Chapter 7.

NOTES CHAPTER 5

1. Cameron, "Early Cult of the Virgin," 2–15; see also Cartlidge, *Art and the Christian Apocrypha*, 21.

2. *Protevangelium*, 4.1–4 (for these verses in the third-century Papyrus Bodmer 5, see Stryker, *Forme la plus ancienne*, 79–80).

3. Epiphanius of Salamis, *Panarion*, 79, 7.2 (Williams, *Panarion*, 626).

4. *Protevangelium of James* 4 (*ANF* 8:362); quotation from *Gospel of Pseudo-Matthew* 3 (*ANF* 8:370).

5. Robinson, *Coptic Apocryphal Gospels*, 7.

6. Robinson, *Coptic Apocryphal Gospels*, 47.

7. Wright, "Departure of My Lady Mary," 156. I cite the sixth-century text because the palimpsest has a gap here. For another recension of this scene where after three days, Mary's body disappears from the cave where it was laid, see John of Thessalonica, *On the Dormition*, 14 (Daley, *On the Dormition of Mary*, 67).

8. Wright, "Departure of My Lady Mary," 157. I cite the sixth-century text because the palimpsest has a gap here.

9. Daley, *On the Dormition of Mary*, 14.

10. Kateusz, "Ascension of Christ," 287–92, Figs. 7 and 8.

11. Vuong, *Gender and Purity*, 88–103.

12. Laurentin, *Maria, Ecclesia, Sacerdotum*, 84–85.

13. Ephrem, *Hymns on the Nativity*, no. 16 (Brock, *Bride of Light*, 21–22).

14. Mango, "Mother of God in Metalwork," 197.

15. Mango, *Silver from Early Byzantium*, 228–30.

16. Piguet-Panayotova, "Attarouthi Chalices," 19–33; and Mango, *Silver from Early Byzantium*, 232–33.

17. Piguet-Panayotova, "Attarouthi Chalices," 19–33; and Mango, *Silver from Early Byzantium*, 230.

18. Jensen, *Understanding Early Christian Art*, 124–28.
19. For the pairs, see Piguet-Panayotova, "Attarouthi Chalices," 19–33, Figs. 1.1 and 1.4, 2.1 and 2.2, 3.1 and 3.4, 4.1 and 4.4, 5.1 and 5.2, 6.1 and 6.2, 7.1 and 7.2, 7.6 and 7.7.
20. Piguet-Panayotova, "Attarouthi Chalices," 25, Fig. 4.4 (Inv. 1986.3.4), 26, Fig. 5.2 (Inv. 1986.3.5), 29, Fig. 6.2 (Inv. 1986.3.7), and 31, Fig. 7.2 (Inv. 1986.3.8). All of these chalices are online at the Metropolitan Museum of Art Web site and good quality photos can be located by inputting their inventory numbers.
21. Piguet-Panyotova, "Attarouthi Chalices," 29.
22. Piguet-Panayotova, "Silver Censers," 648–49, Fig. 21.
23. Weitzmann, *Age of Spirituality*, 625–26; and Piguet-Panayotova, "Silver Censers," Figs. 3 and 6.
24. Mango, *Silver from Early Byzantium*, 256–57.
25. Mango, *Silver from Early Byzantium*, 255–56, Cat. no. 84.
26. Buschhausen, *Spätrömischen Metallscrinia*, 249–52, pl. 58.
27. Mango, "Mother of God in Metalwork," 195–97, Fig. 134.
28. Harvey, *Scenting Salvation*, 66–75; for more on the early sources, see Bradshaw, *Search for the Origins*.
29. Talbot, *Miracle Tales*, 197.
30. Bradshaw, *Search for the Origins*, esp. 146–55.
31. Mango, *Silver from Early Byzantium*, 108–11, Figs. 15.3–15.6.
32. Mango, "Mother of God in Metalwork," 198–99.
33. Mango, "Mother of God in Metalwork," 199–204, Fig. 139 (Musée de Cluny), and Vassilaki, *Mother of God*, 360–61 (Cat. no. 41) for the Benaki Museum cross.
34. Vassilaki, *Mother of God*, 298–99, Cat. nos. 16, and 308–12, Cat. nos. 23–26; and Yeroulanou, "Mother of God in Jewelry," 229, Fig. 173.
35. Mango, *Silver from Early Byzantium*, 249, Fig. 76.
36. Mango, "Mother of God in Metalwork," 198–99, Figs. 132 and 133.
37. Holland, *Cruciana*, 207; and Ricci, *Raccolte artistische di Ravenna*, Fig. 154.
38. Durand, *Armenia Sacra*, 105–7, Cat. no. 32, which shows all four gospel covers. The scene of the Test of Bitter Water is in the second square frame to the left of Mary on the Etchmiadzin and on the first frame on the right on the Saint-Lupicin.
39. Dennison, *Gold Treasure*, 131, Fig. 30.
40. Weitzmann, *Age of Spirituality*, Cat. no. 287.
41. Dennison, *Gold Treasure*, 121–35, plates 15, 16, and 17.
42. Ross, "Objects from Daily Life: Jewelry," 319–21, quotations on 319 and 321, Cat. no. 296; see also Dennison, *Gold Treasure*, 121–35, plates 15–17.

43. Compare, for example, Dennison, *Gold Treasure*, 131, calls the Istanbul Archeological Museum encolpion that depicts Jesus and Mary on opposite sides an "encolpion," but not this one. Similarly, Ross calls the Dunbarton Oaks encolpion that depicts Mary and Jesus on opposite sides an "encolpion," but not this one; Ross, "Objects from Daily Life: Jewelry," Cat. nos. 287 and 296, 312–13 and 319–21.

44. Kateusz, "Ascension of Christ or Ascension of Mary," 287–92, Figs. 7–9.

45. Lowden, *Early Christian and Byzantine Art*, 120–24, Fig. 70.

46. Bovini, *Sant'Apollinare Nuovo*, 24.

47. For details of this controversy, see Spier, *Picturing the Bible*, 259–61. Morey was particularly influential in casting doubt on its date after suggesting its origin in the sixteenth century; Morey, "Silver Casket of San Nazaro," 120.

48. Mango, *Silver from Early Byzantium*, 14–15.

49. Jensen, *Early Christian Art*, 124–27; Cartlidge, *Art and the Christian Apocrypha*, 64–69; and Mathews, *Clash of Gods*, 115–41.

50. Mango, *Silver from Early Byzantium*, 14–15.

51. Cameron explains this; Cameron, "Early Cult of the Virgin," 5.

52. For a recap of the scholarly sea change, see Price, "Marian Piety and the Nestorian Controversy," 31–38; for a recap of the use of *Theotokos* for Mary, see Price, "*Theotokos* and the Council of Ephesus," 89–91; Johnson, *Sub Tuum Praesidium*, 52–75; and Pelikan, *Mary Through the Centuries*, 57–58.

53. Price, "*Theotokos* and the Council of Ephesus," 90.

54. Alexander of Alexandria, *Letter to Alexander of Constantinople*, 12 (*ANF* 6:296); and Price, "*Theotokos* and the Council of Ephesus," 90.

55. Athanasius, *Orations Against the Arians*, 3.29; Julian the Apostate, *Against the Galileans*, 62 D (Wright, *Works of the Emperor Julian*, 3:398–99). See also Price, "*Theotokos* and the Council of Ephesus"; and Shoemaker, *Mary in Early Christian Faith*, 68–73.

56. Shoemaker, *Mary in Early Christian Faith*, 67–73; McGuckin, "Early Cult of Mary," 9–10; and Price, "*Theotokos* and the Council of Ephesus," 89.

57. For an extended recap of the evidence that the veneration of Mary started long before the Council of Ephesus, see Shoemaker, *Mary in Early Christian Faith*.

58. For a recap of the scholarly sea change, see Price, "Marian Piety and the Nestorian Controversy," 31–38; for a recap of the use of Theotokos for Mary, see Price, "*Theotokos* and the Council of Ephesu," 89–91; Johnson, *Sub Tuum Praesidium*, 52–75; Pelikan, *Mary Through the Centuries*, 57–58; and Shoemaker, *Mary in Early Christian Faith*.

59. Grabar, *Christian Iconography*, 47; Brenk, *Apse*, 74; Scholl, "Pelagian Controversy," 197; Spain, "Promised Blessing," 534n69.

60. Lidova, "Imperial *Theotokos*," 64; and Saxer, *Sainte Marie Majeure*, 43.

61. Rubery, "From Catacomb to Sanctuary," 157, Fig. 9; three are titled MARIA and two more MARA, which also usually are identified with Mary, in part because on one of these (Fig. 9e), she is paired with a woman named ANNE, perhaps signifying her mother Anna. Brenk suggests that a halo would be more likely for Mary; Brenk, *Apse*, 67–68.

62. Rubery, "From Catacomb to Sanctuary," 157, Fig. 9b and 9c.

63. Brenk, *Apse*, 72.

64. Lidova, "Embodied Word," forthcoming, cites around 45 on sarcophagi and 19 in catacomb murals.

65. Spier, *Picturing the Bible*, 181, Fig. 10A.

66. Krautheimer, "Publications on S. Maria Maggiore," 373–74.

67. Brenk, *Apse*, 72.

68. For a review of the various identifications, see Lidova, "Imperial *Theotokos*," 71–76.

69. Kearns, *Virgin Mary*, 131.

70. See this register in Lidova, "Imperial *Theotokos*," 62, Fig. 1.

71. See this register in Lidova, "Imperial *Theotokos*," 63, Fig. 1. Apparently, it was so strange for people to see Herod with a throne, three magi, and a *halo*—instead of Mary—that *HERODES* was written over his head to ensure no confusion. In any case, he is the only person named in the mosaics.

72. For details of this arguments, see Lidova, "Imperial *Theotokos*," 62–63, esp. 63n7, as well as 76–79, esp. 78, Figs. 14 and 15, where Lidova compares Mary's gold costume to those of Pharaoh's daughter and Zipporah, Moses' wife. Zipporah, in the scene of her marriage to Moses, wears a bridal dress almost identical to Mary's—gold with white sleeves, pearls in front of her hair bun, and a double row of pearls at the neck. The gold color thus may have signified that Mary was a bride; yellow was the color reserved to brides in Rome, per la Follette, "Costume of the Roman Bride," 55–56. The queen is described dressed in gold in the liturgy through Psalm 44:10; for the antiquity of the use of this psalm in the Marian liturgy, see Fassler, "First Marian Feast in Constantinople," 25–87; also Brown, *Mary and the Art of Prayer*, 175–79.

73. Lidova, "Imperial *Theotokos*," 66.

74. Kondakov, *Iconografia della Madre di Dio*, 307–13, Figs. 218 (cycle), 219 (arms-raised), and 222 (Adoration).

75. Brenk, *Frühchristlichen Mosaiken in S. Maria Maggiore*, 39 and 46.

76. For discussion, see Limberis, *Divine Heiress*, 53–61; Holum, *Theodosian Empresses*, 147–74; Cooper, "Empress and *Theotokos*," 39–51; and Shoemaker, *Mary in Early Christian Faith*, 208–28.

77. For a recap of this evidence, see Shoemaker, *Mary in Early Christian Faith*, 1–208 (although in my opinion, his argument in pages 157–63 deserves more development).

78. Anđelko, "Ranokršćanski relikvijar iz Novalje" (Early Christian Reliquary in Novalja), 283–95.

79. The word PASTOR is in sections and must be read bottom left to top right.

80. On the left is the extracanonical gospel scene of Peter and his jailers; on the right are the canonical gospel scenes of Jesus at the Wedding at Cana and the multiplication of the loaves and fishes (fragment).

81. De Rossi, "Secchia di piombo," 77–87. Discovered in the 1800s, it was exhibited and photographed, but later lost.

82. For a good summary of early writers who described Jesus as a shepherd, see Jensen, *Understanding Early Christian Art*, 37–41. For example, Tertullian, *On Modesty* 7, 10, writing in north Africa where this was found, describes Christians who painted the shepherd to represent Jesus on their cups and chalices.

83. De Rossi, "Secchia di piombo," quotation on 77.

84. McGowan, *Ascetic Eucharists*, 291, 250, for the Marconites, pages 164–67; see also Stewart-Sykes, "Bread and fish," 212–13; and Vinzent, "Marcion's Liturgical Traditions," 211.

85. Jensen, *Early Christian Art*, 32.

86. Torjesen, "Early Christian Orans," 43.

87. Galate "Evangelium," 14–50 gives a good recap of the history of the many varied interpretations of the orante. See also Jensen, *Understanding Early Christian Art*, 32–37; and Snyder, *Ante Pacem*, 19–20.

88. Birk, *Depicting the Dead*, 90–91.

89. Denzey, *Bone Gatherers*, 81–82.

90. Jensen, *Understanding Early Christian Art*, 39.

91. See also Wilpert, *Sarcofagi*, 1:81, Fig. 40 (plaque), pl. 60 (plaque), and for sarcophagi, plates 1.1 (both in middle with shepherd on the men's side and Orante on the women's side), 1.2 (flanking a seated man reading a scroll). Plaque in Marucchi, *Monumenti del museo Cristiano*, plate 57.

92. Wilpert, *Sarcofagi*, plates 2.3, 3.4, 56.1, 56.5, 57.5, 58, 60.4, 61.2, 118.4, 144.5, and 268.1; Garrucci, *Storia*, plate 360.2; and Marucchi, *Monumenti*, plate 36.4.

93. Kateusz, "Ascension of Christ," 298–302, Fig. 12.

94. Wright, "History of the Virgin Mary," 21.
95. González Casado, *Relcaciones Lingüísticas*, 572.
96. This scene sometimes became conflated with the neighborhood scene where both men and women came to Mary. See Smith Lewis, "Transitus Mariae," 24; Wright, "History of the Virgin Mary," 21; and González Casado, *Relcaciones Lingüísticas*, 566–67.
97. Denzey, *Bone Gatherers*, 85; and Huskinson, "Gender and Identity," 203–209.
98. Ambrose, *On Virgins* 2.7 and 2.10 (Ramsey, *Ambrose*, 93, 94); and Jerome, *Letter 107 7*.
99. Kateusz, "Ascension of Christ," 287–92, Fig. 7.
100. Kateusz, "Ascension of Christ," 287; Kantorowicz, "King's Advent," 223–24; Dewald, "Iconography of the Ascension," 285; Herrmann and van den Hoek, "Two Men in White," 302; Watson, *Gospel Writing*, 565; and Maser, "Parusie Christi oder Triumph der Gottesmutter?" 30–51.
101. Kateusz, "Ascension of Christ," 287–92, 289n54, Figs. 7 and 8 for the two adjacent wood panels and Fig. 9 for the ivory plaque with a similar scene of the ascension of Jesus.
102. For more on the tradition of Mary seen as a mediator, see the articles in Peltomaa, *Presbeia Theotokou*; and Horn, "Power of Leadership Through Mediation."

Notes Chapter 6

1. Van Esbroeck, *Vie de la Vierge*, 21 [Geor.] and 22 [Fr.]; and Shoemaker, *Life of the Virgin*, 36–159. Because van Esbroeck alone used the text of Tbilisi A-40 in his edition, I use his, which I translate from his French, unless otherwise noted.
2. Schüssler Fiorenza, *Memory of Her*, 97–241, quote from 95.
3. For evidence that gender parity was strong during the Second Temple period, see Ilan, *Integrating Women into Second Temple History*; Kraemer, "Jewish Women's Judaism(s) at the Beginning of Christianity," 50–79; Levine, "Second Temple Judaism, Jesus and Women," 302–31; and Brooten, *Women Leaders in the Ancient Synagogue*.
4. *Life of the Virgin*, 71, 98; and Shoemaker, "Virgin Mary in the Ministry of Jesus," quotation on 456.
5. *Life of the Virgin*, 96–99.
6. *Life of the Virgin*, 68–70, 72–74, 76 (Mary was inseparable from her son), 69–71 (the women were her disciples and his, and regularly accompanied both).

7. *Life of the Virgin*, 63 (his mother), 69–71 (other women). Although the gospels themselves do not title any of the women with Jesus during his ministry a "disciple," the author of Luke/Acts in Acts 9:36 titled Tabitha a disciple.
8. *Life of the Virgin*, 69 (van Esbroeck, *Vie* [Fr.], 58–59).
9. *Life of the Virgin*, 70 (van Esbroeck, *Vie* [Fr.], 60).
10. It also means that when Jesus sent out disciples, he sent out both men and women, consistent with Joan Taylor's proposal that they went two by two; Taylor, "'Two by Two'," 58–82.
11. Philo of Alexandria, *On the Contemplative Life*, 83–89.
12. *Life of the Virgin*, 74 (van Esbroeck, *Vie* [Fr.], 64: "elle se sacrifi-ait elle-même comme le prêtre et elle était sacrifiée, elle offrait et elle était offerte"). Other than gender, Shoemaker, using later manuscripts, agrees with this translation; and Shoemaker, *Life of the Virgin*, 102.
13. *Life of the Virgin*, 74 (van Esbroeck, *Vie* [Fr.], 63–64).
14. This scholarship was led by the nearly fifteen-year Society of Biblical Literature Seminar on Meals in the Greco-Roman World, 2001 to present. Key books by this Seminar in related groups in the USA and Europe include Klinghardt, *Gemeinschaftsmahl und Mahlgemeinschaft*; Smith, *From Symposium to Eucharist*; Taussig, *In the Beginning Was the Meal*; Smith, *Meals in the Early Christian World*; and Al-Suadi, *Essen als Christusgläubige Ritualtheoretische*.
15. Klinghardt, *Gemeinschaftsmahl und Mahlgemeinschaft*, 45–60; Smith, *From Symposium to Eucharist*, 13–46; and Taussig, *In the Beginning Was the Meal*, 21–54, 178–84.
16. Klinghardt, *Gemeinschaftsmahl und Mahlgemeinschaft*, 29–39, 62–74; Osiek, *Woman's Place*, 68–82; and Taussig, *In the Beginning Was the Meal*, 78–123.
17. Smith, *From Symposium to Eucharist*, 8–22.
18. Corley, *Maranatha*, 89–131; Osiek, *Woman's Place*, 144–250; Standhartinger, "Women in Early Christian Meal Gatherings," 87–108; Bradshaw, "Remembering and Remembered Women," 109–22; and Taussig, "Dealing Under the Table," 264–79.
19. Epiphanius of Salamis, *Panarion*, 49.2.5 (Williams, *Panarion*, 2:22).
20. Both scripture and Philo designate Miriam as a prophetess, and the *Magnificat* in Luke 1:46–55 portrays Mary as a prophet, and gives her more spoken language than any other woman in the New Testament.
21. *Life of the Virgin*, 74 (van Esbroeck, *Vie* [Fr.], 63–64); and Philo, *On the Contemplative Life*, 87 (Younge, *Works of Philo*, 706).
22. Philo of Alexandria, *On the Contemplative Life*, 83–89 and *On Husbandry*, 80–81.

23. Taylor, *Jewish Women Philosophers*, 343. Note that Ross Shepard Kraemer concludes this highly idealized account was probably fictional, but Hal Taussig finds it unlikely that Philo, who otherwise exhibits patriarchal concerns, would invent women in such roles, and Joan E. Taylor argues that it most likely was an actual Judean ritual meal; see Kraemer, *Unreliable Witnesses*, 57–116; Taussig, "Pivotal Place of the Therapeutae"; and Taylor, *Jewish Women Philosophers*, 311–43.

24. Brooten, *Women Leaders in the Ancient Synagogue*, 5–99.

25. Vuong, *Gender and Purity*, 88–103.

26. *Life of the Virgin* 2; van Esbroeck, *Vie* [Fr.], 3.

27. Booth, "On the *Life of the Virgin*," 152–64.

28. Shoemaker, "(Pseudo?-)Maximus *Life of the Virgin*," 116n1. For the story of this battle, see Theodore the Syncellus, *Homily on the Siege of Constantinople in 626 AD*.

29. Booth, "On the *Life of the Virgin*," 164–97; Shoemaker, "(Pseudo?-) Maximus *Life of the Virgin*," 114–42.

30. Booth, "On the *Life of the Virgin*," 167.

31. Booth, "On the *Life of the Virgin*," 167n69.

32. For Mary preaching, see Smith Lewis, "*Transitus*," 47–48 and *Life of the Virgin*, 97, 98. For Mary teaching women, see Smith Lewis, "*Transitus*," 24, 34 (she told them whatever they wanted to know) and *Life of the Virgin*, 69 (if they were her disciples, she taught them), 74 (she was the leader and teacher of the women), 94 (the women also were apostles). For Mary sending evangelists out from Jerusalem, see Smith Lewis, "*Transitus*," 34 and *Life of the Virgin*, 96 (the women also were disciples). For Mary raising her hands in the context of blessing people, see Smith Lewis, "*Transitus*," 24 and *Life of the Virgin*, 106–7.

33. *Life of the Virgin*, 2; and van Esbroeck, *Vie* [Fr.], 3.

34. Van Esbroeck, *Vie* [Fr.], XXII, XXXVI–VIII.

35. *Life of the Virgin*, 128 (van Esbroeck, *Vie* [Fr.], 115, discussion on XXXVII–VIII). Mary called a sacrifice was consistent with the *Protevangelium*, which described Mary as a Temple sacrifice; see Vuong, *Gender and Purity*, 88–103. Shoemaker discusses the passage about Mary being a second sacrifice, but without mentioning van Esbroeck's translation that Mary sacrificed herself at the Last Supper; and Shoemaker, *Life*, 30–35.

36. For Jerusalem 108, see van Esbroeck, *Vie* [Fr.], XXXVI–VIII, 64n74[a], and *Vie* [Geor.], XIV–XVII. For John Geometrician, see *Vie* [Fr.], XIX–XXIX, XXXVII, 64n74[1a], and *Vie* [Geor.], XIII, XV–XVI.

37. For John Geometrician's variant, see van Esbroeck, *Vie* [Fr.], XXII; for Jerusalem 108's variant, see 64n74[a]; for "J" is Jerusalem 108, see XXXVI; for Jerusalem 108's variant being the result of scribal censorship, as is John Geometrician's, see XXXVII.

38. Shoemaker, *Life*, 4–5.
39. Shoemaker, *Life*, 4. His second was Jerusalem 148, dated eleventh/ twelfth century—but lacking Chapters 2–102 (Last Supper is 74). His last mentioned was Mount Sinai 68, dated twelfth century. For manuscript descriptions, see van Esbroeck, *Vie* [Geor.], V–XI.
40. Shoemaker deferred to van Esbroeck for manuscript descriptions; Shoemaker, *Life*, 3n3. For dating, see van Esbroeck, *Vie* [Geor.], V–XI, esp. VI–VII for Tbilisi A-40 (T), and IX–X for Jerusalem 108 (J).
41. Shoemaker, *Life*, 102.
42. Van Esbroeck, *Vie* [Fr.], 64n74ª, and XXXVI–II.
43. Shoemaker, *Life*, 102n1.
44. Shoemaker, "Virgin Mary in the Ministry," 448.
45. Shoemaker, "Virgin Mary in the Ministry," 449.
46. That John Geometrician and Jerusalem 108 were censored versions of the text in Tbilisi A-40, see van Esbroeck, *Vie* [Fr.], XXII and XXXVII. Finally, and most peculiar in my opinion, in support of his argument in this article that John Geometrician's variant undermined van Esbroeck's reading, Shoemaker claimed to footnote John Geometrician's variant— but instead of providing that complex variant, which would hardly support his claim, he provided Jerusalem 108's variant, which is simply a masculinization of Tbilisi A-40's text; Shoemaker, "Virgin Mary in the Ministry," 449n26; that "J" is Jerusalem 108, not John Geometrician, see van Esbroeck, *Vie* [Geor.], IX, and *Vie* [Fr.], XXXVI. For John Geometrician's variant, see van Esbroeck, *Vie* [Fr.], XXII, and for Jerusalem 108's see 64n74ª.
47. *Life of the Virgin*, 98; van Esbroeck, *Vie* [Fr.], 86; and Shoemaker, *Life*, 125.
48. Shoemaker, *Life*, 125n14.
49. *Life of the Virgin*, 14; and van Esbroeck, *Vie* [Fr.], 10. Perhaps the doors of the altar signify the doors which permitted access to relics below the altar, as seen in Fig. 7.6. Perhaps the doors signify the doors of the Ark of the Covenant; from the Torah shrine painted above the Torah niche in the Dura Europos synagogue to torah shrines depicted on gold catacomb glass in Rome, all have two doors which close over the front of the niches holding scrolls.
50. *Life of the Virgin*, 14; and van Esbroeck, *Vie* [Fr.], 11.
51. Shoemaker, *Life*, 46. Other lives of Mary say the same, that of Epiphanios of Kallistros and John Geometrician; Cunningham, "Life of the Virgin Mary," 153.
52. This gospel is dated as early as the second century because it contains docetic narrative elements, for examples, see *Gospel of Bartholomew*, 1.7 and 1.9 [Jesus vanished from the cross]; 2.15–20 [the great angel];

3.17 and 4.61 [Mary gave birth without pain]. For detailed discussion on its archaic elements (some likely second century), and dating (difficult), see Kaestli, *Évangile de Barthélemy*, 45–94. For the third-century dating, see Schneemelcher, *New Testament Apocrypha*, 1:540; and Shoemaker, "Mary the Apostle," 217.

53. *Gospel of Bartholomew*, 2.20 (Schneemelcher, *New Testament Apocrypha*, 1:545).

54. Strycker, *Forme la plus ancienne*, 391. The text in Bodmer 5 is titled in Greek, *Genesis Mariae*, which is usually translated "Birth of Mary".

55. Zervos, "Early Non-Canonical Annunciation Story," 674–84.

56. Zervos, "Early Non-Canonical Annunciation Story," 680–82.

57. θρόνος; see *Protevangelium*, 23.4 (Stryker, *Forme la plus ancienne*, 114); Zervos, "Early Non-Canonical Annunciation Story," 670.

58. Zervos, "Early Non-Canonical Annunciation Story," 677–79.

59. *Protevangelium*, 13.2, 15.2.

60. Zervos, "Early Non-Canonical Annunciation Story," 674; the text contains four passages about where the annunciation took place—which represents significant over-wording, a sign of ideological conflict.

61. Peppard, *World's Oldest Church*, 155–201, esp., 160, and Fig. 5.1 for the wall painting.

62. For more on the iconography of Mary at the well from the *Protevangelium*, see Cartlidge, *Art & the Christian Apocrypha*, 78–88, Fig. 4.2; and Peppard, *World's Oldest Church*, Figs. 5.3, 5.13–5.15.

63. The later scenes differ in that they depict a pitcher in her hand and an angel behind her.

64. Peppard suggested that perhaps the water source represented the spring that Tacitus said was in the Temple area, possibly the same water source later called the "Fountain of the Virgin," and he noted that two fourth-century sculptures of the annunciation—on an ivory diptych in the Milan Cathedral treasury and the Adelphi sarcophagus in Syracuse—depict Mary at a spring looking back over her shoulder; Peppard, *World's Oldest Church*, 160–61, 165–66, Fig. 5.3. Zervos also suggested the water source might be a laver in the Temple courtyard; Zervos, "Early Non-Canonical Annunciation Story," 683.

65. Peppard, *World's Oldest Church*, 161, 179–82, Fig. 5.16.

66. Van Esbroeck, *Vie* [Fr.], 57; and compare Shoemaker, *Life*, 95.

67. Smith Lewis, "Transitus Mariae," 34.

68. Gambero, "Biographies of Mary," 39.

69. *Life of the Virgin*, 68–70, 72–74, 76.

70. *Life of the Virgin*, 63 (van Esbroeck, *Vie* [Fr.], 53; and Shoemaker, *Life*, 90).

71. *Life of the Virgin*, 63 (Shoemaker, *Life*, 90). Emphasis mine.
72. *Life of the Virgin*, 63.13–14 (van Esbroeck, *Vie* [Fr.], 53). Emphasis mine.
73. *Life of the Virgin*, 68 (van Esbroeck, *Vie* [Fr.], 57).
74. *Life of the Virgin*, 68 (Shoemaker, *Life*, 95).
75. Markschies, "Lehrer, Schüler, Schule," 98.
76. For more on this gospel and who used it, see Beatrice, "Gospel According to the Hebrews," 147–95; Edwards, *Hebrew Gospel*, 1–37; and Schneemelcher, *New Testament Apocrypha*, 1:134–78. For the most cautious list, see Gregory, *Gospel According to the Hebrews*.
77. Eusebius, *Ecclesiastical History*, 3.39.16 (Cruse, *Eusebius' Ecclesiastical History*, 106).
78. Irenaeus, *Against Heresies*, 3.1.1 (*ANF* 1:414).
79. Beatrice, "Gospel According to the Hebrews," 147–85. Also see Gregory, *Gospel According to the Hebrews*, 273–79, who considers these passages spurious.
80. Beatrice, "Gospel According to the Hebrews," 147–95, esp. 185–95. Beatrice also suggests that the Hebrew gospel could have been the lost source behind John, Marcion's gospel, and the *Diatessaron* (which Epiphanius called the *Gospel of the Hebrews*).
81. For example, Gregory, *Gospel According to the Hebrews*, 183.
82. Ps.-Cyprian, *On Rebaptism*, 17 (*ANF* 5, 677). For more on this writing, see Schneemelcher, *New Testament Apocrypha*, 2:32.
83. Jerome, *Against the Pelagians*, 3.2 (Schneemelcher, *New Testament Apocrypha*, 1:160). Single quotes to signify the speeches are mine. Affirming the coercion that Ps.-Cyprian suggests, this saying additionally suggests that Jesus initially resisted being baptized: "But he said to them: 'Wherein have I sinned that I should go and be baptized by him?'"
84. Origen, *Commentary on the Gospel of John*, 2.6 and *Homily on Jeremiah*, 15.4; Jerome, *Commentary on Micah*, 7.6, *Commentary on Isaiah*, 40.9, and *Commentary on Ezekial*, 16.13.
85. Origen, *Commentary on the Gospel of John*, 2.6 (*ANF* 9, 329).
86. Origen, *Commentary on the Gospel of John*, 2.6 (*ANF* 9, 330). Compare to Jerome, *Commentary on Isaiah*, 11.24, where he gives a late fourth-century explanation of the gender of Holy Spirit.
87. For Holy Spirit imaged as female and mother, and its change to masculine gender at the end of the fourth century, see Brock, *Holy Spirit in the Syrian Baptismal Tradition*, 19–26; Harvey, "Feminine Imagery for the Divine," 111–22; Murray, *Symbols of Church*, 312–20; and Kateusz, *Finding Holy Spirit Mother*.

88. *Gospel of Thomas*, 101, "My mother gave me death, but my true Mother gave me life" (*NHL*, 124). Also translated as, "My mother gave birth to me, but my true Mother gave me life" (Smith, *Gospel of Thomas*, 172).

89. *Gospel of Philip*, 54.23–26: "Some say Mary conceived by the Holy Spirit. They are in error. They do not know what they are saying. When did a woman ever conceive by a woman?" (*NHL*, 143).

90. *Gospel of the Egyptians*, 41.7–11 and 42.4 describe a trinity of Father, Mother, and Son.

91. *Odes of Solomon*, 19 speaks of the Holy Spirit as "she" and with breasts.

92. *Acts of Thomas*, 27 and 133: "Come, Merciful Mother …Come, Holy Spirit" (Attridge, *Acts of Thomas*, 35).

93. *Acts of Philip Martyrdom*, 10: Mariamne preached, "You are guilty of having forgotten your origins, your Father in heaven, and your spiritual Mother" (Bovon, "Mary Magdalene in the *Acts of Philip*," 82).

94. Notably well over half of the codices in the Nag Hammadi Library describe a female Being, often named as "mother."

95. For one dated 291, see Snyder, *Ante Pacem*, 126; for two more, see Cabrol, *Dictionnaire d'Archéologie Chrétienne*, vol. 3, part 1, 1335, and vol. 7, part 1, 1006.

96. Harvey, "Feminine Imagery for the Divine," 118.

97. Brock, *Holy Spirit in the Syrian Baptismal Tradition*, 19.

98. Kelly, *Early Christian Creeds*, 298.

99. Origen, *Homily on Jeremiah*, 15.4 (Smith, *Origen*, 161). Note that Jerome quoted the same passage from the *Gospel of the Hebrews* in his *Commentary on Micah*, 7:6, *Commentary on Isaiah*, 40:9, and *Commentary on Ezekiel*, 16:13. Quote marks inserted are mine as this is the quote from the Gospel of the Hebrews.

100. Cyril, *Discourse on Mary Theotokos* (Budge, *Miscellaneous Coptic Texts*, 637). Most scholars either accept the passage as genuinely from the Gospel of the Hebrews or at a minimum leave open the possibility that the passage is from the Gospel of the Hebrews, as the author presents it; see Edwards, *Hebrew Gospel*, 59; Schneemelcher, *New Testament Apocrypha*, 150, 177; Klijn, *Jewish-Christian Gospel Tradition*, 135; Burch, "Gospel According to the Hebrews," 310; Waitz, "Neue Untersuchungen," 73; Crone, *Qur-ānic Pagans*, 260; and an exception is van den Broek, *Studies in Gnosticism*, 148–50. Gregory, *Gospel According to the Hebrews*, 280–81, most recently makes the argument that it probably is not.

101. Cyril, *Discourse on Mary Theotokos* (Budge, *Miscellaneous Coptic Texts*, 628).

102. For this bread ritual, see Kateusz, "Collyridian Déjà vu," 86–87; Shoemaker, "Epiphanius of Salamis," 371–401.

103. Cyril, *Discourse on Mary Theotokos* (Budge, *Miscellaneous Coptic Texts*, 640).

104. *Life of the Virgin*, 74. Compare Shoemaker, *Life*, 102; and van Esbroeck, *Vie* [Fr.], 64.

105. Manuscript Bollandist, 196, folio 123.

106. *Gospel of Bartholomew*, 2.15–19 (Schneemelcher, *New Testament Apocrypha*, 1:544–45).

107. Stewart-Sykes, *Didascalia*, 54–55.

108. Ehrman, *Forgery*, 344; and Stewart-Sykes, *Didascalia*, 49–55, esp. 54.

109. Stewart-Sykes, *Didascalia*, 62–69; Ehrman, *Forgery*, 388–90; Schöllgen, "Abfassungszweck," 68; Osiek, "Widow as Altar," 168–69; Methuen, "Widows, Bishops," 200–10; Thurston, "Widows as the 'Altar'," 279–89; and Eisen, *Women Officeholders*, 150–51.

110. *Didascalia Apostolorum*, 9 (Stewart-Sykes, *Didascalia*, 150–51).

111. Ehrman, *Forgery*, 396; and Stewart-Sykes, *Apostolic Church Order*, 78.

112. *Apostolic Church Order*, 26 (Stewart-Sykes, *Apostolic Church Order*, 113).

113. Stewart-Sykes, *Apostolic Church Order*, 49.

114. Ernst, *Martha*, 241–46, 250–51.

115. Ernst, *Martha*, 251; for over-wording likely indicating the focus of an ideological struggle, see Boyarin, "Reading Androcentrism Against the Grain," 31; and Fairclough, *Language and Power*, 96.

116. *Apostolic Church Order*, 26–27 (Stewart-Sykes, *Apostolic Church Order*, 113).

117. Bovon, *New Testament Traditions and Apocryphal Narratives*, 150.

118. Schrader, "Was Martha Added to the Fourth Gospel," 391. Schrader demonstrates that a scribe added "Martha" to John 11:3 in the oldest manuscript of the gospel of John, Papyrus 66, and that the presence of Martha in the entirety of John 11–12 is remarkably unstable in other manuscripts as well.

119. *Apostolic Church Order*, 26 (Stewart-Sykes, *Apostolic Church Order*, 113).

120. Schaberg, *Resurrection of Mary Magdalene*, 144.

121. See discussion, Ernst, *Martha*, 246–50; and Goetz, "Zwei Beiträge," 165–70, who makes this argument from the *ACO's* material about the Lord's Supper.

NOTES CHAPTER 7

1. Faivre, "Place de femmes dans le ritual eucharistique des marcosiens," 310–28, and for the history of *eucharistein*, see 312n6.
2. Irenaeus, *Against Heresies 1*, 13.3–6 (*ANF* 1:334–5).
3. Irenaeus, *Against Heresies 1*, 13.2 (*ANF* 1:334).
4. Council of Nîmes, *Canon 2* (Madigan, *Ordained Women*, 184–85).
5. Gelasius I, *Letter 14* (Madigan, *Ordained Women*, 186–88, quotation on 186).
6. Madigan, *Ordained Women*, 187; Rossi, "Priesthood," 82; and Ramelli, "Colleagues of Apostles, Presbyters, and Bishops," forthcoming.
7. *Letter from Licinius, Melanius, Eustochius* (Madigan, *Ordained Women*, 188–90); "Eucharist" capitalized for consistency.
8. Boretius, *Monumenta Germaniae Historica: Legum sectio 2, Capitularia regum francorum*, vol. 2 (Eisen, *Women Officeholders*, 134).
9. Epiphanius of Salamis, *Panarion*, 49.3.2 (Williams, *Panarion*, 2:22); and for the Greek used for ordain, see Holl, *Epiphanius*, 2:243.
10. Madigan, *Ordained Women*, 168; and Schneemelcher, *New Testament Apocrypha*, 2:458–60.
11. πρεσβύτερος and πρεσβῦτις; see *Martyrdom of Matthew*, 28 (Bonnet, "Martyrium Matthaei," 2.1:259). For the English translations, see James, "Martyrdom of Matthew," 462, which I quote here; and Madigan, *Ordained Women*, 168. For variants in Greek and Latin, including those that demoted the queen to a deaconess, see Bonnet, "Martyrium Matthaei," 2.1:259; and in English, see Madigan, *Ordained Women*, 168–69.
12. *Martyrdom of Matthew*, 28; James, "Martyrdom of Matthew," 462; and Madigan, *Ordained Women*, 168.
13. *Acts of Philip*, 14.9 (Bovon, *Acts of Philip*, 91).
14. *Didascalia Apostolorum*, 16 (Stewart-Sykes, *Didascalia*, 194).
15. *Acts of Philip*, 1.12 (Bovon, *Acts of Philip*, 36). For the Greek, see Bovon, *Acta Philippi*, 29.
16. πρεσβυτέρους and πρεσβύτιδας; see Bovon, "Women Priestesses," 250.
17. Bovon, "Women Priestesses," 248–54.
18. See 1 Corinthians 1:11 for Chloe's house; Colossians 4:15 for Nympha's; Philemon 1:2 for Apphia's; Romans 16:3 for Priscilla listed first and 1 Cor 16:19 for the church in her house; Acts 16:40 for Lydia's; Acts 12:12 for Mary the mother of Mark's; and 2 John 1:1 for the unnamed lady.
19. Madigan, *Women Officeholders*, 193. Eisen alternatively concludes that this *episcopa* probably lived in Umbria north of Rome around the turn of the fifth century; and see Eisen, *Women Officeholders*, 199–200.

20. Council of Tours, Canon 14 (CCSL 148A, 181); quote from Eisen, *Women Officeholders*, 200.

21. Eisen, *Women Officeholders*, 200.

22. Eisen, *Women Officeholders*, 200; Gary Macy concurs with Eisen, in Macy, "Ordination of Women," 490–91; Valerie A. Karras disagrees, but omits mention of *Theodora episcopa*, Pope Paschal's mother, in Karras, "Priestesses or Priest's Wives," 331–32.

23. Epiphanius of Salamis, *Panarion*, 49.3.2–3 (Williams, *Panarion*, 2:22–23).

24. Schaefer, *Women in Pastoral Office*, 227–29; for a photo of the mosaic, see the cover of Torjesen, *When Women Were Priests*.

25. Schaefer, *Women in Pastoral Office*, 106–110, Fig. 2.8.

26. Eisen, *Women Officeholders*, 200–205.

27. That one or both were a deacon, see Foletti, "Des femmes à l'autel," 76; Bisconti, "Volti degli aristocratici," 45; Liccardo, "Donne e madonne," 235; Ciavolino, "Nuovi affreschi," 378; and Ciavolino, "Scavi e scoperte di archeologia Cristiana in Campania," 615–69, esp. 657. That Bitalia was a priest, see Kroeger, "Bitalia," 11–12.

28. Ciavolino, "Scavi e scoperte," 653.

29. For the symbols on the inside walls of the arcosolium, see Braconi, "Arcosolio di *Cerula*," Fig. 2.

30. Braconi, "Arcosolio di *Cerula*," Fig. 1.

31. For Bitalia's portrait, see Braconi, "Arcosolio di *Cerula*," 137, Fig. 6.

32. For the fresco of San Gennaro, see Bisconti, "Napoli," Fig. 18.

33. For this arcosolium, see Braconi, "Arcosolio di *Cerula*," Fig. 15. This girl, flanked by her mother and father, who are dressed much less finely, has a remarkable resemblance in both dress and posture to the mosaic of Mary Orante in the Oratory of Pope John 7 in Old Saint Peter's dated 706; for the image, see de Rossi, *Musaici cristiani*, pl. "Frammenti du musaici dell'oraorio di Giovanni VII." Also see Rubery, "Pope John VII's Devotion to Mary," 158–59, Figs. 2 and 17.

34. Schaefer, *Women in Pastoral Office*, 199.

35. Braconi, "Arcosolio di *Cerula*," Fig. 13; also see encircled crosses on the *pænula* of Eleusinius as well as on the intrados of his arcosolium, which is just down the hall from the chapel, in Garucci, *Storia*, Fig. 2:102.1. Many of these encircled crosses appear to have been poorly restored.

36. Regarding its identification as the Parousia, see Nasrallah, "Empire and Apocalypse," 506; for the dancing feet, see Kiilerich, *Rotunda in Thessaloniki*, quote on 16, plus Figs. 9 and 13, plus see 46, Figs. 37 and 38, for the pencil drawing of Christ beneath the lost dome mosaic.

37. By contrast, Vatican specialist Matteo Braconi—who even rejects other scholars' suggestion that Cerula could have been a deacon or catechist—ignores all the Christian symbology around Cerula and repeatedly suggests this procession was pagan, not Christian: "Bacchanal," "frenzied," "satyrs and maenads." See Braconi, "Arcosolio di *Cerula*," 136 (not a deaconess), 139–45 (design), quotations from 140.

38. Braconi, for example, calls this iconography "una scelta iconografia estemamente singulare"; Braconi, "Arcosolio di *Cerula*," 136. The closest similar iconography in the same catacomb are two open books painted on the intrados of the nearby arcosolium of Eleusinius, a portrait that various commentators have commented could be that of a bishop or is similar to that of the bishops identified in the so-called bishops' crypt, all of whom hold a book or scroll; see Liccardo, *Redemptor*, 68; Fasola, "Tombe Privilegiate," 207; and Delehaye, *Sanctus*, 264.

39. Bisconti, "Napoli," 14–28, Figs. 9, 11, 13, 14, also 16 regarding that only *Scs Johannes* (John) is named. Bisconti describes these men dressed in togas as philosophers. Roman magistrates also wore togas. Fabrizio Braconi does not mention the association of gospel books with bishops, yet assumes that men depicted with a closed book or scroll are a bishop; see Braconi, "Arcosolio di *Cerula*," 136.

40. Schaefer, *Women in Pastoral Office*, 224–26, photo on 225; and Ramelli, "Colleagues of Apostles."

41. Wilpert associated Petronella with Peter's daughter (from the *Acts of Peter*) for why she in particular was depicted wearing the long strip of folded cloth that he saw as the earliest episcopal pallium. Wilpert, *Capitolo di storia del vestiario*, 24–35, esp. 31–32, Fig. 24; Wilpert, *Gewandung der Christen in den ersten Jahrhunderten*, 47–49; and Wilpert, *Malereien der Katakomben Roms*, 1:466. At the time, Wilperet's theory was widely accepted, as seen in Lowrie, *Christian Art and Architecture*, 403–9, esp. 407 for Petronella. Wilpert's detailed proposal later was rebutted by another Vatican specialist, Braun, *Liturgische Gewandung im Occident und Orient*, 659–64. So far, however, no one has explained the origin of the episcopal pallium as well as Wilpert, nor can anyone explain why no male bishops are seen wearing the pallium until the sixth century—and at the very same time, Mary and Elizabeth are also seen wearing it in the Euphrasiana Basilica apse mosaics.

42. Bradshaw, *Ordination Rites of the Ancient Churches*, 39–43. Although there is some question about when this ritual came to Rome, see my detail associated with Fig. 4.16 above regarding the mosaics at the very top of the Maria Maggiore Basilica triumphal arch, which depict

Peter and Paul holding open books on either side of an empty bishop's throne, as if waiting to hold the gospel books over the head of the new Bishop of Rome. This iconography was particularly poignant, because as discussed in Chapter 6, Pope Celestine (r. 422–432), who most likely started construction on the basilica, died before its completion.

43. See note above. For other interpretations related to the empty throne itself, see Ivan Foletti, "Cicut in caelo et in terra."

44. Kroeger, "Bitalia," 11–12, esp. 12.

45. I first proposed this in the documentary film, *Jesus' Female Disciples: The New Evidence*, which aired on Channel 4 in the UK on April 8, 2018. To me they suggest flames more than they suggest any surviving combination of bookstrap, flap, bookmarker, toggle, etc., although it is not inconceivable that they may have been intended to suggest both. More details are addressed in Kateusz, "Women Church Leaders."

46. Bradshaw, *Ordination Rites of the Ancient Churches*, 40; Bradshaw, *Rites of Ordination*, 70; and Lecuyer, "Note sur la liturgie," 370–71 and 370n6.

47. Bradshaw, *Ordination Rites of the Ancient Churches*, 40.

48. For the Rabbula Gospel illumination of Pentecost, see Spier, *Picturing the Bible*, 276–82, Fig. 82F. Although the illuminations have recently been assessed to have been made separately from the Rabbula gospels and attached later, these illuminations employ very old iconography; I have elsewhere argued that the iconography in the Ascension illumination, for example, closely reflects the Six Books narrative that was so popular in Ancient Syria; Kateusz, "Ascension of Christ or Ascension of Mary," 274–77. In addition, instead of a Trinitarian halo, Jesus is depicted with a regular halo, which is exceedingly rare in art after the sixth century. For the image, see Spier, *Picturing the Bible*, Fig. 82D.

49. In making this claim, I considered two candidates. The first is the lower register of the dome mosaics in the fourth- to sixth-century Rotunda Church of Thessaloniki. These depict only men—bishops, presbyters, soldiers, musicians—but the key liturgical element, the *altar table*, is not present. Nor do any of these arms-raised men hold a chalice or paten. The general view is that these are portraits of martyrs in the heavenly realm. (For details on the Rotuda church, see Nasrallah, "Empire and Apocalypse in Thessaloniki, 465–509, esp. 488–90; Kleinbauer, "Orantes in the Mosaic Decoration," 25–45; Kiilerich, *Rotunda in Thessalonki*, 22–45; Bakirtzis, *Mosaics of Thessaloniki*, 55–114.) The second candidate is the lost apse mosaic of the fifth-century San Giovanni Evangelista church in Ravenna—but this mosaic has not survived, and we have only second-hand descriptions of it, descriptions which suggest that it included two imperial couples flanking two

other people at an altar, perhaps Bishop Peter Chrysologus and an angel, or perhaps, symbolizing the imperial priesthood, Melchizedek and another person. Due to the multiplicity of possible interpretations about an artifact after it has been destroyed, and the tendency of some interpreters to imagine only modern constructs, I restrict my argument to art that has *survived*. For San Giovanni Evangelista, see Deliyannis, *Ravenna*, 68–69, 68n163; and Zangara, "Predicazione alla presenza," 289–92.

50. Deckers and Serdaroğlu, "Hypogäum beim Silivri-Kapi," 140–63, esp. 147–52.

51. Given the dating of the sarcophagus, this boy may have depicted the young emperor Theodosius II, who became emperor at the age of seven. The *Letter to Cosmas* suggests that he had a role in the Holy of Holies. See below.

52. Deckers, "Hypogäum," 160–63. Their dating continues to be accepted; see Török, *Transfigurations of Hellenism*, 215; and Koch, *Frühchristliche Sarkophage*, 408. Mathews dated the panel a little later but without addressing any of Deckers' dating criteria; Mathews, "Sarcophagi di Costantinopoli," 313–35, esp. 320.

53. Sozomen, *Ecclesiastical History*, 9.1. Sozomen was favorable toward Pulcheria, but unfortunately today his history stops at the year 425, having lost its ending, which originally included the Nestorian conflict; we thus do not know what he wrote about Pulcheria's role in it.

54. *Letter to Cosmas*, 6 (Nau, *Histoire de Nestorius*, 275–86, esp. 278); *Barhadbeshabba*, 20 (Nau, *Barhadbeshabba Abaya*, 515–70, esp. 565).

55. For the view that the *Letter to Cosmas* has little historical value, see Price, "Marian Piety and the Nestorian Controversy," 31–38, 34. Also see Cooper, "Contesting the Nativity," 31–43. For the view that the *Letter of Cosmas* as one of several witnesses regarding the historical conflict between Nestorius and Pulcheria, see Holum, *Theodosian Empresses*, 147–74; Limberis, *Divine Heiress*, 53–61.

56. *Letter to Cosmas*, 6 (Nau, *Histoire de Nestorius*, 279).

57. Zosimus, *New History*, 4.36 describes Gratian refusing the honor, to which Zosimus attributes his death not long after; Ridley, Zosimus, 115–16.

58. Taft, "Byzantine Imperial Communion Ritual," 1–27, esp. 5–8 for earlier reports of the emperor taking communion like the priest, 9–17 for the *Book of Ceremonies* descriptions of the emperor taking the bread and wine in his own hands, 17–20 for later reports, and 20–21 for a report of the empress taking communion in the sanctuary. This later report of an empress in the Holy of Holies may reflect the tip of the iceberg considering the early report in the *Letter to Cosmas* about Pulcheria.

The lack of intervening reports could be due to later censorship or simply by the way Byzantine historians and scribes often overlooked the empress, despite how much power she wielded. Procopius, for example, almost ignored Theodora in his official histories, but described her exercising enormous power in his *Secret History*. For more detail on the extent to which some Byzantine empresses wielded actual power, see Herrin, *Unrivaled Influence*, esp. 161–207. For more on the intersection of *imperium* and *sacerdotium*, see Dagron, *Emperor and Priest*, esp. 84–191.

59. *Letter to Cosmas*, 6 (Nau, *Histoire de Nestorius*, 279). Nestorius later wrote that his conflict with Pulcheria was so "that I might not be the chief celebrant of the sacrifice among those whom she had unrighteously chosen," a statement for which the *Letter to Cosmas* provides context; Nestorius, *Bazaar of Heracleides*, 1.3 (Driver, *Bazaar of Heracleides*, 96–97).

60. For a recap, see Kate Cooper, "Empress and *Theotokos*," 39–51; and Constas, *Proclus of Constantinople*, 46–73.

61. For a detailed analysis, see Foster, "Giving Birth to God," 48–114. See also, Harrison, "Male and Female in Cappadocian Theology," 465; Crouzel, *Origen*, 124; McVey, "Ephrem the Syrian's Theology," 458–60; and Constas, *Proclus*, 246.

62. Gregory of Nazianzus, *Oration on the Nativity*, 38.1 (Peltomaa, *Image of the Virgin Mary*, 73). See also, Harrison, "Male and Female in Cappadocian Theology," 465.

63. *Gospel of Bartholomew*, 2.8 (Schneemelcher, *New Testament Apocrypha*, 1:544).

64. Crystostom said: "The divine law excluded women from the ministry, but they forcibly push themselves in"; Chrysostom, *Six Books on the Priesthood*, 3.9 (Neville, *Six Books*, 78). See also John reforming the order of widows, Palladius, *Dialogue on the Life of St. John Chrysostom*, 4 (Meyer, *Palladius*, 38–40).

65. See Holum, *Theodosian Empresses*, 69–77.

66. Longhi, *Capsella*, 112; Guarducci, *Capsella*, 123; Buddensieg, "Coffret en ivoire de Pola," 192; and Elsner, "Closure and Penetration," 183. See Angiolini, *Capsella*, 101–4 for a review of various scholars' dating.

67. Longhi, *Capsella*, 110; and Guarducci, *Capsella*, 121.

68. Angiolini, *Capsella*, 104–6.

69. Gnirs, "Basilica," 34, 36–37, Fig. 28.

70. For scholars who have identified them as women, see Toesca, *Storia dell'arte italiana*, 322; Ducati, *Arte in Roma*, 380; Soper, "Italo-Gallic School of Early Christian Art," 157; Leclercq, "Pola," col. 1345; Wilpert, "Due più antiche rappresentazioni," 148; Cecchelli, *Vita di*

Roma, 208; Guarducci, *Capsella eburnea*, 126–27; Elsner, *Closure and Penetration*, 187; Bisconti, "Capsella di Samagher," 230–31; and Longhi, *Capsella*, 109–12. For a good recap, see Angiolini, *Capsella*, 12–14, 22–30.

71. Philo of Alexandria, *On the Contemplative Life*, 83–89 (Yonge, *Philo*, 706). Emphasis added.

72. Leclercq, "Pola," coll. 1342–1346, esp. col. 1345, Fig. 10429.

73. Kirschbaum, *Tombs of St. Peter and St. Paul*, 52; and Guarducci, *Tomb of St. Peter*, Fig. 23.

74. Kirschbaum, *Tombs*, 55, Fig. 7 (stack of altars); 67, Fig. 12 (slab); 56, and plate 26 (shrine).

75. Toynbee, "Shrine of St. Peter," 22.

76. For identification of these as steps, see Cecchelli, *Vita di Roma nel Medioevo*, 1:208; and Klauser, "Römische Petrustradition," 111. See also Ruysschaert, "Réflexions sur les fouilles vaticanes," 46n2 regarding the steps being natural striations in the ivory. These same striations appear as bricks in the column base to the right of the steps and in the pediment to the left, and the artist seems to have incorporated them into the design; in any case, the woman is depicted either standing or kneeling on top. Ghetti, *Esplorazioni*, vol. 1, Fig. 90-a shows a four-foot height from the Constantinian pavement to the tabletop. This is about the height of the altar table depicted in San Vitale, which is shown shoulder high to both Melchisedek and Abel; for that mosaic, see von Simson, *Sacred Fortress*, plate 15.

77. Kirschbaum, *Tombs*, 81–94, 113–19.

78. Gregory of Tours, *Glory of the Martyrs*, 27 (van Dam, *Glory of the Martyrs*, 24).

79. Gregory of Tours, *Glory of the Martyrs*, 27 (van Dam, *Glory of the Martyrs*, 24). For Latin, see Krusch, *Gregorii episcopi Turonensis*, 54.

80. Jerome, *Contra Vigilantium*, 1.8 (*NPNF-2* 6, 420): "Does the bishop of Rome do wrong when he offers sacrifices to the Lord over the venerable bones of the dead men Peter and Paul, as we should say, but according to you, over a worthless bit of dust, and judges their tombs worthy to be Christ's altars?" At about the same time, Augustine was similarly equating the *mensa* on Cyprian's tomb as God's altar table; for discussion, see Jensen, "Dining with the Dead," 137–38. For more on altars above saints' relics, see Brown, *Cult of the Saints*, 1–22; and Crook, *Architectural Setting of the Cult of Saints*, 6–67, esp. 11–12.

81. Hassett, "Altar," 1:362–67, esp. 363.

82. Toynbee, *Shrine of St. Peter*, 216, note that the excavators also found some small holes in line with the back of the shrine and from these hypothesized a barrier around the entire ciborium, but which is not

seen on the ivory. See the relative elevations and a reconstruction of Gregory the Great's raised altar and presbytery in Ghetti, *Esplorazioni*, vol. 1, 124–25, Figs. 90-a, 91; 186, Fig. 141. Also see Kirschbaum, *Tombs*, 143–144, Figs. 12, 13.

83. Kirschbaum, *Tombs*, 60.

84. For ampoules with staggered columns or three triangular roof panels indicating a hexagon structure, see Grabar, *Ampoules*, plates 9, 11 (Monza 5), 14, 22, 34, 45 (Bobbio 15); and Biddle, *Tomb of Christ*, Figs. 17, 18, and 23. For the hexagonal glass vessels, see Barag, "Glass Pilgrim Vessels from Jerusalem, Part 1," Figs. 1, 2A–2F, 8, and Fig. A I–VIII; and Barag, "Glass Pilgrim Vessels from Jerusalem, Parts 2 and 3," 51–63.

85. For spiral columns, see Grabar, *Ampoules*, plates 9, 11, 14, 22, 24–28, 33, 35, 40 (Bobbio 6; and Biddle, *Tomb of Christ*, Fig. 18. For the hexagonal glass vessels, see Barag, "Glass Pilgrim Vessels from Jerusalem, Part 1," Figs. 1, 2A–2F, 8, and Fig. A I–VIII; and Barag, "Glass Pilgrim Vessels from Jerusalem, Parts 2 and 3," 51–63. For ivory pyxides, see St. Clair, "Visit to the Tomb," Figs. 1, 7–10.

86. This quote is from the museum's online description of the pyx. https://www.metmuseum.org/toah/works-of-art/17.190.57/ (accessed May 9, 2018).

87. Noga-Banai, *Sacred Stimulus*.

88. The shrine over Christ's tomb appears most likely to have had a hexagon shape, although the three elements of the Anastasis—the ornate gated doorway to the shrine, the hexagonal monument, and the rotunda dome above—are shown together only on one artifact, a frame on the Sancta Sanctorum painted reliquary box; see Biddle, *Tomb of Christ*, 22, Fig. 17. Nonetheless, for ampoules that depict the hexagonal front, or at least, the three triangular panels of its hexagonal roof, see Grabar, *Ampoules*, pl. 9, 11, 14, 34, and 35. Also see the hexagonal glass pilgrim vessels from Jerusalem that Barag argues represented the architecture of the Anastasis shrine, see Barag, "Glass Pilgrim Vessels from Jerusalem, Parts 2 and 3," 51–63. For mosaics depicting the monument as hexagonal, see Biddle, *Tomb of Christ*, Figs. 22 and 23. Note also that four frontal columns on an artifact may represent the four columns visible on a hexagon when seen from the front, especially as the middle two, representing the shorter front face, are often depicted as if closer to the viewer than the outside two; see Biddle, *Tomb of Christ*, Figs. 18, 23, 24, and 26; and Grabar, *Ampoules*, 9, 14, 22, 13, 34, 35, 36, and 45.

89. Ghetti, *Esplorazioni sotto la confessione di San Pietro*, vol. 1, Fig. 121, plate H; and Kirschbaum, *Tombs*, Fig. 10, plate 29, where with careful

inspection one can see that everything in front of the shrine in Fig. 10s "reconstruction" is a dotted line, in other words, hypothetical.

90. Kirschbaum, *Tombs*, 61. Emphasis added.

91. Ghetti, *Esplorazioni*, vol. 1, plate H; and Kirschbaum, *Tombs*, plate 29.

92. Toynbee, *Shrine*, 201.

93. Grabar, *Martyrium*, 1:293–94. Grabar was familiar with the excavations and published before the excavators' final report.

94. Ruysschaert, "Réflexions sur les fouilles vaticanes," 46–48. Ruysschaert later recanted, after which he was appointed Vice-Prefect of the Library; and see Ruysschaert, "Découverte d'une grande tradition romaine," 401–11, esp. 411

95. Toynbee, *Shrine*, 208n28; Kirschbaum, *Gräber der Apostelfürsten*, 57n13; and see also Kirschbaum's 1959 English translation, Kirschbaum, *Tombs*, 61n13.

96. Kirschbaum, *Tombs*, 157. Compare with Gregory of Tours, *Glory of the Martyrs* 27.

97. Kirschbaum, *Tombs*, 158. Kirschbaum paraphrased Jerome as saying that the sacrifice was "at" Peter's tomb (instead of "over" it), and then in a footnote argued that "at" the tomb was "reasonably" consistent with the *Liber Pontificalis* (*Tombs*, 61n13). Recent research, however, shows the *Liber Pontificalis* is remarkably unreliable with respect to Old Saint Peter's; see Westall, "Constantius II and the Basilica of St. Peter," 205–42; and Gem, "From Constantine to Constans," 35–64.

98. Toynbee, *Shrine*, 212, for Gregory of Tours.

99. Perkins, "Memoria, Martyr's Tomb," 20–37, quotation on 23.

100. Brown, *Cult of the Saints*, 9.

101. Crook, *Architectural Setting of the Cult of Saints*, 11–12.

102. Bogdanović, *Framing of Sacred Space*, 185.

103. Noga-Banai, *Sacred Stimulus*, 130.

104. Kleinbauer, "Orants in the Mosaic Decoration," 36, 38; Bogdanović, *Framing of Sacred Space*, 185.

105. Those who identified the man and woman at the altar prior to the Vatican excavations include Gnirs, "Basilica ed il reliquiario d'avorio," 33–34, Fig. 28; Toesca, *Storia dell'arte italiana*, 322; Ducati, *Arte in Roma*, 380, Soper, "Italo-Gallic School," 157; and Leclercq, "Pola," col. 1345; also Cecchelli, *Vita*, 208, in 1952 still saw a married couple at an altar. For a good recap of the different male and female pairs that various scholars have proposed since the excavations, see Angiolini, *Capsella*, 12–14, 22–30.

106. Elsner, *Closure and Penetration*, 187.

107. Guarducci, *Capsella eburnea*, 126–27 (Constantine and Helena); and Longhi, *Capsella*, 109–12 (Galla Placidia and Valentinian II); and Bisconti, "Capsella di Samagher," 230–31.
108. Guarducci, *Capsella eburnea*, 126–27.
109. Geertman, "Genesi del *Liber Pontificalis*," 37–107, esp. 37.
110. For recent recaps, see Westall, "Constantius II and the Basilica of St. Peter," 205–42; and Gem, "From Constantine to Constans," 35–64; for a detailed study on the later appropriation of Peter in order to assert the primacy of the bishop of Rome, see also Demacopoulos, *Invention of Peter*.
111. Longhi, *Capsella*, 109–12.
112. Ambrose, *On Theodosius*, 40–47 (Deferrari, "On Theodosius," 325–28).
113. Longhi, *Capsella*, 109–12, 145–48; and Guarducci, *Capsella*, 106–16. But see also Bisconti, "Capsella di Samagher," 217–31, esp. 231, where he disputes that these can be identified as Guarducci proposed.
114. Deliyannis, *Ravenna in Late Antiquity*, 62–84.
115. Andrew Gillett, "Rome, Ravenna and the Last Western Emperors," 142–47; and Sivan, *Galla Placidia*, 134–41.
116. Leo, *Letter 56* (*NPNF-2* 12, 58).
117. Longhi, *Capsella*, 100; Angiolini, *Capsella*, 29; Buddensieg, "Coffret en ivoire de Pola," 163; and Bogdanović, *Framing of Sacred Space*, 185.
118. Gregory the Great, *Epistle*, 4.30. Jensen, Saints' Relics, 162–63, gives a good recap of his letter to the *Empress Constantina*.
119. Bogdanović, *Framing of Sacred Space*, 185, suggests that the veiled figure could have been the high priest, with the figure on the left the assistant priest.
120. What event these two mosaics were intended to commemorate has resulted in heated discussion; for a recap of some of the opinions, see Deliyannis, *Ravenna in Late Antiquity*, 242–43, but as is often the case with heated discussions, she does not present all sides equally; most notably she omits von Simson's view that this is a Eucharistic scene; for example, von Simson, *Sacred Fortress*, 36: "The entire cycle of mosaics thus culminates in the apse of San Vitale, where the sacrifice offered by Justinian as emperor and priest …"
121. Theodora herself was the focus of considerable sexual slander, best known from the writer Procopius, but recently the accuracy of this slander has been seriously questioned; for the positive Syriac tradition that Theodora was the daughter of Syriac priest, see Harvey, "Theodora the 'Believing Queen'"; see also McClanan, "Empress Theodora and the Tradition of Women's Patronage."

122. Von Simson, *Sacred Fortress*, 30–31. See also Elsner, "Closure and Penetration," 183–227, esp. 222–24, with respect to the visual parallels between this scene and the iconography of the ivory box from Pola discussed below.

123. Lidov, "Priesthood of the Virgin Mary," 17, Fig. 18.

124. Lidov, "Priesthood of the Virgin Mary," 17.

125. Harvey, "Theodora the 'Believing Queen,'" 209–34.

126. Meier, *Andere Zeitalter Justinians*, 489–528, 570–86 (Mary); 528–60, esp. 546–50 (divine analogies).

127. See Justinian without a halo in Weitzmann, *Age of Spirituality*, 33–35, plate 28.

128. *Protevangelium*, 7.2, 10.1–2. Lafontaine-Dosogne, *Iconographie de l'enfance de la Vierge*, 1:136–67.

129. Taylor, "Christian Archeology in Palestine," forthcoming.

130. Jensen, *Understanding Early Christian Art*, 57.

131. See also Jensen, *Understanding Early Christian Art*, Fig. 14 for a nearby meal scene in the Callistus Catacomb that depicts some of the seven diners as more clearly feminine; another very similar seven-person meal scene in the third-century Capella Greca in the Priscilla Catacomb clearly depicts a women wearing a veil; another at the end of the table has a long skirt and appears to be breaking bread; see Torjesen, *When Women Were Priests*, 52; and Tulloch, "Women Leaders," 182, 182n67; for the best image of both these scenes, see Wilpert, *Malereien*, pl. 15.

132. *Didascalia Apostolorum*, 26 (Connolly, *Didascalia*, 253)

133. Tulloch, "Women Leaders in Family Funerary Banquets," 164–93, esp. 181–85, Figs. 8.2–8.5, quote from 182. Note that Tulloch does not mention that these meals have often been identified as Eucharistic; she proposes that these meals scenes depict a family funerary banquet with a woman offering a toast. For yet more such meal scenes with women, see du Bourguet, *Early Christian Painting*, Figs. 87 and 100.

134. Tulloch, "Women Leaders in Family Funerary Banquets," 182.

135. Tulloch, "Women Leaders in Family Funerary Banquets," 181–85.

136. Nicolai, *Christian Catacombs of Rome*, 116, Fig. 132

137. Virtually all scholars agree the veiled arms-raised person is a woman; for recap, see Finney, *Invisible God*, 214–16, Fig. 6.47; also Torjesen, "Early Christian *Orans*," 51, Fig. 2.1.

138. Finney, *Invisible God*, 214.

139. Finney, *Invisible God*, 214–16.

140. Finney, *Invisible God*, 216.

141. Torjesen, "Early Christian *Orans*," 51.

142. Reta Halteman Finger chose this fresco for the cover of her book, *Of Widows and Meals*, and some of these quickly painted diners likely represented women, because women are clearly identifiable in other more detailed catacomb meal scenes. See also, Wilpert, *Malereien*, pl. 15.
143. For discussion, see Jensen, *Early Christian Art*, 52–59; for the Marcionites and fish, see Stewart-Sykes, "Bread and Fish," 214–18.
144. Mitchell, "Looking for Abercius," 303; Snyder, *Ante-Pacem*, 139–40.
145. Mitchell, "Looking for Abercius," 303.
146. *Life of the Virgin*, 2; and van Esbroeck, *Vie* [Fr.], 3.

NOTES CHAPTER 8

1. Markschies, "Lehrer, Schüler, Schule," 98.
2. King, *Gospel of Mary*, 9–11.
3. Flowers, *Art of Forgetting*, 1.
4. Athanasius, *Festal Letter 39*, 23 (Brakke, "New Fragment," 62). Emphasis mine.
5. Schneemelcher, *New Testament Apocrypha*, 1:38–40.
6. Flowers, *Art of Forgetting*, 2.
7. Hedrick, *History and Silence*, 93–94.
8. See the "Works of Tertullian" condemned in the Gelasianum Decree, in Schneemelcher, *New Testament Apocrypha*, 1:39. For discussion on Tertullian's conversion to New Prophecy, aka "Montanism," see Epiphanius, *Panarion*, 48 and 49, esp. 49.2.5 and 49.3.2; and Trevett, *Montanism*, 14–15, 68–76.
9. Schneemelcher, *New Testament Apocrypha*, 1:39–40.
10. Castelli, "Romans," 279.
11. Epp, *Junia*, 53–59.
12. Parrott, "*Eugnostos the Blessed* (III, 3 and V, 1) and *The Sophia of Jesus Christ* (III, 4 and BG 8502, 3)," 222; for the side-by-side Coptic and English translation of NHC III, *The Sophia of Jesus Christ*, see Parrott, "Nag Hammadi Codices III, 3–4 and V, 1 with Papyrus Berolinensis 8502, 3 and Oxyrhynchus Papyrus 1081," 37. Emphasis mine.
13. Experts who earlier had identified a man and a woman at an altar include Gnirs, "Basilica," 34, 36–37, Fig. 28; Toesca, *Storia dell'arte italiana*, 322; Ducati, *Arte in Roma*, 380; Soper, "Italo-Gallic School of Early Christian Art," 157; Leclercq, "Pola," col. 1345; Wilpert, "Due più antiche rappresentazioni," 148; and Cecchelli, *Vita di Roma*, 208.
14. Ghetti, *Esplorazioni sotto la confessione di San Pietro*, 1:171.
15. Bradshaw, *Search for the Origins*, 3–4.
16. Cross, "Early Western Liturgical Manuscripts," 63–64. Emphasis added.

17. See my note at the end of Chapter 6 regarding the fifth-century Rotunda Church mosaics in Thessaloniki (no altar present) and the lost apse mosaic in San Giovanni Evangelista church in Ravenna (uncertain and destroyed). With respect to artifacts potentially dated to Justinian's reign or earlier, a sixth-century ivory pyx depicts the Anastasis altar and men on opposite sides of the ciborium, but compositionally these men are part of two adjacent gospel scenes—they are oriented towards those scenes, not the altar; see the Cleveland pyx in St. Clair, "Visit to the Tomb," 131–32, Fig. 9. The oldest artifacts to depict a Christian man *without a woman* at an altar appear to be two Eucharistic patens silver stamped between the years 565 and 574, thus dating to the reign of Justin II, the emperor who followed Justinian. These two patens recreate the Last Supper ritual with a two-headed Jesus—that is, two torsos, each with Jesus's head and a Trinitarian halo—behind a large cloth-covered altar table. Twelve male disciples flank the table, six to a side. This representation of a double-Jesus at the altar table is novel to say the least, and the entire composition, pointedly displayed on Eucharistic patens, was arguably an attempt to undermine the older tradition that both Mary and Jesus had officiated at the Last Supper. Instead of Mary and her son officiating at the altar table, the artist Mary with a *second* Jesus. Instead of women on one side of the table and men on the other, the artist depicted men on both. For these two patens, see Mango, *Silver from Early Byzantium*, 159–70, Figs. 34.3 and 35.4.

Abbreviations

ANF   Ante-Nicene Fathers
CSCO   Corpus Scriptorum Christianorum Orientalium
JFSR   Journal of Feminist Studies in Religion
NHS   Nag Hammadi Studies
SBL   Society of Biblical Literature

References

Note on Primary Sources: Where possible I have used editions and translations of the ancient sources that are widely accessible, many of which are out of copyright and online. I cite each when I first reference the source, and thereafter when quoted.

Abrahamsen, Valerie. "Human and Divine: The Marys in Early Christian Tradition." Pages 164–81 in *A Feminist Companion to Mariology*. Edited by Amy-Jill Levine. Cleveland: Pilgrim Press, 2005.

Aitken, Ellen Bradshaw. "Remembering and Remembered Women in Greco-Roman Meals." Pages 109–22 in *Meals in the Early Christian World: Social Formation, Experimentation, and Conflict at the Table*. Edited by Dennis E. Smith and Hal Taussig. New York: Palgrave Macmillan, 2012.

Al-Suadi, Soham. *Essen als Christusgläubige Ritualtheoretische Exegese paulinischer Texte*. Tübingen: Francke, 2011.

Ambrose. *On Theodosius*. In *Funeral Orations by Saint Gregory Nazianzen and Saint Ambrose*. Translated by Roy J. Deferrari. Fathers of the Church 22. Baltimore, MD: Catholic University Press, 1953.

———. *On Virgins*. In *Ambrose*. Translated by Boniface Ramsey, O. P. London: Routledge, 1997.

Angert-Quilter, Theresa. "A Commentary on the Shorter Text of the Acts of Thecla and Its New Testament Parallels." Dissertation. Australian Catholic University, 2014.

Angiolini, Anna. *La capsella eburnea di Pola*. Bologna: Pàtron, 1970.

Arentzen, Thomas. *The Virgin in Song: Mary and the Poetry of Romanos the Melodist*. Philadelphia: University of Pennsylvania Press, 2017.

Armitage, David, and Jo Guldi. "*The History Manifesto*: A Reply to Deborah Cohen and Peter Mandler." *The American Historical Review* 120, no. 2 (April 2015): 543–54.

Arras, Victor. *De Transitus Mariae Aethiopice*. Vol. 1. CSCO 342–343. Louvain: Secrétariat du CSCO, 1973.

Athanasius. *Orations Against the Arians*. In *The Orations of St. Athanasius against the Arians*. Translated by William Bright. Eugene, OR: Wipf & Stock, 2005.

Attridge, Harold, W. *The Acts of Thomas*. Edited by Julian V. Hills. Early Christian Apocrypha 3. Salem, OR: Polebridge, 2010.

Badurina, Anđelko. "Ranokršćanski relikvijar iz Novalje." (Early Christian Reliquary in Novalja). *Materijali* 12 (1976): 283–95.

Bagatti, Bellarmino. "La verginità di Maria negli apocrifi del II–III secolo." *Marianum* 33 (1971): 281–92.

Bagatti, Bellarmino, Michele Piccirillo, and Alberto Prodromo. *New Discoveries at the Tomb of the Virgin Mary in Gethsemane*. Jerusalem: Franciscan Printing Press, 1975.

Bagnoli, Martina. *Treasures of Heaven: Saints, Relics, and Devotion in Medieval Europe*. London: British Museum Press, 2011.

Bakirtzis, Charalambos, Eftychia Kourkoutidou-Nikolaidou, and Chrysanthi Mavropoulou-Tsioumi. *Mosaics of Thessaloniki: 4th–14th century*. Edited by Charalambos Bakirtzis. Translated by Alexandra Doumas. Athens: Kapon, 2012.

Baldi, Donato, and Anacleto Mosconi. "L'Assunzione di Maria SS. negli apoc- rifi." Pages 75–125 in *Atti del congresso nazionale mariano dei Fratei Minori d'Italia*. Studia Mariana 1. Rome: Commissionis Marialis Franciscanae, 1948.

Barag, Dan. "Glass Pilgrim Vessels from Jerusalem, Part 1." *Journal of Glass Studies* 13 (1971): 35–63.

———. "Glass Pilgrim Vessels from Jerusalem, Parts II and III." *Journal of Glass Studies* 13 (1971): 45–63.

Barag, Dan, and John Wilkinson. "The Monza-Bobbio Flasks and the Holy Sepulchre." *Levant* 6 (1974): 179–87.

Barker, Margaret. *The Great Angel: A Study of Israel's Second God*. Louisville, KY: Westminster John Knox, 1992.

———. *The Mother of the Lord, Volume 1: The Lady in the Temple*. London: Bloomsbury, 2012.

Bauckham, Richard. *The Fate of the Dead: Studies on Jewish and Christian Apocalypses*, Leiden: Brill, 1998.

———. *Gospel Women: Studies of the Named Women in the Gospels*. Grand Rapids, MI: William B. Eerdmans, 2002.

Bauer, A., V. Golenishchev, and J. Strzygowski. *Eine Alexandrinische weltchronik: text und miniaturen eines griechischen papyrus der sammlung W. Goleniščev*. Vienna: C. Gerold, 1905.

Bauer, Franz Alto. "St. Peter's as a Place of Collective Memory in Late Antiquity." Pages 155–70 in *Rom in der Spätantike: Historische Erinnerung im städtischen Raum. Heidelberger althistorische Beiträge und epigraphische Studien*. Edited by Ralf Behrwald and Christian Witschel. Stuttgart: Franz Steiner, 2012.

Beattie, Tina. "Mary in Patristic Theology." Pages 75–105 in *Mary: The Complete Resource*. Edited by Sarah Jane Boss. Oxford: Oxford University Press, 2007.

Beavis, Mary Ann. "Mary of Bethany and the Hermeneutics of Remembrance." *Catholic Biblical Quarterly* 75 (2013): 739–55.

———. "Reconsidering Mary of Bethany." *Catholic Biblical Quarterly* 74, no. 2 (April 2012): 281–97.

Becker, Adam H., and Annette Yoshiko Reed, eds. *The Ways That Never Parted: Jews and Christians in Late Antiquity and the Early Middle Ages*. Minneapolis: Fortress, 2007.

Beckwith, John. *Early Christian and Byzantine Art*. 2nd edn. New Haven: Yale University Press, 1993.

Bell, Susan Groag. "Medieval Women Book Owners: Arbiters of Lay Piety and Ambassadors of Culture." In *Women and Power in the Middle Ages*. Edited by Mary Erler and Maryanne Kowalski. Athens, GA: University of Georgia Press, 1988.

Bellet, P. "Testimonios Coptos de la aparicion de Christo resuscitato a la Virgen." *Estudios Biblicos* 13 (1954): 199–205.

Benko, Stephen. *The Virgin Goddess: Studies in the Pagan and Christian Roots of Mariology.* Leiden: Brill, 2004.

Bernabò, Massimo, ed. *Il Tetravangelo di Rabbula. Firenze, Biblioteca Medicea Laurenziana, plut. 1.56: L'illustrazione del Nuovo Testamento nella Siria del VI secolo.* Rome: Edizioni di Storia e Letteratura, 2008.

Bernstein, Moshe J. "Women and Children in Legal and Liturgical Texts from Qumran." *Dead Sea Discoveries* 11, no. 2 (2004): 191–211.

Bertetto, D. "Madre sacerdotale." *Miles Immaculatae* 21 (1985): 205–20.

Bertonière, Gabriel. *The Historical Development of the Easter Vigil and Related Services in the Greek Church.* Orientalia Christiana Analecta 193. Rome: Pontificum Institutum Studiorum Orientalium, 1972.

Biddle, Martin. *The Tomb of Christ.* Thrupp, UK: Sutton, 1999.

Birk, Stine. *Depicting the Dead: Self-Representation and Commemoration on Roman Sarcophagi with Portraits.* Aarhus Studies in Mediterranean Antiquity 11. Denmark: Aarhus University Press, 2013.

Bisconti, Fabrizio. "La Capsella di Samagher: Il quadro delle interpretazioni." *Il cristianesimo in Istria fra tarda antichità e alto Medioevo* (2009): 217–31.

———. "Napoli. Catacombe di S. Gennaro. Cripta dei Vescovi. Restauro ultimi." *RACr* 91 (2015): 7–34.

———. "I volti degli aristocratici nella tarda antichità: fisionomie e ritratti nelle catacombe romane e napoletane." Pages 27–46 in *Aristocrazie e società fra transizione romano-germanica e alto medioevo. Atti del Convegno internazionale di studi Cimitile-Santa Maria Capua Vetere, 14–15 giugno 2012.* Edited by Carlo Ebanista and Marcello Rotili. Cimitile: Tavolario Edizioni, 2015.

Bogdanović, Jelena. *The Framing of Sacred Space: The Canopy and the Byzantine Church.* New York: Oxford University Press, 2017.

Bonnet, Maximilien, trans. "Martyrium Matthaei." Pages 1.2:217–62 in *Acta Apostolorum Apocrypha*, 2 vols. in 3. Edited by Richard Albert Lipsius and Maximilien Bonnet. Leipzig: Mendelssohn, 1891–1903.

Booth, Philip. "On the *Life of the Virgin* Attributed to Maximus the Confessor." *Journal of Theological Studies*, NS, 66, no. 1 (April 2015): 149–200.

Borella, Pietro. *Il Rito Ambrosiano.* Brescia: Nuova Cartographica, 1964.

Boretius, Alfred. *Monumenta Germaniae Historica: Legum sectio 2, Capitularia regum Francorum.* 2 2. Hannover: Hahn, 1897.

Bosio, Antonio, and Paulo Aringhi. *Roma subterranea.* 2 vols. Paris: Fredericum Leonard, 1659. Reprint. Portland, OR: Collegium Graphicum, 1972.

Bovini, Giuseppe. *Sant'Apollinare Nuovo in Ravenna.* Translated by J. Templeton. Milan: "Silvana" Editoriale d'Arte, 1961.

Bovon, François. *New Testament Traditions and Apocryphal Narratives.* Translated by Jane Haapiseva-Hunter. Allison Park, PA: Pickwick, 1995.

———. "Byzantine Witnesses for the Apocryphal Acts of the Apostles." Pages 87–98 in *The Apocryphal Acts of the Apostles*. Edited by François Bovon, Ann Graham Brock, and Christopher R. Matthews. Cambridge: Harvard University Press, 1999.

———. "Editing the Apocryphal Acts of the Apostles." Pages 1–35 in *The Apocryphal Acts of the Apostles*. Edited by François Bovon, Ann Graham Brock, and Christopher R. Matthews. Cambridge: Harvard University Press, 1999.

———. "Mary Magdalene in the *Acts of Philip*." Pages 75–89 in *Which Mary? The Marys of Early Christian Tradition*. Edited by F. Stanley Jones. Atlanta: Society of Biblical Literature, 2002.

———. "From Vermont to Cyprus: A New Witness of the *Acts of Philip*." *Apocrypha* 20 (2009): 9–27.

———. "Women Priestesses in the Apocryphal Acts of Philip." Pages 246–58 in *New Testament and Christian Apocrypha*. Edited by Glenn E. Snyder. Grand Rapids, MI: Baker Academic, 2009.

———. "An Introduction to the *Acts of Philip*." Pages 1–30 in *The Acts of Philip: A New Translation*. Edited by François Bovon and Christopher R. Matthews. Waco: Baylor University Press, 2012.

Bovon, François, and Christopher R. Matthews, eds. and trans. *The Acts of Philip: A New Translation*. Waco, TX: Baylor University Press, 2012.

Bovon, François, Bertrand Bouvier, and Frédéric Amsler, eds. *Acta Philippi: Textus*. Corpus Christianorum, Series Apocryphorum 11. Turnhout: Brepols, 1999.

Boyarin, Daniel. *Border Lines: The Partition of Judaeo-Christianity*. Philadelphia: University of Pennsylvania Press, 2004.

———. "Reading Androcentricism against the Grain: Women, Sex, and Torah-Study." *Poetics Today* 12 (1991): 29–53.

Bozóky, Edina. *Le livre secret des Cathares: Interrogatio Johannis*. Paris: Beauchesne, 1980.

Braake, David. "A New Fragment of Athanasius's Thirty-Ninth *Festal Letter*: Heresy, Apocrypha, and the Canon." *Harvard Theological Review* 103, no. 1 (2010): 47–66.

Braconi, Matteo. "L'arcosolio di *Cerula* nelle catacombe di San Gennaro a Napoli: Prime intuizioni e recenti scoperte." *Campania Sacra: Rivista di Storia Sociale e Religiosa del Mezzogiorno* 46–47 (2015–2016): 129–146, and Figs. 1–21a–b.

Bradshaw Aitken, Ellen. "Remembering and Remembered Women in Greco-Roman Meals." Pages 109–22 in *Meals in the Early Christian World*. Edited by D. E. Smith and Hal Taussig. New York: Palgrave Macmillan, 2012.

Bradshaw, Paul F. *Ordination Rites of the Ancient Churches of East and West*. New York: Pueblo Publishing Company, 1990.

————. *The Search for the Origins of Christian Worship: Sources and Methods for the Study of Early Liturgy.* Oxford: Oxford University Press, 2002.

————. *Rites of Ordination: Their History and Theology.* Collegeville, MN: Liturgical, 2013.

Braun, Joseph. *Die liturgische Gewandung im Occident und Orient: nach Ursprung und Entwicklung, Verwendung und Symbolik.* Freiburg: Herder, 1907.

————. "Maniple." Pages 601–602 in *The Catholic Encyclopedia: An International Work of Reference on the Constitution, Doctrine, Discipline, and History of the Catholic Church.* Vol. 9. Edited by Charles G. Herbermann, Edward A. Pace, Condé Bénoist Pallen, Thomas J. Shahan, John J. Wynne, and Andrew Alphonsus MacErlean. New York: Encyclopedia, 1910.

Breatnach, Caoimhín. "An Irish Homily on the Life of the Virgin Mary." *Ériu* 51 (2000): 23–58.

Breck, Joseph. "Two Early Christian Ivories of the Ascension." *The Metropolitan Museum of Art Bulletin* 14, no. 11 (November 1919): 242–44.

Breckenridge, J. D. "'Et prima vidit': The Iconography of the Appearance of Christ to His Mother." *The Art Bulletin* 39 (1957): 9–32.

Bremmer, Jan N. "The Representation of Priests and Priestesses in the Pagan and Christian Greek Novel." Pages 136–61 in *Priests and Prophets Among Pagans, Jews and Christians.* Studies in the History and Anthropology of Religion 5. Edited by Beate Dignas, Robert Parker and Guy G. Stroumsa. Leuven: Peeters, 2013.

————. *Maidens, Magic and Martyrs in Early Christianity.* Tubingen: Mohr Siebert, 2017.

Brenk, Beat. *Die Frühchristlichen Mosaiken in S. Maria Maggiore zu Rom.* Wiesbaden: Franz Steiner Verlag, 1975.

————. *The Apse, the Image and the Icon: An Historical Perspective of the Apse as a Space for Images.* Wiesbaden: Reichert Verlag, 2010.

Bright, William. *The Orations of St. Athanasius against the Arians.* Eugene, OR: Wipf & Stock, 2005.

Brock, Ann Graham. "Setting the Record Straight—The Politics of Identification: Mary Magdalene and Mary the Mother in *Pistis Sophia.*" Pages 43–52 in *Which Mary?: The Marys of Early Christian Tradition.* Edited by F. Stanley Jones. SBLSymS 19. Atlanta: Society of Biblical Literature, 2002.

————. *Mary Magdalene, the First Apostle: The Struggle for Authority.* Harvard Theological Series 51. Cambridge, MA: Harvard University Press, 2003.

————. "The Identity of the Blessed Mary, Representative of Wisdom in *Pistis Sophia.*" Pages 122–50 in *Walk in the Ways of Wisdom: Essays in Honor of Elisabeth Schüssler Fiorenza.* Edited by Shelly Matthews, Cynthia Briggs Kittredge, and Melanie Johnson-Debaufre. Harrisburg, PA: Trinity Press International, 2003.

————. "Apostleship—The Claiming and Bestowing of Authority." Pages 31–44 in *Rivista di storia del cristianesimo: Modi della comunicazione e rapporti di potere nel cristianesimo antico*. Edited by Enrico Norelli. Brescia, Italy: Morcelliana, 2006.

Brock, Sebastian. "Mary at the Eucharist: An Oriental Perspective." *Sobornost* 1, no. 2 (1979): 50–59.

————. *Bride of Light: Hymns on Mary from the Syriac Churches*. Kottayam, India: St. Joseph's Press, 1994.

————. *Holy Spirit in the Syrian Baptismal Tradition*. The Syrian Churches 9. Enlarged 2nd edn. Pune, India: Anita Printers, 1998.

Broek, Roelof van den. "Das Bericht des koptischen Kyrillos von Jerusalem über dal Hebräerevangelium." Pages 142–56 in *Studies in Gnosticism and Alexandrian Christianity*. NHS 39. Leiden: Brill, 1996.

Brooks, E. W., trans. "John of Ephesus, Lives of the Eastern Saints." *Patrologia Orientalis* 17. Edited by R. Graffin and F. Nau. Paris, 1923.

Brooten, Bernadette J. *Women Leaders in the Ancient Synagogue: Inscriptional Evidence and Background Issues*. Brown Judaic Studies 36. Chico, CA: Scholars Press, 1982.

Brown, Peter. *The World of Late Antiquity: AD 150–750*. London: Norton, 1971.

————. *The Cult of the Saints: Its Rise and Function in Latin Christianity*. Haskell Lectures on History. Chicago: University of Chicago Press, 1981.

————. *Power and Persuasion in Late Antiquity: Towards a Christian Empire*. Madison: University of Wisconsin Press, 1992.

————. *Authority and the Sacred: Aspects of the Christianisation of the Roman World*. Cambridge: Cambridge University Press, 1997.

Brown, Rachel Fulton. *From Judgment to Passion: Devotion to Christ and the Virgin Mary, 800–1200*. New York: Columbia Press, 2002.

————. *Mary and the Art of Prayer: The Hours of the Virgin in Medieval Christian Life and Thought*. New York: Columia University Press, 2018.

Brubaker, Leslie, and Mary B. Cunningham. *The Cult of the Mother of God in Byzantium: Texts and Images*. Birmingham Byzantine and Ottoman Studies. Farnham Surrey: Ashgate, 2011.

Buddensieg, Tilmann. "Le coffret en ivoire de Pola: Saint-Pierre et le Latran." *Cahiers archéologiques* 10 (1959): 157–95.

Budge, E. A. Wallis. "The History of the Blessed Virgin Mary." Pages 1–168 in *The History of the Blessed Virgin Mary and the History of the Likeness of Christ which the Jews of Tiberias Made to Mock at*. Luzac's Semitic Text and Translation Series 5. Edited by E. A. Wallis Budge. London: Luzac, 1899.

————. *Miscellaneous Coptic Texts in the Dialect of Upper Egypt*. London: Oxford University Press, 1915.

————. "The History of the Holy and Pure Mary." Pages 168–201 in *Legends of Our Lady Mary, The Perpetual Virgin and Her Mother, Hanna Translated from the Ethiopic Manuscripts Collected by King Theodore at Makdalâ and Now in the British Museum*. Edited by E. A. Wallace Budge. London: Oxford University Press, 1933.

Burch, Vacher. "The Gospel According to the Hebrews: Some New Matter Chiefly from Coptic Sources." *Journal of Theological Studies* 21, no. 84 (July 1920): 310–15.

Burghardt, Walter J. *The Image of God in Man: According to Cyril of Alexandria*. Washington, DC: Catholic University Press, 1957.

Burris, Catharine. "The Reception of the *Acts of Thecla* in Syriac Christianity: Translation, Collection, and Reception." Dissertation. University of North Carolina at Chapel Hill, 2010.

Burrus, Virginia. "The Heretical Woman as a Symbol in Alexander, Athanasius, Epiphanius, and Jerome." *Harvard Theological Review* 84, no. 3 (July 1991): 229–48.

Buschhausen, Helmut. *Die spätrömischen Metallscrinia und frühchristlichen Reliquiare. 1. Teil: Katalog*. Weiner Byzantinische Studien 9. Vienna: Hermann Böhlaus Nachf., 1971.

Butts, Aaron Michael. "Manuscript Transmission as Reception History: The Case of Ephrem the Syrian (d. 373)." *Journal of Early Christian Studies* 25, no. 2 (2017): 281–306.

Buxton, Bridget A. "A New Reading of the Belvedere Altar." *American Journal of Archeology* 118, no. 1 (January 2015): 91–111.

Cabrol, Fernand, and Henri LeClerq. *Dictionnaire d'archéologie chrétienne et de liturgie*. Paris: Letouzey et Ane, 1907–1953.

Cameron, Averil. "The Early Cult of the Virgin." Pages 2–15 in *Mother of God: Representations of the Virgin in Byzantine Art*. Edited by Maria Vassilaki. Milan: Skira editore, 2000.

———. "Jews and Heretics—A Category Error?" Pages 345–60 in *The Ways that Never Parted: Jews and Christians in Late Antiquity and the Early Middle Ages*. Edited by Adam H. Becker and Annette Yoshiko Reed. Minneapolis: Fortress, 2007.

Cardile, P. Y. "Mary as Priest: Mary's Sacerdotal Position in the Visual Arts." *Arte Cristiana* 72 (1984): 199–208.

Cartlidge, David R., and J. Keith Elliott. *Art and the Christian Apocrypha*. New York: Routledge, 2001.

Cassuto, U. *The Goddess Anath: Canaanite Epics of the Patriarchal Age: Texts, Hebrew Translation, Commentary, and Introduction*. Translated by Israel Abrahams. Jerusalem: Magnes Press, The Hebrew University, 1971.

Castelli, Elizabeth A. "Romans." Pages 272–300 in *Searching the Scriptures, Volume Two: A Feminist Commentary*. Edited by Elisabeth Schüssler Fiorenza. New York: Crossroad, 1994.

Castelli, Elizabeth, and Hal Taussig. 1997. *Reimagining Christian Origins*. Valley Forge: Trinity Press International.

Cecchelli, Carlo. *La vita di Roma nel Medioevo, volume 1: Le arti minori e il costume*. Rome: Palandi, 1951–52.

———. *La vita di Roma nel medio evo*. Roma: F. lli Palombi, 1951–1952.

Cerrito, Alessandra. "Sull'oratorio di S. Felicita presso le terme di Traiano a Roma." Pages 155–84 in *Domum tuam dilexi; miscellanea in onore di Aldo Nestori*. Edited by Aldo Nestori. Città del Vaticano: Pontificio Istituto di archeologia cristiana, 1998.

Chadwick, Henry. "Rufinus and the Tura Papyrus of Origen's Commentary on Romans." *JBL*, New Series 10, no. 1 (April 1959), 10–42.

Chaine, Marius. *Apocrypha de Beata Maria Virgine*. Rome: Karolus de Luigi, 1909.

Charles, R. H. *The Apocrypha and Pseudepigrapha of the Old Testament*. Vol. 2. [Place of publication not identified]: Oxford/Clarendon, 1913.

Chrysostom. *On the Priesthood*. In *The Six Books of the Priesthood of St. John Chrysostom, Translated from the Greek*. Translated by F. W. Hohler. Cambridge: Talboys, 1837.

Ciavolino, Nicola. "Nuovo affreschi delle catacombe di S. Gennaro." *Campania Sacra* 20 (1989): 357–78.

———. "Scavi e scoperte di archeologia Cristiana in Campania dal 1983 al 1993." Pages 615–69 in *1983–1993: diece anni di archeolgia cristiana in Italia: atti del 7. Congresso nazionale di archeologia cristiana, Cassino, 20–24 settembre 1993*. Edited by Eugenio Russo. Cassino: Edizione dell'Università degli Studi di Cassino, 2003.

Clark, Elizabeth A. "Holy Women, Holy Words: Early Christian Women, Social History, and the 'Linguistic Turn'." *Journal of Early Christian Studies* 6, no. 3 (1998): 413–30.

———. "The Lady Vanishes: Dilemma of a Feminist Historian After the 'Linguistic Turn'." *Church History* 67, no. 1 (March 1998): 1–31.

Clauss, Manfred. *The Roman Cult of Mithras: The God and His Mysteries*. Translated by Richard Gordon. New York: Routledge, 2000.

Clédat, Jean. *Le monastère et la nécropole de Baouît*, Mèmoires publiés par les membres de l'Institut français d'archéologie orientale de Caire. Vol. 12. Cairo: L'Institut Français d'Archéologie Orientale, 1904.

Cohen, Deborah, and Peter Mandler. "*The History Manifesto*: A Critique." *The American Historical Review* 120, no. 2 (April 2015): 530–42.

Cohen, Shaye D. *The Beginnings of Jewishness: Boundaries, Varieties, Uncertainties*. Berkeley: University of California Press, 1999.

Cohn, Norman. *Europe's Inner Demons: The Demonization of Christians in Medieval Christendom*. London: Pimlico, 2005.

Connolly, R. Hugh. *Didascalia Apostolorum: The Syriac Version Translated and Accompanied by the Verona Latin Fragments*. Oxford: Clarendon, 1929.

Constas, Nicholas. *Proclus of Constantinople and the Cult of the Virgin in Late Antiquity: Homilies 1–5, Texts and Translations.* Supplements to Vigiliae Christianae 66. Boston: Brill, 2003.

Coon, Lynda L. *Sacred Fiction: Holy Women and Hagiography in Late Antiquity.* Philadelphia: University of Pennsylvania Press, 1997.

Cooper, Kate. "Contesting the Nativity: Wives, Virgins, and Pulcheria's *imitatio Mariae.*" *Scottish Journal of Religious Studies* 19 (1998): 31–43.

———. "Empress and *Theotokos*: Gender and Patronage in the Christological Controversy." Pages 39–51 in *The Church and Mary.* Edited by R. N. Swanson. Woodbridge, Suffolk: Boydell, 2004.

———. *Band of Angels: The Forgotten World of Early Christian Women.* New York: Overlook, 2013.

Congar, Yves. *I Believe in Holy Spirit.* Milestones in Catholic Theology. Translated by David Smith. New York: Crossroad, 2001.

Corley, Kathleen E. *Maranatha: Women's Funerary Rituals and Christian Origins.* Minneapolis: Fortress Press, 2010.

Cormack, Robin S. "The Mosaic Decoration of S. Demetrios, Thessaloniki: A Re-examination in the Light of the Drawings of W. S. George." *The Annual of the British School at Athens* 64 (1969): 17–52.

———. "The Mother of God in Apse Mosaics." Pages 91–105 in *Mother of God: Representations of the Virgin in Byzantine Art.* Edited by Maria Vassilaki. Milan: Skira editore, 2000.

———. "The Mother of God in the Mosaics of Hagia Sophia at Constantinople." Pages 107–23 in *Mother of God: Representations of the Virgin in Byzantine Art.* Edited by Maria Vassilaki. Milan: Skira editore, 2000.

Cothenet, Édouard. "Marie dans les Apocryphes." Pages 71–156 in *Maria: études sur la Sainte Vierge.* Edited by Hubert du Manoir de Jaye. Paris: Beauchesne, 1952.

———. "Traditions bibliques et apocalyptiques dans les récits anciens de la Dormition." Pages 155–75 in *Marie dans les récits apocryphes chrétiens.* Edited by Édouard Cothenet et al. Paris: Médiaspaul, 2004.

Coxe, A. Cleveland, trans. "The Book of John Concerning the Falling Asleep of Mary." Pages 587–91 in *Ante-Nicene Fathers.* Vol. 8. Edited by Alexander Roberts and James Donaldson. Reprint. Peabody, MA: Hendrickson, 2004.

Crone, Patricia. *The Qur-ānic Pagans and Related Matters.* Islamic History and Civilization 129. Leiden: Brill, 2016.

Crook, John. *The Architectural Setting of the Cult of Saints in the Early Christian West, c. 300–1200.* Oxford: Oxford University Press, 2000.

Cross, F. L. "Early Western Liturgical Manuscripts." *Journal of Theological Studies* 16 (1965): 61–67.

Crouzel, Henri. *Origen*. Translated by A. S. Worall. San Francisco: Harper & Row, 1989.

Cruze, C. F., trans. *Eusebius' Ecclesiastical History: Complete and Unabridged*. Peabody, MA: Hendrickson Publishers, 1998.

Cullmann, Oscar, trans. "The Protevangelium of James." Pages 414–39 in *New Testament Apocrypha*. Vol. 1. Edited by Wilhelm Schneemelcher. Translated by Robert McL. Wilson. Cambridge: James Clarke, 1991.

Cunningham, Mary B. "The Life of the Virgin Mary According to Middle Byzantine Preachers and Hagiographers: Changing Contexts and Perspectives." *Apocrypha* 27 (2016): 137–59.

Cutler, Anthony. "The Mother of God in Ivory." Pages 167–75 in *Mother of God: Representations of the Virgin in Byzantine Art*. Edited by Maria Vassilaki. Milan: Skira editore, 2000.

Dagron, Gilbert. *Vie et miracles de Sainte Thècle: Texte grec, traduction et commentaire*. Subsidia Hagiographica 62. Brussels: Société des Bollandistes, 1978.

———. *Emperor and Priest: The Imperial Office in Byzantium*. Translated by Jean Birrell. Cambridge: Cambridge University Press, 2003.

Daley, Brian E. *On the Dormition of Mary: Early Patristic Homilies*. Popular Patristics Series 18. Crestwood, NY: St. Vladimir's Seminary Press, 1998.

Dalton, Ormonde M. *Catalogue of the Ivory Carvings of the Christian Era with Examples of Mohammedan Art and Carvings in Bone*. London: Longmans and Co., 1909.

———. *Byzantine Art and Archaeology*. Oxford: Clarendon Press, 1911.

Dam, Raymond van, trans. *Glory of the Martyrs*. Liverpool: Liverpool University Press, 2004, 1–102.

Davis, J. *The History of Count Zosimus*. London: Green & Chaplin, 1814.

Davies, Stevan L. "Women, Tertullian and the Acts of Paul." *Semeia* 38 (1986): 139–43.

Davis, Stephen J. *The Cult of St Thecla: A Tradition of Women's Piety in Late Antiquity*. Oxford Early Christian Studies. Oxford: Oxford University Press, 2001.

———. "An Arabic *Acts of Paul and Thecla*: Text Translation, with Introduction and Critical Commentary." Pages 106–51 in *Thecla: Paul's Disciple and Saint in East and West*. Edited by Jeremy W. Barrier, Jan N. Bremmer, Tobias Nicklas, and Amand Puig i Tàrrech. Leuven: Peeters, 2017.

de Boer, Esther. *The Mary Magdalene Cover-Up: The Sources Behind the Myth*. London: T&T Clark, 2007.

Deckers, Johannes G., and Ümit Serdaroğlu. "Das Hypogäum beim Silivri-Kapi in Istanbul." *Jahrbuck für Antike und Christentum* 36 (1993): 140–63.

DeConick, April D. *Holy Misogyny: Why the Sex and Gender Conflicts in the Early Church Still Matter*. New York: Bloomsbury, 2013.

Delehaye, Hippolyte. *The Legends of the Saints: An Introduction on Hagiography.* New York: Longmans, Green, 1907.

———. *Sanctus: essai sur le culte des saints dans l'antiquité.* Subsidia hagiographica 17. Mons: G. Delporte, 1954.

Deliyannis, Deborah Mauskopf. *Ravenna in Late Antiquity.* Cambridge: Cambridge University Press, 2010.

Dennison, Walter. *A Gold Treasure of the Late Roman Period.* New York: Macmillan, 1918.

Dennison, Walter, and Charles R. Morey. *Studies in East Christian and Roman Art.* University of Michigan Studies, Humanistic Series 12. New York: Macmillan, 1918.

Denzey, Nicola. *The Bone Gatherers: The Lost Worlds of Early Christian Women.* Boston: Beacon, 2007.

———. "A New Gnosticism: Why Simon Gathercole and Mark Goodacre on the Gospel of Thomas Change the Field." *Journal of the Study of the New Testament* 36, no. 3 (2014): 240–50.

Dever, William G. *Did God Have a Wife?: Archeology and Folk Religion in Ancient Israel.* Grand Rapids, MI: Eerdmans, 2005.

Donahue, Charles. *The Testament of Mary: The Gaelic Version of the Dormitio Mariae Together with an Irish Latin Version.* New York: Fordham University Press, 1942.

Drake, Susanna. *Slandering the Jew: Sexuality and Difference in Early Christian Texts.* Philadelphia: University of Pennsylvania Press, 2013.

Driver, Godfrey Rolles, and Leonard Hodgson, trans. *Nestorius: The Bazaar of Heracleides.* Oxford: Clarenton, 1925.

Ducati, Pericle. *L'arte in Roma dalle origini al sec. VIII.* Bologna: Cappelli, 1938.

Durand, Jannic, Ioanna Rapti, and Dorota Giovannoni, eds. *Armenia Sacra: Mémoire chrétienne des Arméniens (IVᵉ–XVIIIᵉ siècle).* Paris: Musée du Louvre Éditions, 2007.

Ebertshäuser, Caroline H., Herbert Haag, Joe H. Kirchberger, and Dorothee Sölle. *Mary: Art, Culture, and Religion Through the Ages.* Translated by Peter Heinegg. New York: Crossroad, 1998.

Ehrman, Bart D. *Forgery and Counterforgery: The Use of Literary Deceit in Early Christian Polemics.* New York: Oxford University Press, 2013.

Eisen, Ute E. *Women Officeholders in Early Christianity: Epigraphical and Literary Studies.* Translated by Linda M. Maloney. Collegeville, MN: Liturgical, 2000.

Elliott, J. K. *The Apocryphal New Testament: A Collection of Apocryphal Christian Literature in an English Translation Based on M. R. James.* Edited by J. K. Elliott. Oxford: Clarendon Press, 1993.

Elsner, Jaś. *Art and the Roman Viewer: The Transformation of Art from the Pagan World to Christianity*. Cambridge: Cambridge University Press, 1995.

———. "Closure and Penetration: Reflections on the Pola Casket." Pages 183–227 in *From Site to Sight: The Transformation of Place in Art and Literature*. Edited by V. P. Tschudi and T. K. Seim. Rome: Scienze e Lettere, 2013.

Epiphanius. *Panarion*. In the *Panarion of Epiphanius of Salamis*, 2 vols. Translated by Frank Williams. Leiden: Brill, 1997, 1994.

Epp, Eldon J. *Junia: The First Woman Apostle*. Minneapolis: Fortress, 2005.

Epp, Eldon J., and Gordon D. Fee. *Studies in the Theory and Method of New Testament Textual Criticism*. Studies and Documents 45. Grand Rapids, MI: Eerdmans, 1993.

Ernst, Allie M. *Martha from the Margins: The Authority of Martha in the Early Christian Tradition*. Leiden: Brill, 2009.

Esbroeck, Michel-Jean van. "Les textes littéraires sur l'Assomption avant le Xe siècle." Pages 265–85 in *Les actes apocryphes des apôtres*. Publications de la faculté de théologie de l'Université de Genève 4. Edited by François Bovon. Geneva: Labor et Fides, 1981.

———, trans. *Maxime le Confesseur: Vie de la Vierge*. Scriptores Iberici 21 [Geor.] and 22 [Fr.]. CSCO 478 and 479. Louvain: Peeters, 1986.

Evangelatou, Maria. "The Symbolism of the Censer in Byzantine Representations of the Dormition of the Virgin." Pages 117–31 in *Images of the Mother of God: Perceptions of the Theotokos in Byzantium*. Edited by Maria Vassilaki. Aldershot: Ashgate, 2005.

Evans, Helen C., and Brandie Ratliff, ed. *Byzantium and Islam: Age of Transition*. New York: The Metropolitan Museum of Art, 2012.

Fairclough, Norman. *Language and Power*. 2nd edn. Harlow, Essex: Pearson Education Ltd., 2001.

———. *Discourse and Social Change*. Cambridge, UK: Polity, 2010.

Faivre, Cécile, and Alexandre. "La place des femmes dans le ritual eucharistique des marcosiens: déviance ou archaïsme?" *Revue des sciences religieuses* 71 (1997): 310–28.

Fasola, Umberto Maria. "Le tombe privilegiate dei vescovi dei duchy di Napoli nelle catacombe di S. Gennaro." Pages 205–12 in *L'inhumation privilégiée du IVe au VIIIe siècle en occident*. Actes du colloque tenu à Créteil les 16–18 mars 1984. Edited by Yvette Duval and J.-C. Picard. Paris: De Boccard, 1986.

Feltoe, Charles Lett, trans. *The Letters and Sermons of Leo the Great*. Nicene and Post-Nicene Fathers 2. Vol. 12. New York: Christian Literature, 1895.

Ferguson, Everett. *Baptism in the Early Church: History, Theology, and Liturgy in the First Five Centuries*. Grand Rapids, MI: William B. Eerdmans, 2009.

Fine, Steven, ed. *Sacred Realm: The Emergence of the Synagogue in the Ancient World*. New York: Oxford University Press, 1996.

———. *Art and Judaism in the Greco-Roman World: Toward a New Jewish Archeology*. Cambridge: Cambridge University Press, 2005.

Finger, Reta Halteman. *Of Widows and Meals: Communal Meals in the Book of Acts*. Grand Rapids, MI: Eerdmans, 2007.

Finney, Paul Corbey. *The Invisible God: The Earliest Christians on Art*. New York: Oxford University Press, 1994.

Fixot, Michel. *La Crypte de Saint-Maximin La-Sainte-Baume: Basilique Sainte-Marie Madeleine*. Aix-en-Provence: Edisud, 2001.

Flowers, Harriet I. *The Art of Forgetting: Disgrace and Oblivion in Roman Political Culture*. Chapel Hill: The University of North Carolina Press, 2006.

Foletti, Ivan. "*Cicut in caelo et in terra*. Osservazioni sulla *cathedra vacua* della basilica sistina di Santa Maria Maggiore a Roma," *Iconographica* 10–11 (2011–2012): 33–46.

———. "Des femmes à l'autel? Jamais! Les diaconesses (veuves et prêtresses) et l'iconographie de la Théotokos." Pages 51–92 in *Féminité et masculinité altérées: transgression et inversion des genres au Moyen Age*. Micrologus' Library 77. Edited by Eva Pibiri and Fanny Abbott. Florence: SISMEL Edizioni del Galluzzo, 2017.

Förster, Hans. "'Sich des Gebrauchs der Frauen enthalten': Eine Anfrage an die grammatikalische Struktur einer Interzession für Verstorbene im Grossen Euchologion aus dem Weissen Kloster." *Zeitschrift für Antikes Christentum/Journal of Ancient Christianity* 9 (2006): 584–91.

———. *Transitus Mariae: Beiträge zur koptischen Überlieferung mit einer Edition von P. Vindob. K 7589, Cambridge Add 1876 8 und Paris BN Copte 12917 ff. 28 und 29*. Berlin: Walter de Gruyter, 2006.

Foster, Judith Mary. "Giving Birth to God: The Virgin Empress Pulcheria and the Imitation of Mary in Early Christian Greek and Syriac Traditions." Dissertation. Concordia University, Montreal, 2008.

Francis, James A. "Biblical not Scriptural: Perspectives on Early Christian Art from Contemporary Classical Scholarship." *Sacra Pagina* 44 (2010): 3–6.

Frazer, Margaret E. "Holy Sites Representations." Pages 564–91 in *Age of Spirituality: Late Antique and Early Christian Art, Third to Seventh Century*. Edited by Kurt Weitzmann. New York: Metropolitan Museum of Art in association with Princeton University Press, 1979.

Frend, W. H. C. "The Gnostic Origins of the Assumption Legend." *Modern Churchman* 43 (1953): 23–28.

Foucault, Michel. *The History of Sexuality: Volume 1: An Introduction*. Translated by Robert Hurley. New York: Vintage, 1990.

Fulton, Rachel. *From Judgment to Passion: Devotion to Christ and the Virgin Mary, 800–1200*. New York: Columbia University Press, 2002.

Gaborit-Chopin, Danielle, ed. *Ivoires médiévaux: V–XV siècle*. Paris: Éditions de la Réunion des musées nationaux, 2003.

Galante, Gennaro Aspreno. "I nuovi scavi nelle catacombe di S. Gennaro in Napoli." *Atti della Reale Accademia di archologia, lettere e belle arti di Napoli* 25 (1908): 115–69.

Galinsky, Karl. *Augustan Culture: An Interpretive Introduction*. Princeton: Princeton University Press, 1996.

Gambero, Luigi. "Biographies of Mary in Byzantine Literature." *Marian Studies* 60 (2009): 31–50.

Garrucci, Raffaele. *Vetri ornati di figure in oro trovati nei cimiteri dei cristiani primitivi di Roma*. Rome: Tipografia Salviucci, 1858.

———. *Storia della arte cristiana nei primi otto secoli della chiesa*. 5 vols. Prato: Gaetano Guasti, 1872–1881.

Gathercole, Simon. *The Composition of the Gospel of Thomas: Original Language and Influences*. Cambridge: Cambridge University Press, 2012.

Geertman, Herman. "La genesi del Liber Pontificalis romano. Un processo di organizzazione della memoria." Pages 37–107 in *Liber, Gesta, histoire. Écrire l'histoire des evêques et des papes, de l'antiquité au XXIe siècle*. Edited by François Bougard and Michel Sots. Turnhout: Brepols, 2009.

Gem, Richard, "From Constantine to Constans: The Chronology of the Construction of Saint Peter's Basilica." Pages 35–64 in *Old Saint Peter's, Rome*. Edited by Rosamond McKitterick, John Osborne, Carol M. Richardson, and Joanna Story. Cambridge: Cambridge University Press, 2013.

Ghetti, Bruno M. Apollonj, Antonio Ferrua, Enrico Josi, and Engelbert Kirschbaum. *Esplorazioni sotto la confessione di San Pietro in Vaticano, eseguite negli anni 1940–1949*. 2 vols. Vatican City: Città del Vaticano, 1951.

Gianelli, C. "Témoignages patristiques grecs en faveur d'une apparition du Christ ressuscité à la vierge." *Revista eclesiástica brasileira* 11 (1953): 106–19.

Gibson, Elsie. "Mary and the Protestant Mind." *Review for Religious* 24 (1965): 396–98.

Gillett, Andrew. "Rome, Ravenna and the Last Western Emperors." *Papers of the British School at Rome* 69 (2001): 131–67.

Gnirs, Anton. "La basilica ed il reliquiario d'avorio di Samagher presso Pola." *Atti e memorie della società istriana di archeologia e storia patria* 24 (1908): 5–48.

Goetz, K. G. "Zwei Beiträge zur synoptischen Quellenforschung." *ZNW* 20 (1921): 165–70.

Goldschmidt, A. "Mittelstüke fünfteiliger Elfenbeintafeln des V–VI Jahrhunderts." *Jahrbuch fur Kunstwissenschaft* (1923): 30–33.

González, José María Salvador. "La iconografía de la Asunción de la Virgen María en la pintura del quattrocento italiano a la luz de sus fuentes patrísticas y teológicas." Dissertation. Institut D'Estudis Medievals, Universitat Autònoma de Barcelona, 2011.

González Casado, Pilar. "Las relaciones lingüísticas entre el siríaco y el árabe en textos religiosos árabes cristianos." Dissertation. Universidad Complutense de Madrid, 2013.

Goodacre, Mark. *Thomas and the Gospels: The Case for Thomas's Familiarity with the Synoptics.* Grand Rapids, MI: Eerdmans, 2012.

Grabar, André. *Martyrium, recherches sur le culte des reliques et l'art chrétien antique.* 2 vols. Paris: Collège de France, 1946.

———. *Les ampoules de Terre Sainte (Monza – Bobbio).* Paris: C. Klincksieck, 1958.

———. *Christian Iconography: A Study of its Origins.* Bollingen Series 35: The A. W. Mellon Lectures in the Fine Arts 10. Princeton: Princeton University Press, 1980.

Grant, Robert M., and Glen W. Menzies. *Joseph's Bible Notes (Hypomnestikon).* Atlanta: Society of Biblical Literature, 1996.

Gregory, Andrew. *The Gospel According to the Hebrews and the Gospel According to the Ebionites.* Edited by Christopher Tuckett and Andrew Gregory. Oxford Early Christian Texts. Oxford: Oxford University Press, 2017.

Gregory of Tours, and Lewis Thorpe. *The History of the Franks.* London: Penguin, 1974.

Gregory of Tours, and Raymond van Dam. *Glory of the Martyrs.* Liverpool: Liverpool University Press, 2004.

Gregory, and John R. C. Martyn. *The Letters of Gregory the Great.* Toronto: Pontifical Institute of Mediaeval Studies, 2004.

Grisar, Hartmann. *Die römische Kapelle Sancta Santorum und ihr Schatz: Meine Entdeckungen und Studien in der Palastkapelle der mittelalterlichen Päpste.* Rome: Laterano, 1908.

Guarducci, Margherita. *The Tomb of St. Peter: The New Discoveries in the Sacred Grottoes of the Vatican.* Translated by Joseph McLellan. New York: Hawthorne, 1960.

———. *La capsella eburnea di Samagher: un cimelio di arte paleocristiana nella storia del tardo impero.* Trieste: Società istriana di archeologia, 1978.

Guerra Gómez, M. "La Virgen María y su 'sacerdocio' auxiliar del unico sacerdote, Jesucristo: algunas cosideraciones filosóficoteológicas en torno a un texto patrístico." *Burgense* 37 (1996): 125–55.

Gutmann, Joseph. *Hebrew Manuscript Painting.* New York: Braziller, 1978.

Guyon, Jean, and Marc Heijmans. *D'un monde à l'autre: Naissance d'une Chrétienté en Provence, IVᵉ–VIᵉ siècle. Catalogue de l'exposition 15 septembre 2001–6 janvier 2002, Musée de l'Arles antique.* Arles: Musée de l'Arles antique, 2002.

Hadley, Judith M. *The Cult of Asherah in Ancient Israel and Judah: Evidence for a Hebrew Goddess*. University of Cambridge Oriental Publications 57. Cambridge: University of Cambridge Press, 2000.

Haeperen, François van. "Les prêtresses de *Mater Magna* dans le monde romain occidental." Pages 299–322 in *Sacerdos: Figure del sacro nella società romana*. Edited by Gianpaolo Urso. Pisa: ETS, 2014.

Haibach-Reinisch, Monika. *Ein neuer "Transitus Mariae" des Pseudo-Melito*. Rome: Pontificia Academia Mariana Internationalis, 1962.

Haines-Eitzen, Kim. *The Gendered Palimpsest: Women, Writing, and Representation in Early Christianity*. Oxford: Oxford University Press, 2012.

Hamarneh, Sami K. "Cosmas and Damian in the Near East: Earliest Extant Monument." *Pharmacy in History* 27, no. 2 (1985): 78–83.

Hammer, Jill, and Taya Shere. *The Hebrew Priestess: Ancient and New Visions of Jewish Women's Spiritual Leadership*. Teaneck, NJ: Ben Yehuda Press, 2015.

Harnack, Adolf von, Lyle D. Bierma, and John E. Steely. *Marcion: The Gospel of the Alien God*. Eugene, OR: Wipf & Stock, 1990.

Harrison, Verna E. F. "Male and Female in Cappadocian Theology." *Journal of Theological Studies* 41, no. 2 (1990): 441–71.

———. "Women and the Image of God according to St. John Chrysostom." Pages 236–71 in *In Dominico Eloquio/In Lordly Eloquence: Essays in Patristic Exegesis in Honor of Robert L. Wilken*. Edited by Paul Blowers. Grand Rapids: Eerdmans, 2001.

———. "Women, Human Identity, and the Image of God: Antiochene Interpretations." *Journal of Early Christian Studies* 9, no. 2 (2001): 205–49.

Harvey, Susan Ashbrook. "Feminine Imagery for the Divine: The Holy Spirit, the Odes of Solomon, and Early Syriac Tradition." *St. Vladimir's Theological Quarterly* 37, no. 2 and no. 3 (1993): 111–39.

———. "Theodora the 'Believing Queen': A Study in Syriac Historiographical Tradition." *Hugoye: Journal of Syriac Studies* 4, no. 2 (2001): 209–34.

———. *Scenting Salvation: Ancient Christianity and the Olfactory Imagination*. Berkeley: University of California Press, 2006.

Haskins, Susan. *Mary Magdalen: Myth and Metaphor*. New York: Riverhead, 1993.

Hassett, Maurice M. "Altar." Pages 362–67 in *The Catholic Encyclopedia: An International Work of Reference on the Constitution, Doctrine, Discipline, and History of the Catholic Church*. Vol. 1. Edited by Charles G. Herbermann, Edward A. Pace, Condé Bénoist Pallen, Thomas J. Shahan, John J. Wynne, and Andrew Alphonsus MacErlean. New York: Encyclopedia, 1907.

Hedrick, Charles W., Jr. *History and Silence: Purge and Rehabilitation of Memory in Late Antiquity*. Austin: University of Texas Press, 2000.

Herrin, Judith. *Unrivaled Influence: Women and Empire in Byzantium*. Princeton: Princeton University Press, 2013.

Herrmann, John, and Annewies van den Hoek. "'Two Men in White': Observations on an Early Christian Lamp from North Africa with the Ascension of Christ." Pages 293–318 in *Early Christian Voices: In Texts, Traditions, and Symbols, Essays in Honor of François Bovon*. Edited by David H. Warren, Ann Graham Brock, and David W. Pao. Biblical Interpretation Series 66. Boston: Brill, 2003.

Hilhorst, A. "Tertullian on the Acts of Paul." Pages 150–63 in *The Apocryphal Acts of Paul*. Edited by Jan N. Bremmer. Studies on the Apocryphal Acts of the Apostles 2. Kampen: Kok Pharos, 1996.

Himmelmann, Nikolaus. *Über Hirten-Genre in der antiken Kunst*. Opladen: Westdeutscher, 1980.

Hock, Ronald F. *The Infancy Gospels of James and Thomas*. Scholars Bible 2. Santa Rosa, CA: Polebridge, 1995.

———. "Response: Luke and the Protevangelium of James." Pages 253–78 in *Jesus and Mary Reimagined in Early Christian Literature*. Edited by Vernon K. Robbins and Jonathan M. Potter. Writings from the Greco-Roman World Supplement Series. Atlanta: SBL Press, 2015.

Hoffmann, R. Joseph, trans. *Celsus on the True Doctrine: A Discourse Against the Christians*. New York: Oxford University Press, 1987.

———. *Marcion: On the Restitution of Christianity*. Eugene, OR: Wipf & Stock Publishers, 2016.

Holl, Karl, ed. *Epiphanius*. Vol. 2. Leipzig: J. C. Henrichs, 1915.

Holland, John. *Cruciana: Illustrations of the Most Striking Aspects Under Which the Cross of Christ, and Symbols Derived from It, Have Been Contemplated by Piety, Superstition, Imagination, and Taste*. Liverpool: D. Marples, 1835.

Hollman, Meredith Elliott. "Temple Virgin and Virgin Temple: Mary's Body as Sacred Space in the Protevangelium of James." Pages 103–28 in *Jesus and Mary Reimagined in Early Christian Literature*. Edited by Vernon K. Robbins and Jonathan M. Potter. Atlanta: SBL Press, 2015.

Holum, Kenneth G. *Theodosian Empresses: Women and Imperial Dominion in Late Antiquity*. Berkeley: University of California Press, 1982.

Horn, Cornelia B. "St. Nino and the Christianization of Pagan Georgia." *Medieval Encounters; Jewish, Christian, and Muslim Culture in Confluence and Dialogue* 4, no. 3 (1998): 242–64.

———. "The Power of Leadership Through Mediation, or How Mary Exercises Overlapping Authority." In *Maria, Marianne, Miriam: Rediscovering the Marys*. Edited by Mary Ann Beavis and Ally Kateusz. New York: T&T Clark, 2019, forthcoming.

Horner, George William. *The Statutes of the Apostle; Or, Canones Ecclesiastici*. London: Williams and Norgate, 1904.

Horner, Tim. "Jewish Aspects of the *Protevangelium of James*." *Journal of Early Christian Studies* 12, no. 3 (2004): 313–35.

Hubai, Peter. *Koptische apokryphen aus Nubien: der Kasr el-Wizz kodex.* Göttingen: Walter de Gruyter, 2009.

Humble, Susan Elizabeth. *A Divine Round Trip the Literary and Christological Function of the Descent/Ascent Leitmotiv in the Gospel of John.* Leuven: Peeters, 2016.

Hunter, David G. "The Paradise of Patriarchy: Ambrosiaster on Woman as (Not) God's Image." *Journal of Theological Studies,* NS, 43 (1992): 447–69.

Hurtado, Larry W. "The *Pericope Adulterae*: Where from Here?" Pages 147–58 in *The Pericope of the Adulteress in Contemporary Research.* Edited by David Alan Black and Jacob N. Cerone. Library of New Testament Studies 551. London: Bloomsbury T&T Clark, 2016.

Huskinson, Janet. "Gender and Identity in Scenes of Intellectual Life on Late Roman Sarcophagi." Pages 190–213 in *Constructing Identities in Late Antiquity.* Edited by Richard Miles. London: Routledge, 1999.

Hylen, Susan E. "'Domestication' of Saint Thecla: Characterization of Thecla in the *Life and Miracles of Saint Thecla*." *Journal of Feminist Studies in Religion* 30, no. 2 (2014): 5–21.

———. *A Modest Apostle: Thecla and the History of Women in the Early Church.* Oxford: Oxford University Press, 2015.

Ilan, Tal. "Notes and Observations on a Newly Published Divorce Bill from the Judaean Desert." *Harvard Theological Review* 89, no. 2 (1968): 195–202.

———. *Integrating Women into Second Temple History.* Tübingen: Mohr Siebeck, 1999.

Innemée, Karel. "Deir al-Surian, a Treasure Chest in the Desert." *Past Horizons: Adventures in Archeology.* http://www.pasthorizonspr.com/index.php/archives/06/2013/deir-al-surian-a-treasure-chest-in-the-desert (accessed December 16, 2013).

———. "Dayr al-Suryan: New Discoveries." In *Claremont Coptic Encyclopedia.* Online. Claremont: Claremont Graduate University, 2016, 1–50. http://ccdl.libraries.claremont.edu/cdm/singleitem/collection/cce/id/2137/rec/1 (accessed April 20, 2018).

Innemée, Karel, and Youhanna Nessim Youssef. "Virgins with Censers: A 10th Century Painting of the Dormition in Deir Al-Surian." *Bulletin de la Société d'archéologie copte* 46 (2007): 69–85.

Irenaeus. *Against Heresies.* In *The Apostolic Fathers with Justin Martyr and Irenaeus.* Translated by A. Cleveland Coxe. Ante-Nicene Fathers 1. Buffalo, NY: Christian Literature, 1885.

Irwin, Dorothy. "The Ministry of Women in the Early Church." *Duke Divinity School Review* 45, no. 2 (1980): 76–86.

James, Montague Rhodes, trans. *The Apocryphal New Testament: Being the Apocryphal Gospels, Acts, Epistles, and Apocalypses with Other Narratives and Fragments.* Oxford: Clarendon, 1945.

————. "The Martyrdom of Matthew." Pages 460–62 in *The Apocryphal New Testament: Being the Apocryphal Gospels, Acts, Epistles, and Apocalypses with Other Narratives and Fragments.* Oxford: Clarendon, 1945.

Janos, Stephen, trans. "The Holy Great-Martyress Irene." http://www.holytrinityorthodox.com/calendar/los/May/05-01.htm (accessed January 26, 2014).

Jansen, Katherine Ludwig. *The Making of the Magdalen: Preaching and Popular Devotion in the Later Middle Ages.* Princeton: Princeton University Press, 2000.

Jensen, Anne. *God's Self-Confident Daughters: Early Christianity and the Liberation of Women.* Translated by O. C. Dean, Jr. Louisville: Westminster, 1996.

Jensen, Robin M. "Dining with the Dead." Pages 107–43 in *Commemorating the Dead: Texts and Artifacts in Context, Studies of Roman, Jewish, and Christian Burials.* Edited by Laurie Brink and Deborah Green. Berlin: Walter de Gruyter, 2008.

————. "Recovering Ancient Ecclesiology: The Place of the Altar and the Orientation of Prayer in the Early Latin Church." *Worship* 89 (March 2015): 99–124.

————. "Saints' Relics and the Consecration of Church Buildings in Rome." Pages 153–69 in *Studia Patristica. Vol. LXXI—Including Papers Presented at the Conferences on "Early Roman Liturgy to 600" (14.11.2009 and 27.02.2010) at Blackfriars Hall, Oxford, UK.* Edited by Juliette Day and Markus Vinzent. Leuven: Peeters, 2014.

————. *Understanding Early Christian Art.* New York: Routledge, 2000.

Jerome. *Contra Vigilantium.* In *The Principle Works of St. Jerome.* Translated by William Henry Freemantle. Nicene and Post-Nicene Fathers 2. Vol. 6. New York: Christian Literature, 1893.

————. *Letter 107.* In *Select Letters of St. Jerome.* Translated by F. A. Wright. Reprint. Cambridge: Harvard University Press, 1954.

John of Ephesus. *Lives of Eastern Saints.* In *Patrologia Orientalis* 17. Translated by E. W. Brooks. Edited by René Graffin and François Nau. Paris, 1923.

John of Thessalonica. *On the Dormition.* In *On the Dormition of Mary: Early Patristic Homilies.* Popular Patristics Series 18. Edited by Brian E. Daley. Crestwood, NY: St. Vladimir's Seminary Press, 1998.

Johnson, Maxwell, E. *The Rites of Christian Initiation: Their Evolution and Interpretation.* Collegeville, MN: Liturgical Press, 2007.

————. "*Sub Tuum Praesidium*: The *Theotokos* in Christian Life and Worship Before Ephesus." *Pro Ecclesia* 17, no. 1 (2008): 52–75.

Johnson, Scott Fitzgerald. *The Life and Miracles of Thekla: A Literary Study.* Hellenic Studies 13. Cambridge: Harvard University Press, 2006.

Julian the Apostate. *Against the Galileans.* In *The Works of the Emperor Julian.* Vol. 3. Translated by Wilmer Cave Wright. Cambridge, MA: Harvard University Press, 2014.

Kaestli, Jean-Daniel, trans. *L'évangile de Barthélomy d'après deus écrits apocryphes.* Belgium: Brepols, 1993.

Kantorowicz, Ernst H. "The 'King's Advent' and the Enigmatic Panels in the Doors of Santa Sabina." *The Art Bulletin* 26, no. 4 (December 1944): 207–31.

Karras, Valerie A. "Female Deacons in the Byzantine Church." *Church History* 73, no. 2 (June 2004): 272–316.

———. "The Liturgical Functions of Consecrated Women in the Byzantine Church." *Theological Studies* 66 (2005): 96–116.

———. "Priestesses or Priest's Wives: *Presbytera* in Early Christianity." *St Vladimir's Theological Quarterly* 51, nos. 2–3 (2007): 321–45.

Kateusz, Ally. "Collyridian Déjà Vu: The Trajectory of Redaction of the Markers of Mary's Liturgical Leadership." *Journal of Feminist Studies in Religion* 29, no. 2 (Fall 2013): 75–92.

———. *Finding Holy Spirit Mother.* Holt, MO: Divine Balance Press, 2014.

———. "Ascension of Christ or Ascension of Mary?: Reconsidering a Popular Early Iconography." *Journal of Early Christian Studies* 23, no. 2 (Summer 2015): 273–303.

———. "'She Sacrificed Herself as the Priest': Early Christian Female and Male Co-Priests." *Journal of Feminist Studies in Religion* 33, no. 1 (Spring 2017): 45–67.

———. "Dormition Urtext? Earliest Dormtion Wall Painting Combines the Great Angel and Women with Censers." In *Maria, Mariamne, Miriam: Rediscovering the Maries.* Edited by Mary Ann Beavis and Ally Kateusz. New York: Bloomsbury, 2019, forthcoming.

———. "Two Women Leaders: 'Mary and the Other Mary Magdalene'." In *Maria, Mariamne, Miriam: Rediscovering the Marys.* Edited by Mary Ann Beavis and Ally Kateusz. New York: Bloomsbury, 2019, forthcoming.

Kearns, Cleo McNelly. *The Virgin Mary, Monotheism, and Sacrifice.* Cambridge: Cambridge University Press, 2008.

Kelly, J. N. D. *Early Christian Creeds.* 3rd edn. New York: Longman's, 1986.

Kessler Herbert L. "The Christian Realm: Narrative Representations." Pages 449–512 in *Age of Spirituality: Late Antique and Early Christian Art, Third to Seventh Century, Catalogue of the Exhibition at The Metropolitan Museum of Art, November 19, 1977, Through February 12, 1978.* Edited by Kurt Weitzmann. New York: Metropolitan Museum of Art in association with Princeton University Press, 1979.

———. "Bright Gardens of Paradise." Pages 111–39 in *Picturing the Bible: The Earliest Christian Art.* Edited by Jeffrey Spier. New Haven: Yale University Press in association with the Kimbell Art Museum, 2007.

Kienzle, Beverly Mayne, and Pamela J. Walker, eds. *Women Preachers and Prophets Through Two Millennia of Christianity*. Berkeley: University of California Press, 1998.

Kiilerich, Bente, and Hjalmar Torp. *The Rotunda in Thessaloniki and Its Mosaics*. Athens: Kapon Editions, 2017.

King, Karen L. trans. *The Gospel of Mary of Magdala: Jesus and the First Woman Apostle*. Santa Rosa, CA: Polebridge, 2003.

Kirschbaum, Engelbert. *Die Gräber der Apostelfürsten*. Frankfurt: Heinrich Scheffler, 1957.

———. *The Tombs of St. Peter and St. Paul*. Translated by John Murray. New York: St. Martin's, 1959.

Klausner, Theodor. *Die römische Petrustradition im Lichte der neuen Ausgrabungen unter der Peterskirche*. Arbeitsgemeinschaft für Forschung des Landes Nordrhein-Westfalen 24. Cologne: Westdeutscher, 1956.

———. "Pallium." Columns 7–9 in *Lexikon für Theologie und Kirche*. Vol. 8. Edited by Michael Buchberger, Michael, Josef Höfer, and Karl Rahner. Freiburg: Herder, 1963.

Kleinbauer, W. Eugene. "The Orants in the Mosaic Decoration of the Rotunda at Thessaloniki: Martyr Saints or Donors?" *Cahiers archéologiques* 30 (1982): 25–45.

Klijn, Albertus Frederik Johannes. *Jewish-Christian Gospel Tradition*. Leiden: E. J. Brill, 1992.

Klinghardt, Matthias. *Gemeinschaftsmahl und Mahlgemeinschaft: Soziologie und Liturgie frühchristlicher Mahlfeiern*. Tübingen: Francke, 1996.

Knust, Jennifer, and Tommy Wasserman. *To Cast the First Stone: The Transmission of a Gospel Story*. Princeton: Princeton University Press, 2018.

Knust, Jennifer Wright. *Abandoned to Lust: Sexual Slander and Ancient Christianity*. New York: Columbia University Press, 2006.

Koch, Guntram. *Frühchristliche Sarkophage*. Munich: Beck, 2000.

Koester, Helmut. *History and Literature of Early Christianity. Volume Two: Introduction to the New Testament*. 2nd edn. New York: Walter de Gruyter, 2000.

Kondakov, Nikolaj Petrovič. *Ikonografija Bogomateri*. Vols. 1 and 2. St. Petersburg: Akademija nauk, 1914–1915.

———. *Iconografia della Madre di Dio*. Vol. 1. Edited and Translated by Ivan Foletti. Rome: Viella Libreria Editrice, 2014.

Kraemer, Ross Shepard. "Jewish Women and Women's Judaism(s) at the Beginning of Christianity." Pages 50–79 in *Women and Christian Origins*. Edited by Ross Shepard Kraemer and Mary Rose D'Angelo. New York: Oxford University Press, 1999.

———. *Unreliable Witnesses: Religion, Gender, and History in the Greco-Roman Mediterranean*. Oxford: Oxford University Press, 2011.

Krautheimer, Richard. "Recent Publications on S. Maria Maggiore in Rome." *American Journal of Archaeology* 46, no. 3 (1942): 373–79.

Kristeva, Julia. "Stabat Mater." Pages 160–86 in *The Kristeva Reader*. Edited by Toril Moi. New York: Columbia University Press, 1986.

Kroeger, Catharine. "Bitalia, The Ancient Woman Priest." *Priscilla Papers* 7, no. 1 (Winter 1993): 11–12.

Krusch, Bruno, ed. *Gregorii episcopi Turonensis: Miracula et opera minora*. Scriptores rerum Merovingicarum. Vol. 1, part 2. Hannover: Impensis Bibliopolii Hahniani, 1885.

Ladouceur, Paul. "Old Testament Prefigurations of the Mother of God." *St. Vladimir's Theological Quarterly* 50, nos. 1–2 (2006): 5–57.

La Follette, Laetitia. "The Costume of the Roman Bride." Pages 54–64 in *The World of Roman Costume*. Edited by Judith Lynn Sebesta and Larissa Bonfante. Madison, WI: University of Wisconsin Press, 2001.

Lafontaine, Jacqueline. *Peintures Médiévales dans le temple dit la Fortune Virile a Rome*. Brussels: Imprimerie Universa Wetteren, 1959.

———. *Iconographie de l'Enfance de la Vierge dans l'Empire byzantine et en Occident*. Vol. 1. Brussels: Académie Royale de Belgique, 1992.

Larsen, Matthew D. C. *Gospels before the Book*. Oxford: Oxford University Press, 2018.

Lauer, Philippe. *Le trésor du Sancta Sanctorum*. Paris: E. Leroux, 1906.

Laurentin, René. *Maria, Ecclesia, sacerdotium: Essai sur le développement d'une idée religieuse*. Paris: Nouvelles Éditiones Latines, 1952.

Le Blant, Edmond. *Les sarcophages chrétiens de la Gaule*. Paris: Imprimerie Nationale, 1886.

Leclercq, Henri. "Pola." Columns 1342–1346 in *Dictionnaire d'archéologie chrétienne et de liturgie*. Vol. 14, Part 1. Edited by Fernand Cabrol and Henri Leclercq. Paris: Letouzey et Ané. 1939.

Lecuyer, Joseph. "Note sur la liturgie du sacre des evêques." *Ephemerides liturgicae* 66 (1952): 369–72.

Leloup, Jean-Yves. *The Gospel of Mary Magdalene*. Translated by Joseph Rowe. Rochester, VT: Inner Traditions, 2002.

Lerner, Constantine B. *The Wellspring of Georgian Historiography: The Early Medieval Historical Chronicle: The Conversion of K'art'li and The Life of Nino*. London: Bennett and Bloom, 2004.

———. "Conversion of K'art'li." Pages 139–93 in *The Wellspring of Georgian Historiography: The Early Medieval Historical Chronicle: The Conversion of K'art'li and The Life of Nino*. Translated by Constantine B. Lerner. London: Bennett and Bloom, 2004.

Levine, Amy-Jill. "Second Temple Judaism, Jesus and Women: Yeast of Eden." *Biblical Interpretation* 2 (1994): 302–31.

Levine, Lee I. *Visual Judaism in Late Antiquity: Historical Contexts of Jewish Art.* New Haven: Yale University Press, 2012.

Liccardo, Giovanni. "Donne e madonne nelle pitture delle catacombe di Napoli." *Marianum* 55 (1993): 225–43.

———. *Redemptor meus vivit: Iscrizioni cristiane antiche dell'area napoletana.* Trapani: Il Pozzo di Giacobbe, 2008.

Liddell, Robert Scott, Henry Stuart Jones, and Roderick McKenzie, eds. *A Greek-English Lexicon.* Oxford: Oxford University Press, 1996.

Lidov, Alexei. "The Priesthood of the Virgin Mary as an Image-Paradigm of Christian Visual Culture." *IKON* 10 (2017): 9–26.

Lidova, Maria. "Embodied Word: Telling the Story of Mary in Early Christian Art." In *The Reception of the Mother of God in Byzantium: Marian Narratives in Texts and Images.* Edited by Mary Cunningham and Thomas Arentzen. Cambridge: Cambridge University Press, forthcoming.

———. "The Imperial *Theotokos*: Revealing the Concept of Early Christian Imagery in Santa Maria Maggiore in Rome." *Convivium* 2, no. 2 (2015): 59–81.

Lilienfeld, Fairy von. "Amt und geistliche Vollmacht der heiligen Nino, 'Apostle und Evanglist,' von Ostgeorgien, nach den ältesten georgischen Quellen." Pages 224–49 in *Horizonte der Christenheit. Festschrift für Friedrich Heyer zu seinem 85. Geburtstag.* Edited by Michael Kohlbacher and Markus Lesinski. Series *Oikonomia-Quellen und Studien zur orthodoxen Theologie* 34. Erlangen, 1994.

Limberis, Vasiliki. *Divine Heiress: The Virgin Mary and the Creation of Christian Constantinople.* London: Routledge, 1994.

Longhi, Davide. *La capsella eburnea di Samagher: iconografia e committenza.* Ravenna: Girasole, 2006.

Lowden, John. *Early Christian and Byzantine Art.* London: Phaidon, 2003.

Lowe, Malcolm. "ΙΟΥΔΑΙΟΙ of the Apocrypha: A Fresh Approach to the Gospels of James, Pseudo-Thomas, Peter and Nicodemus." *Novum Testamentum* 23, no. 1 (1981): 56–90.

Lowrie, Walter. *Christian Art and Architecture: Being a Handbook to the Monuments of the Early Church.* New York: Macmillan, 1901.

Mackie, Gillian. "The San Venanzio Chapel in Rome and the Martyr Shrine Sequence." *Revue d'Art Canadienne/Canadian Art Review* 23 (1996): 1–13.

MacLean, Arthur John. *The Ancient Church Orders.* Cambridge: Cambridge University Press, 1910.

Macy, Gary. "The Ordination of Women in the Early Middle Ages." *Theological Studies* 61, no. 3 (September 2000): 481–507.

———. *The Hidden History of Women's Ordination: Female Clergy in the Medieval West.* Oxford: Oxford University Press, 2008.

Madigan, Kevin, and Carolyn Osiek, trans. *Ordained Women in the Early Church: A Documentary History*. Baltimore, MD: John Hopkins University Press, 2011.

Maguire, Richard. "A Fertile Crescent? Some Sources for the Orant Virgin in Livadia in Cyprus." Pages 434–53 in *PoCa (Postgraduate Cypriot Archaeology) 2012*. Edited by Hartmut Matthäus, Bärbel Morstadt, and Christian Vonhoff. Newcastle upon Tyne: Cambridge Scholars Press, 2015.

Maier, Walter A. *Aserah: Extrabiblical Evidence*. Harvard Semitic Monographs 37. Atlanta: Scholars Press, 1986.

Mancinelli, Fabrizio. *Catacombs and Basilicas: The Early Christians in Rome*. Florence: Scala, 1981.

Mango, Cyril, ed. *The Oxford History of Byzantium*. Oxford: Oxford University Press, 2001.

Mango, Marlia Mundell. *Silver from Early Byzantium: The Kaper Koraon and Related Treasures*. Baltimore, MD: Trustees of the Walters Art Gallery, 1986.

———. "The Mother of God in Metalwork: Silver Plate and Revetments." Pages 194–207 in *Mother of God: Representations of the Virgin in Byzantine Art*. Edited by Maria Vassilaki. Milan: Skira, 2000.

Manns, Frédéric. "La mort de Marie dans le texte de la Dormition de Marie." *Augustinianum* 19, no. 3 (1979): 507–15.

Marchiori, Laura. "Medieval Wall Painting in the Church of Santa Maria in Pallara, Rome: The Use of Objective Dating Criteria." *Papers of the British School at Rome* 77 (2009): 225–55, 344.

Margalit, Baruch. *A Matter of "Life" and "Death": A Study of the Baal-Mot Epic (CTA 4-5-6)*. Alter Orient und Altes Testament 206. Kevelaer: Butzon und Bercker, 1980.

Markschies, Christoph. "Lehrer, Schüler, Schule: Zur Bedeutung einer Institution für das antike Christentum." Pages 97–120 in *Religiöse Vereine in der römischen Antike. Untersuchungen zu Organisation, Ritual und Raumordnung*. Edited by Ulrike Egelhaaf-Gaiser and Alfred Schäfer. Tubingen: Mohr Siebeck, 2002.

Marmorstein, Arthur. *Studies in Jewish Theology: The Arthur Marmorstein Memorial Volume*. Edited by Joseph Rabbinowitz and Meyer S. Lew. London: Oxford University Press, 1975.

Martimort, Aimé Georges. *Deaconesses: An Historical Study*. Translated by K. D. Whitehead. San Francisco: Ignatius, 1986.

Marucchi, Orazio. *I Monumenti del Museo Cristiano Pio-Lateranense riprodotti in atlante di XCVI. tavole con testo illustrativo di Orazio Marucchi ... Contributo allo studio degli antichi Cimiteri cristiani di Roma*. Rome: Cathedral Church of St. John Lateran, 1910.

———. *Manuale di archeologia cristiana*. Roma: Desclée & C, 1933.

Maser, Peter. "Parusie Christi oder Triumph der Gottesmutter? Anmerkungen zu einem Relief der Tür von S. Sabina in Rom." *RQ* 77 (1982): 30–51.

Mathews, Thomas F. "I sarcophagi di Costantinopoli come fonte iconografica." *Corso di cultura sull'arte ravennate e bizantina* 41 (1994): 313–35.

———. *The Clash of Gods: A Reinterpretation of Early Christian Art.* Rev. edn. Princeton: Princeton University Press, 2003.

Mattingly, Harold. *Coins of the Roman Empire in the British Museum.* 6 vols. London: Trustees of the British Museum, 1936.

Mavropoulou-Tsioumi, Chrysanthi. *Hagia Sophia: The Great Church of Thessaloniki.* Translated by Nicola Wardle. Athens: Kapon, 2017.

McClanan, Anne L. "The Empress Theodora and the Tradition of Women's Patronage in the Early Byzantine Empire." Pages 50–72 in *The Cultural Patronage of Medieval Women.* Edited by June Hall McCash. Athens, GA: University of Georgia Press, 1996.

McEnerney, John I. *St. Cyril of Alexandria: Letters 1–50.* Washington, DC: Catholic University of America Press, 1987.

McGowan, Andrew B. *Ancient Christian Worship: Early Church Practices in Social, Historical, and Theological Perspective.* Grand Rapids, MI: Baker Academic, 2014.

———. "Changing Courses: Eucharistic Origins." Westar Institute Fall 2017 Meeting, Society of Biblical Literature, Annual Meeting, Christianity Seminar.

McVey, Kathleen E. "Ephrem the Syrian's Theology of Divine Indwelling and Aelia Pulcheria Augusta." *Studia Patristica* 35 (2001): 458–65.

Megaw, Arthur, and E. Hawkins. "A Fragmentary Mosaic of the Orante Virgin in Cyprus." *XIVe CEB* [held 1971, Bucharest] 3, no. 3 (1976): 363–66 (with Figures 1–2 and Photos A–D).

Meeks, Wayne A. "The Image of the Androgyne: Some Uses of a Symbol in Earliest Christianity." *History of Religions* 13, no. 2 (1974): 165–208.

Meer, Frederik van der. *Maiestas Domini. Théophanies de l'apocalypse dans l'art chrétien: Étude sur les origines d'une iconographie spéciale du Christ.* Studi di antichità cristiana 13. Vatican City: PIAC, 1938.

Meier, Mischa. *Das andere Zeitalter Justinians: Kontingenzerfahrung und Kontingenzbewaltigung im 6. Jahrhundert n. Chr.* Göttingen: Vandenhoeck & Ruprecht, 2003.

Methuen, Charlotte. "Widows, Bishops and the Struggle for Authority in the *Didascalia Apostolorum*." *JEH* 46 (1995): 197–213.

Metzger, Bruce M. *The Text of the New Testament: Its Transmission, Corruption, and Restoration.* 2nd edn. New York: Oxford University Press, 1968.

Meyer, Robert T., trans. *Palladius: Dialogue on the Life of St. John Chrysostom.* New York: Newman, 1985.

Milliner, Matthew. "Giving Birth to God: The Virgin Empress Pulcheria and the Imitation of Mary in Early Christian Greek and Syriac Traditions." Dissertation. Concordia University, Montreal, 2008.

Mimouni, Simon Claude. *Dormition et Assomption de Marie: Histoire des traditions anciennes.* Théologie Historique 98. Paris: Beauchesne, 1995.

———. *Les traditions anciennes sur la Dormition et l'Assomption de Marie: Études littéraires, historiques et doctrinales.* Supplements to Vigiliae Christianae: Texts and Studies of Early Christian Life and Language 104. Leiden: Brill, 2011.

Miner Dorothy, Eugenia, and Marvin Chauncey Ross. *Early Christian and Byzantine Art: An Exhibition Held at the Baltimore Museum of Fine Art, April 25 to June 22, 1947.* Baltimore: Trustees of the Walters Art Gallery, 1947.

Mitchell, Leonel L. *Baptismal Anointing.* London: University of Notre Dame, 1978.

Mitchell, Margaret M. "Looking for Abercius: Reimagining the Contexts of Interpretation of the 'Earliest Christian Inscription.'" Pages 303–35 in *Commemorating the Dead: Texts and Artifacts in Context. Studies of Roman, Jewish and Christian Burials.* Edited by Laurie Brink and Deborah Green. Berlin: Walter de Gruyter, 208.

Montevecchim, Orsolina. "Una donna 'prostatis' del figlio minorenne in un papiro del IIᵃ." *Aegyptus* 61 (1981): 103–15.

Moor, J. C. de. *The Rise of Yahwism: The Roots of Israelite Monotheism.* 2nd edn. Leuven: Peeters, 1997.

Morey, C. R. "The Silver Casket of San Nazaro in Milan." *American Journal of Archaeology* 23, no. 2 (1919): 101–25.

Morris, Colin. *The Sepulchre of Christ and the Medieval West: From the Beginning to 1600.* Oxford: Oxford University Press, 2005.

Morris, Joan. *The Lady Was a Bishop: The Hidden History of Women with Clerical Ordination and the Jurisdiction of Bishops.* New York: Macmillan, 1973.

Mullooly, Joseph. *Saint Clement, Pope and Martyr, and His Basilica in Rome.* Rome: G. Barbèra, 1973.

Murray, Peter, and Linda Murray. *Oxford Dictionary of Christian Art.* Oxford: Oxford University Press, 1996.

Murray, Robert. *Symbols of Church and Kingdom: A Study in Early Syriac Tradition.* Rev. edn. Piscataway, NJ: Gorgias Press, 2004.

Myslivec, J. "Tod Mariens." Columns 333–38 in *Lexikon der christlichen Ikonographie* IV. Edited by Engelbert Kirschbaum, Günter Bandmann, Wolfgang Braunfels, Johannes Kollwitz, Wilhelm Mrazek, Alfred A. Schmid, and Hugo Schnell. Rome: Herder, 1972.

Nasrallah, Laura. "Empire and Apocalypse in Thessaloniki: Interpreting the Early Christian Rotunda." Journal of Early Christian Studies 13, no. 4 (2005): 465–508.

Nau, François, trans. *Barhadbeshabba Abaya: Histoire ecclésiastique*, Patrologia Orientalis 9. Paris, 1913.

———. *Histoire de Nestorius d'après la lettre à Cosme et l'Hymne de Sliba de Mansourya sur les docteurs grecs.* Patrologia Orientalis 13. Paris: Firmin-Didot, 1916.

Neville, Graham, trans. *St. John Chrysostom: Six Books on the Priesthood.* Crestwood, NT: St. Vladimir's Seminary Press, 1977.

Nicolai, Vincenzo Fiocchi, Fabrizio Bisconti, and Danilo Mazzoleni. *The Christian Catacombs of Rome: History, Decoration, Inscriptions.* Translated by Cristina Carlo Stella and Lori-Ann Touchette. Regensburg: Schnell & Steiner, 2009.

Nilgen, Ursula. "Die grosse Reliquieninschrift von Santa Prassede: Eine quellenkritische Untersuchung zur Zeno-Kapelle." *RQ* 69 (1974): 7–29.

Noga-Banai, Galit. *Sacred Stimulus: Jerusalem in the Visual Christianization of Rome.* Oxford: Oxford University Press, 2018.

Norelli, Enrico. *Marie des apocryphes: Enquête sur la mere de Jésus dans le christianisme antique.* Christianismes Antiques. Geneva: Labor et Fides, 2009.

———. "La letteratura apocrifa sul transito di Maria e il problema delle sue origini." Pages 121–65 in *Il dogma dell'assunzione di Maria: problemi attuali e tentativi di ricomprensione.* Edited by Ermanno M. Toniolo. Rome: Edizioni Marianum, 2010.

Nutzman, Megan. "Mary in the Protevangelium of James: A Jewish Woman in the Temple?" *Greek, Roman, and Byzantine Studies* 53 (2013): 551–78.

Oakeshott, Walter. *The Mosaics of Rome from the Third to the Fourteenth Centuries.* New York, 1967.

Olyan, Saul M. *Asherah and the Cult of Yahweh in Israel.* SBL Monograph Series 34. Atlanta: Scholars Press, 1988.

———. "What Do We Really Know About Women's Rites in the Israelite Family Context?" *Journal of Near Eastern Religions* 10 (2010): 55–67.

Omanson, Roger. *A Textual Guide to the Greek New Testament.* Stuttgart: Deutsche Bibelgesellschaft, 2006.

Onofrio, Mario de. *Romei e Giubilei: Il pellegrinaggio medievale a San Pietro (350–1350).* Milan: Electa, 1999.

Origen. *Homily on Jeremiah.* In *Origène: Homélies sur Jérémie.* Translated by Pierre Husson and Pierre Nautin. Paris: Éditions du Cerf, 1977.

Orlandi, Tito. "Coptic Literature." Pages 51–81 in *The Roots of Egyptian Christianity.* Edited by Birger A. Pearson and James E. Goehring. Philadephia: Fortress, 1986.

Osiek, Carolyn. "The Widow as Altar: The Rise and Fall of a Symbol." *Second Century* 3 (1983): 159–69.

Osiek, Carolyn, Margaret Y. MacDonald, and Janet H. Tulloch. *A Woman's Place: House Churches in Earliest Christianity.* Minneapolis: Fortress, 2006.

Paap, A. H. R. E. *Nomina Sacra in the Greek Papyri of the First Five Centuries A.D.: The Sources and Some Deductions.* Leiden: E. J. Brill, 1959.

Papadopoulos-Kerameus, Athanasios. *Analekta hierosolymtikēs stachyologias.* Vol. 2. St. Petersburg: V. Kirsbaoum, 1894.

Parker, Pierson. "A Proto-Lukan Basis for the Gospel According to the Hebrews." *Journal of Biblical Literature* 59, no. 4 (1940): 471–78.

Parlby, Geri. "The Origins of Marian Art in the Catacombs and the Problems of Identification." Pages 41–56 in *The Origins of the Cult of the Virgin Mary.* Edited by Christ Maunder. New York: Burns & Oates, 2008.

Parrott, Douglas M. "*Eugnostos the Blessed* (III,3 and V,1) and *The Sophia of Jesus Christ* (III, 4 and BG 8502,3)." Pages 220–43 in *The Nag Hammadi Library in English.* Edited by James M. Robinson. 3rd rev. edn. San Francisco: Harper, 1988.

————. "Nag Hammadi Codices III, 3–4 and V,1 with Papyrus Berolinensis 8502,3 and Oxyrhynchus Papyrus 1081." Pages 1–216 in *The Coptic Gnostic Library: A Complete Edition of the Nag Hammadi Codices.* Vol. 3. Edited by James M. Robinson. Leiden: Brill, 2000.

Patai, Raphael. *The Hebrew Goddess.* 3rd enlarged edn. Detroit: Wayne State University Press, 1990.

Payne, Philip B. *Man and Woman, One in Christ: An Exegetical and Theological Study of Paul's Letters.* Grand Rapids, MI: Zondervan, 2009.

Pearce, Sarah, ed. *The Image and Its Prohibition in Jewish Antiquity.* Oxford: Oxford University Press, 2013.

Pelikan, Jaroslav. *Mary Through the Centuries: Her Place in the History of Culture.* New Haven: Yale University Press, 1996.

Peltomaa, Leena Mari. *The Image of the Virgin Mary in the Akathistos Hymn.* Leiden: Brill, 2001.

Peltomaa, Leena Mari, Andreas Külzer, and Pauline Allen, ed. *Presbeia Theotokou: The Intercessory Role of Mary across Times and Places in Byzantium (4th—9th Century).* Veröffentlichungen zur Byzanzforschung 39. Denkschriften der philosophisch-historischen Klasse 481. Vienna: Verlag der Österreichischen Akademie der Wissenschaften, 2015.

Peppard, Michael. *The World's Oldest Church: Bible, Art, and Ritual at Dura-Europos, Syria.* New Haven, CT: Yale University Press, 2016.

Perkins, John Ward. "Memoria, Martyr's Tomb and Martyr's Church." *Journal of Theological Studies* 17, no. 1 (1966): 20–37.

Perret, Louis. *Catacombes de Rome.* 5 vols. Paris: Gide et J. Baudry, 1851.

Pesthy, Monika. "Thecla among the Fathers." Pages 164–78 in *The Apocryphal Acts of Paul and Thecla.* Edited by Jan N. Bremmer. Studies on the Apocryphal Acts of the Apostles 2. Kampen, The Netherlands: Kok Pharos, 1996.

Petersen, Heinz. *Bucheinbände.* Graz: Academische Druck, 1991.

Philo of Alexandria. *On the Contemplative Life*. In *The Works of Philo*. Translated by C. D. Yonge. Peabody, MA: Hendrickson, 2004.

Piguet-Panayotova, Dora. "Silver Censers. A Hexagonal Decorated Silver Censer in the Bayerisches Nationalmuseum, Munich." Pages 639–60 in *Radovi XIII. medunarodnog kongresa za starokršćansku arheologiju = Acta XIII congressus internationalis archaeologiae christianae : Split - Pore}c, 25. 9.–1.10. 1994*. Edited by Nenad Cambi. Studi di antichità cristiana 54. Vatican: Pontificio Istituto di archeologia christiana, 1998.

———. "The Attarouthi Chalices." *Mitteilungen zur spätantiken Archäologie und byzantinischen Kunstgeschichte* 6 (2009): 9–76.

Prescott, Andrew. *The Benedictional of St. Æthelwold: A Masterpiece of Anglo-Saxon Art*. London: The British Library, 2002.

Price, Richard, and Michael Gaddis, trans. *The Acts of the Council of Chalcedon*. Vol. 3. Liverpool: Liverpool University Press, 2005.

Price, Richard. "Marian Piety and the Nestorian Controversy." Pages 31–38 in *The Church and Mary*. Edited by R. N. Swanson. Studies in Church History 39. Woodbridge, Suffolk: Boydell, 2004.

———. "Theotokos: The Title and Its Significance in Doctrine and Devotion." Pages 56–74 in *Mary: The Complete Resource*. Edited by Sarah Jane Boss. Oxford: Oxford University Press, 2007.

———. "The *Theotokos* and the Council of Ephesus." Pages 89–109 in *Origins of the Cult of Mary*. Edited by Chris Maunder. London: Burns and Oates, 2008.

Pseudo-Melito. *The Assumption of the Virgin*. In *The Apocryphal New Testament: A Collection of Apocryphal Christian Literature in an English Translation Based on M. R. James*. Edited by J. K. Elliott. Oxford: Clarendon Press, 1993.

Puglisi, James F. *The Process of Admission to Ordained Ministry, a Comparative Study: Epistemological Principles and Roman Catholic Rites*. Vol. 1. Translated by Michael S. Driscoll and Mary Misrahi. Collegeville, MN: Liturgical, 1996.

Rahmani, L. Y. "Eulogia Tokens from Byzantine Bet She'an." *Atiqot* 22 (1993): 109–19.

Ramelli, Ilaria L. E. "Colleagues of Apostles, Presbyters, and Bishops: Women *Syzygoi* in Ancient Christian Communities." In *Patterns of Women's Ministry and Authority Within Ancient Christianity and Judaism*. Edited by Ilaria L. E. Ramelli and Joan E. Taylor. London: Oxford University Press, 2019, forthcoming.

Rebillard, Éric. *The Care of the Dead in Late Antiquity*. Cornell Studies in Classical Philology 69. Translated by Elizabeth Trapnell Rawlings and Jeanine Routier-Pucci. London: Cornell University Press, 2009.

Ricci, Corrado. *Raccolte artistiche di Ravenna*. Bergamo: Istituto Italiano d'Arti Grafiche, 1905.

———. *Ravenna (Translated from the Italian)*. Bergame: Istituto d'Arti Grafiche, 1907.

Roberts, C. H. *Catalogue of Greek and Latin Papyri in the John Rylands Library, III: Theological and Literary Texts*. Manchester: John Rylands Library, 1938.

Robinson, Forbes, trans. *Coptic Apocryphal Gospels*. Cambridge: Cambridge University Press, 1896.

Robinson, James M., ed. *The Nag Hammadi Library in English*. Rev. edn. San Francisco, 1990.

Robbins, Vernon K. "Priestly Discourse in Luke and Acts." Pages 13–40 in *Jesus and Mary Reimagined in Early Christian Literature*. Edited by Vernon K. Robbins and Jonathan M. Potter. Atlanta: SBL Press, 2015.

———. "Bodies and Politics in Luke 1–2 and Sirach 44–50: Men, Women, and Boys." Pages 41–63 in *Jesus and Mary Reimagined in Early Christian Literature*. Edited by Vernon K. Robbins and Jonathan M. Potter. Atlanta: SBL Press, 2015.

Ross, Marvin C. "Objects from Daily Life: Jewelry." Pages 302–28 in *Age of Spirituality: Late Antique and Early Christian Art, Third to Seventh Century*. Edited by Kurt Weitzmann. New York: Metropolitan Museum of Art in association with Princeton University Press, 1979.

Rossi, Giovanni Battista de. "Secchia di piombo trovata nella Reggenza di Tunisi." *Bullettino di Archeologia Cristiana* 5, no. 6 (1867): 77–87.

———. *Musaici cristiani e saggi dei pavimenti delle chiese di Roma anteriori al secolo XV. Tavole cromo-lithografiche con cenni storici e critici*. Rome: Spithöver di G Haass, 1899.

Rossi, Mary Ann, and Giorgio Otranto. "Priesthood, Precedent, and Prejudice: On Recovering the Women Priests of Early Christianity." *Journal of Feminist Studies in Religion*, 7, no. 1 (1991): 73–94.

Rotelle, John E., and Roland J. Teske. *Arianism and Other Heresies*. The Works of Saint Augustine, a Translation of the 21st Century. Vol. 18. Hyde Park, NY: New City Press, 2007.

Rubery, Eileen. "Pope John VII's Devotion to Mary: Papal Images of Mary from the Fifth to the Early Eighth Centuries." Pages 155–99 in *The Origins of the Cult of the Virgin Mary*. Edited by Chris Maunder. London: Burns & Oates, 2008.

———. "From Catacomb to Sanctuary: The Orante Figure and the Cult of the Mother of God and S. Agnes in Early Christian Rome, with Special Reference to Gold Glass." *Studia Patristica* 73 (2014): 129–74.

Rubin, Miri. *Mother of God: A History of the Virgin Mary*. New Haven: Yale University Press, 2009.

Rubinstein, Richard E. *When Jesus Became God: The Struggle to Define Christianity During the Last Days of Rome*. San Diego: Harcourt, 1999.

Ruysschaert, José. "Réflexions sur les fouilles vaticanes, le rapport officiel et la critique." *Revue d'histoire ecclésiastique* 49 (1954): 5–58.

————. "À la découverte d'une grande tradition romaine." *Revue du Clergé Africain* (1961): 401–11.

Sassoon, Isaac S. D. *The Status of Women in Jewish Tradition*. Cambridge: Cambridge University Press, 2011.

Saxer, Victor. *Sainte-Marie-Majeure: une basilique de Rome dans l'histoire de la ville de son église (V^e–XIII^esiècle)*. Rome: École Française de Rome, 2001.

Schaberg, Jane. "*The Father, the Son and the Holy Spirit: The Triadic Phrase in Matthew 28:19b.*" SBL Dissertation Series 61. Chico, CA: Scholars Press, 1982.

————. *The Resurrection of Mary Magdalene: Legend, Apocrypha, and the Christian Testament*. New York: Continuum, 2003.

Schaefer, Mary M. *Women in Pastoral Office: The Story of Santa Prassede, Rome*. New York: Oxford University Press, 2013.

Schlatter, Fredric W. "The Two Women in the Mosaic of Santa Pudienza." *Journal of Early Christian Studies* 3, no. 1 (1995): 1–24.

Scheid, John. "The Religious Roles of Roman Women." Pages 377–408 in *A History of Women: From Ancient Goddesses to Christian Saints*. Edited by Pauline Schmitt Pantel. Translated by Arthur Goldhammer. Cambridge, MA: Belknap, 1994.

Schenk, Christine. *Crispina and Her Sisters: Women and Authority in Early Christianity*. Minneapolis: Fortress, 2017.

Schiller, Gertrud. *Ikonographie der christlichen Kunst*. Vol. 4.2, Maria. Gütersloh: Mohn, 1980.

Schneemelcher, Wilhelm, ed. *New Testament Apocrypha*. Vols. 1 and 2. Translated by R. McL. Wilson. Rev. edn. Cambridge: James Clark, 1991, 1992.

————, trans. "The Acts of Paul and Thecla." Pages 2:239–46 in *New Testament Apocrypha*, Vols. 1 and 2. Translated by R. McL. Wilson. Rev. edn. Cambridge: James Clark, 1991, 1992.

Scholl, Lindsey Ann. "The Pelagian Controversy: A Heresy in its Intellectual Context." Dissertation. University of California at Santa Barbara, 2011.

Schöllgen, Georg. "Der Abfassungszweck der frühchristlichen Kirchenordnungen: Anmerkungen zu den Thesen Bruno Steimers." *Journal of Ancient Christianity* 40 (1997): 55–77.

Schrader, Elizabeth. "Was Martha Added to the Fourth Gospel in the Second Century?" *Harvard Theological Review* 110, no. 3 (2017): 360–92.

Schrader, J. L. "Antique and Early Christian Sources for the Riha and Stuma Patens." *Gesta* 18, no. 1 (1979): 147–56.

Schultz, Celia E. *Women's Religious Activity in the Roman Republic*. Edited by Robin Osborne, P. J. Rhodes, and Richard J. A. Talbert. Studies in the History of Greece and Rome. Chapel Hill: The University of North Carolina Press, 2006.

Schüssler Fiorenza, Elisabeth. *In Memory of Her: A Feminist Theological Reconstruction of Christian Origins.* New York: Crossroad, 1983.

———. *Jesus: Miriam's Child, Sophia's Prophet: Critical Issues in Feminist Christology.* New York: Continuum: 1994.

Sellew, Philip. "An Early Coptic Witness to the *Dormitio Mariae* at Yale: P.CtYBR inv. 1778 Revisited." *Bulletin of the America Society of Papyrologists* 37 (2000): 37–69.

Shoemaker, Stephen J. "'Let Us Go and Burn Her Body': The Image of the Jews in the Early Dormition Traditions." *Church History* 68, no. 4 (December 1999): 775–823.

———. "The (Re?)Discovery of the Kathisma Church and the Cult of the Virgin in Late Ancient Palestine." *Maria: A Journal of Marian Studies* 2 (2001): 21–72.

———. "Rethinking the 'Gnostic Mary': Mary of Nazareth and Mary of Magdala in Early Christian Tradition." *Journal of Early Christian Studies* 9, no. 4 (2001): 555–95.

———. "Gender at the Virgin's Funeral: Men and Women as Witnesses to the Dormition." *Studia Patristica* 34 (2001): 552–58.

———. *Ancient Traditions of the Virgin Mary's Dormition and Assumption.* Oxford Early Christian Studies. Oxford: Oxford University Press, 2002.

———. "The Ethiopic *Liber Requiei*." Pages 290–350 in *Ancient Traditions of the Virgin Mary's Dormition and Assumption.* Oxford Early Christian Studies. Oxford: Oxford University Press, 2002.

———. "The *Ethiopic Six Books*." Pages 375–96 in *Ancient Traditions of the Virgin Mary's Dormition and Assumption.* Oxford Early Christian Studies. Oxford: Oxford University Press, 2002.

———. "A Case of Mistaken Identity? The Marys of Early Christian Tradition." Pages 5–30 in *Which Mary? The Marys of Early Christian Tradition.* Edited by F. Stanley Jones. Atlanta: Society of Biblical Literature, 2002.

———. "Jesus' Gnostic Mom: Mary of Nazareth and the Gnostic Mary Traditions." Pages 153–82 in *Mariam, the Magdalen, and the Mother.* Edited by Deirdre Good. Bloomington: Indiana University Press, 2005.

———. "The Virgin Mary in the Ministry of Jesus and the Early Church According to the Earliest *Life of the Virgin*." *Harvard Theological Review* 98, no. 4 (2005): 441–67.

———. "The Georgian *Life of the Virgin* attributed to Maximus the Confessor: Its Authenticity (?) and Importance." Pages 307–28 in *Mémorial R. P. Michel van Esbroeck, S. J.* Edited by Alexey Muraviev and Basil Lourié. Scrinium 2. St. Petersburg: Byzantinorossica, 2006.

———. "A Peculiar Version of the *Inventio Crucis*." *Studia patristica* 41 (2006): 75–81.

————. "Epiphanius of Salamis, the Kollyridians, and the Early Dormition Narratives: The Cult of the Virgin in the Fourth Century." *Journal of Early Christian Studies* 16 (2008): 371–401.

————. "The Cult of the Virgin in the Fourth Century: A Fresh Look at Some Old and New Sources." Pages 71–87 in *The Origins of the Cult of the Virgin Mary*. Edited by Christ Maunder. New York: Burns & Oates, 2008.

————. "Apocrypha and Liturgy in the Fourth Century: The Case of the 'Six Books' Dormition Apocryphon." Pages 153–63 in *Jewish and Christian Scriptures: The Function of 'Canonical' and 'Non-canonical' Religious Texts*. London: T&T Clark, 2010.

————. "From Mother of Mysteries to Mother of the Church: The Institutionalization of the Dormition Apocrypha." *Apocrypha* 22 (2011): 11–47.

————. "Mary the Apostle: A New Dormition Fragment in Coptic and Its Place in the History of Marian Literature." Pages 203–29 in *Bibel, Byzanz und Christlicher Orient: Festschrift für Stephen Gerö*. Edited by Dmitrij F. Bumazhnov, Emmanouela Grypeou, Timothy B. Sailors, and Alexander Toepel. Leuven: Peeters, 2011.

————. "New Syriac Dormition Fragments from Palimpsests in the Schøyen Collection and the British Library." *Le Muséon* 124 (2011): 259–78.

————. *The Life of the Virgin*. New Haven: Yale University Press, 2012.

————. *Mary in Early Christian Faith and Devotion*. New Haven: Yale University Press, 2016.

————. "The (Pseudo?-)Maximus *Life of the Virgin* and the Byzantine Marian Tradition." *Journal of Theological Studies*, NS, 67, no. 1 (April 2016): 114–42.

Simson, Otto G. von. *Sacred Fortress: Byzantine Art and Statecraft in Ravenna*. Princeton, NJ: Princeton University Press, 1987.

Sivan, Hagith. *Galla Placidia: The Last Roman Empress*. Oxford: Oxford University Press, 2011.

Slater, Richard N. "An Inquiry into the Relationship between Community and Text: The Apocryphal *Acts of Philip* 1 and the Encratites of Asia Minor." Pages 281–306 in *The Apocryphal Acts of the Apostles*. Edited by François Bovon, Ann Graham Brock, and Christopher R. Matthews. Cambridge: Harvard University Press, 1999.

Smend, Ursula. *Die Kirche Sainte-Marie-Madeleine und der Dominikanerkonvent in Saint-Maximin (Provence): Studien zur Baugeschichte, Bauorganisation und Architektur am Beispiel einer königlichen Stiftung (1225–1550)*. Frankfurt am Main: Lang, 1990.

Smid, H. R. *Protevangelium Jacobi: A Commentary*. ANT 1. Assen: van Gorcum, 1965.

Smith, Andrew Philip. *The Gospel of Thomas*. Apollo, CA: Ulysses Books, 2002.

Smith, Christopher. "*Virgo Sacerdos*: Mary and the Priesthood of the Faithful." Thesis. Pontificia Universitas Gregoriana, Rome, 2005.

Smith, Dennis E. *From Symposium to Eucharist: The Banquet in the Early Christian World*. Minneapolis: Fortress Press, 2003.

Smith, Dennis E., and Hal E. Taussig. *Meals in the Early Christian World Social Formation, Experimentation, and Conflict at the Table*. New York: Palgrave Macmillan, 2012.

Smith, John Clark, and Origen. *Origen: Homilies on Jeremiah and I Kings 28*. Washington, DC: Catholic University of America Press, 1998.

Smith Lewis, Agnes, ed. and trans. *Apocrypha Syriaca: The Protevangelium Jacobi and Transitus Mariae*. Studia Sinaitica 11. London: C. J. Clay, 1902.

———. "Eugenia." Pages 1–25 in *Select Narratives of Holy Women from the Syro-Antiochene or Sinai Palimpsest as Written Above the Old Syriac Gospels by John the Stylite, of Beth-Mari-Qanūn in A.D. 778*. Studia Sinaitica 10. London: C. J. Clay, 1900.

———. "Irene." Pages 94–148 in *Select Narratives of Holy Women from the Syro-Antiochene or Sinai Palimpsest as Written Above the Old Syriac Gospels by John the Stylite, of Beth-Mari-Qanūn in A.D. 778*. Studia Sinaitica 10. London: C. J. Clay, 1900.

———. *Light on the Four Gospels from the Sinai Palimpsest*. London: Williams and Norgate, 1913.

———. *The Old Syriac Gospels; Or, Evangelion Da-Mepharreshê: Being the Text of the Sinai or Syro-Antiochene Palimpsest, Including the Latest Additions and Emendations, with the Variants of the Curetonian Text, Corroborations from Many Other Mss., and a List of Quotations from Ancient Authors*. London: Williams and Norgate, 1910.

———. *Select Narratives of Holy Women from the Syro-Antiochene or Sinai Palimpsest as Written Above the Old Syriac Gospels by John the Stylite, of Beth-Mari-Qanūn in A.D. 778*. Studia Sinaitica 10. London: C. J. Clay, 1900.

———. "Transitus Mariae." Pages 12–69 in *Apocrypha Syriaca: The Protevangelium Jacobi and Transitus Mariae*. Studia Sinaitica 11. Edited by Agnes Smith Lewis. London: C. J. Clay, 1902.

———. *A Translation of the Four Gospels from the Syriac*. London: C. J. Clay and Sons, 1896.

Snyder, Graydon F. *Ante-Pacem: Archeological Evidence of Church Life Before Constantine*. Macon: Mercer University Press, 1985.

Socrates. *Ecclesiastical History*. In *Socrates, Sozomenus: Church Histories*. Translated by Chester David Hartranft. Nicene and Post-Nicene Fathers 2. Vol. 2. Oxford: Parker, 1891.

Soper, Alexander Coburn. "The Italo-Gallic School of Early Christian Art." *The Art Bulletin* 20, no. 2 (June 1938): 145–92.

Sozomen. *Ecclesiastical History*. In *Socrates, Sozomenus: Church Histories*. Translated by Chester David Hartranft. Nicene and Post-Nicene Fathers 2. Vol. 2. Oxford: Parker, 1891.

Spain, Suzanne. "'The Promised Blessing': The Iconography of the Mosaics of S. Maria Maggiore." *The Art Bulletin* 61, no. 4 (December 1979): 518–40.

Sperling, Harry, and Maurice Simon. *The Zohar*. Vol. 1. London: Soncino Press, 1970.

Spier, Jeffrey, ed. *Picturing the Bible: The Earliest Christian Art*. New Haven: Yale University Press in association with the Kimbell Art Museum, 2007.

St. Clair, Archer. "The Visit to the Tomb: Narrative and Liturgy on Three Early Christian Pyxides." *Gesta* 18, no. 1 (1979): 127–35.

Standhartinger, Angela. "Women in Early Christian Meal Gatherings: Discourse and Reality." Pages 87–108 in *Meals in the Early Christian World: Social Formation, Experimentation, and Conflict at the Table*. Edited by Dennis E. Smith and Hal Taussig. New York: Palgrave Macmillan, 2012.

Stegmüller, Otto. "*Sub tuum praesidium*: Bemerkungen zur ältesten Überlieferung." *Zeitschrift für katholische Theologie* 74 (1952): 76–82.

Steigerwald, Gerhard. *Die frühchristlichen Mosaiken des Triumphbogens von S. Maria Maggiore in Rom*. Berlin: Schnell and Steiner, 2016.

Stewart-Sykes, Alistair, trans. "Bread and Fish, Water and Wine: The Marcionite Menu and the Maintenance of Purity." Pages 207–20 in *Marcion und seine kirchengeschichtliche Wirkung* [Marcion and His Impact on Church History]. Edited by Martin Meiser, Katharina Greschat, and Gerhard May. Berlin: Walter de Gruyter, 2002.

———. *The Apostolic Church Order: The Greek Text with Introduction, Translation and Annotation*. Strathfield, NSW, Australia: St. Paul's Publications, 2006.

———. *The Didascalia apostolorum: An English Version with Introduction and Annotation*. Studia Traditionis Theologiae, Explorations in Early and Medieval Theology 1. Turnhout: Brepols, 2009.

Strycker, Émile de. *La forme la plus ancienne du Protévangile de Jacques: Recherches sur le papyrus Bodmer 5*. Brussels: Société des Bollandistes, 1961.

Strzygowski, Josef. *Byzantinische Denkmäler: I. Das Etschmiadzin-Evangeliar*. Vienna: Mechitharisten-Congregation, 1891.

Swanson, Reuben, ed. *New Testament Greek Manuscripts: Romans*. Wheaton, IL: Tyndale House, 2001.

Szirmai, J. A. *The Archeology of Medieval Bookbinding*. London: Routledge, 1999.

Taft, Robert F. "The Byzantine Imperial Communion Ritual." Pages 1–27 in *Ritual and Art: Byzantine Essays for Christopher Walter*. Edited by Pamela Armstrong. London: Pindar, 2006.

Talbot, Alice-Mary, and Scott Fitzgerald Johnson, trans. *Miracle Tales from Byzantium*. Dumbarton Oaks Medieval Library 12. Cambridge: Harvard University Press, 2012.

Taussig, Hal. "Dealing under the Table: Ritual Negotiation of Women's Power in the Syro-Phoenician Woman Pericope." Pages 264–79 in *Reimagining Christian Origins*. Edited by Elizabeth Castelli and Hal Taussig. Valley Forge: Trinity, 1997.

———. *In the Beginning Was the Meal: Social Experimentation & Early Christian Identity*. Minneapolis: Fortress Press, 2009.

———. "The Pivotal Place of the Therapeutae in Understanding the Meals of Early Judaism." Pages 117–28 in *Meals in Early Judaism: Social Formation at Table*. Edited by Susan Marks and Hal Taussig. New York: Palgrave Macmillan, 2014.

———. "A Brief Technical History of the Mansucripts Concerning Thecla." https://d1cam0bj22fh80.cloudfront.net/wp-content/uploads/2017/03/Taussig-Technical-History-Thecla.pdf (accessed October 15, 2018).

Taylor, Joan E. *Jewish Women Philosophers of First-Century Alexandria: Philo's 'Therapeutae' Reconsidered*. Oxford: Oxford University Press, 2003.

———. "'Two by Two': The Ark-etypal Language of Mark's Apostolic Pairings." Pages 58–82 in *The Body in Biblical, Christian and Jewish Texts*. Library of Second Temple Studies 85. Edited by Lester Grabbe. London: T&T Clark Bloomsbury, 2014.

———. "Christian Archaeology in Palestine: the Roman and Byzantine Periods." In *Oxford Handbook of Early Christian Archeology*. Edited by David K. Pettegrew and William Caraher. Oxford: Oxford University Press, 2018, forthcoming.

Teravanotko, Hanna K. *Denying Her Voice: The Figure of Miriam in Ancient Jewish Literature*. Bristol, CT: Göttingen/Vandenhoeck & Ruprecht, 2016.

Terry, Ann, and Henry Maguire. *Dynamic Splendor: The Wall Mosaics in the Cathedral of Eufrasius in Poreč*. 2 vols. University Park, PA, 2007.

Tertullian. *On Prescription against Heretics*. In *The Ante-Nicene Fathers*. vol. 3. Edited by Alexander Roberts and James Donaldson. Translated by Peter Holmes. Reprint. Peabody, MA: Hendrickson, 2004.

———. *On Baptism*. In *The Ante-Nicene Fathers*. Vol. 3. Edited by Alexander Roberts and James Donaldson. Translated by S. Thelwall. Reprint. Peabody, MA: Hendrickson, 2004.

———. *On the Veiling of Virgins*. In *The Ante-Nicene Fathers*. Vol. 4. Edited by Alexander Roberts and James Donaldson. Translated by S. Thelwall. Reprint. Peabody, MA: Hendrickson, 2004.

Thompson, Thomas A. "Vatican II and Beyond." Pages 401–55 in *Mary: A History of Doctrine and Devotion*. Notre Dame, IN: Ave Maria, 2009.

Thunø, Erik. "Looking at Letters: 'Living Writing' in S. Sabina in Rome." *Marburger Jahrbuch für Kunstwissenschaft* 34 (2007): 19–41.

Thurston, Bonnie Bowman. "The Widows as the 'Altar of God." SBL *Seminar Papers* 24 (1985): 279–89.

Tkacz, Catharine Brown. *The Key to the Brescia Casket: Typology and the Early Christian Imagination.* Notre Dame, IN: University of Notre Dame Press, 2002.

Toesca, Pietro. *Storia dell'arte italiana* I. Turin: Unione, 1927.

Torjesen, Karen Jo. *When Women Were Priests: Women's Leadership in the Early Church & the Scandal of Their Subordination in the Rise of Christianity.* San Francisco: HarperSanFrancisco, 1995.

———. "The Early Christian *Orans*." Pages 42–56 in *Women Preachers and Prophets Through Two Millennia of Christianity.* Edited by Beverly Mayne Kienzle and Pamela J. Walker. Berkeley: University of California Press, 1998.

Török, László. *Transfigurations of Hellenism: Aspects of Late Antique Art in Egypt AD 250–700.* Leiden: Brill, 2005.

Toynbee, Jocelyn, and John Ward Perkins. *The Shrine of St. Peter and the Vatican Excavations.* New York: Pantheon, 1957.

Toynbee, J. M. C. "The Shrine of St. Peter and its Setting." *Journal of Roman Studies* 43 (1953): 1–26.

Trevett, Christine. *Montanism: Gender, Authority and the New Prophecy.* Cambridge: Cambridge University Press, 1996.

Tulloch, Janet H. "Women Leaders in Family Funerary Banquets." In *A Woman's Place: House Churches in Earliest Christianity.* Edited by Carolyn Osiek, Margaret Y. MacDonald, and Janet H. Tulloch. Minneapolis: Fortress, 2006, 164–93.

Turcan, Robert. *The Gods of Ancient Rome.* Translated by Antonia Nevill. New York: Routledge, 2001.

Turner, Peter. *Truthfulness, Realism, Historicity: A Study in Late Antique Spiritual Literature.* Burlington, VT: Ashgate, 2012.

Uspenskij, A. I. "O vnov' otkrytych mosaikach v cerkvi Sv. Dimitrija v San Demetrio a Salonico (with Plates 1–XX)." *Izvestija Russkogo Archeologičeskogo Instituta v Konstantinopole* 14 (1909): 1–61.

Van Esbroeck, Michel-Jean. "Les textes littéraires sur l'Assomption avant le Xe siècle." Pages 265–85 in *Les actes apocryphes des apôtres.* Publications de la faculté de théologie de l'Université de Genève 4. Edited by François Bovon. Geneva: Labor et Fides, 1981.

———, trans. *Maxime le Confesseur: Vie de la Vierge.* Scriptores Iberici 21 [Geor.] and 22 [Fr.]. CSCO 478 and 479. Louvain: Peeters, 1986.

Vikan, Gary. *Early Byzantine Pilgrimage Art.* Dumbarton Oaks Byzantine Collection Publications 5. Washington, DC: Dumbarton Oaks Research Library and Collection, 2010.

Vio, Ettore, ed. *St. Mark's Basilica in Venice*. London: Thames & Hudson, 1999.

Volbach, Wolfgang Fritz. *Early Christian Art*. Translated by Christopher Ligota. New York: Harry N. Abrams, Inc., 1962.

Vossius, G. J., trans. *The History of Count Zosimus, Sometime Advocate and Chancellor of the Roman Empire*. London: Green and Chaplin, 1814.

Vuong, Lily C. "Let Us Bring Her Up to the Temple of the Lord." Pages 418–32 in *Infancy Gospels: Stories and Identities*. Edited by Claire Clivaz, Andreas Dettwiler, Luc Devillers, and Enrico Norelli. Tübingen: Mohr Siebeck, 2011.

———. *Gender and Purity in the Protevangelium of James*. Wissenschaftliche Untersuchungen zum Neuen Testament 2. Reihe 358. Tübingen: Mohr Siebeck, 2013.

Walker, Alexander, trans. "The Book of John Concerning the Falling Asleep of Mary." Pages 587–91 in *The Twelve Patriarchs, Excerpts and Epistles, The Clementina, Apocrypha, Decretals, Memoirs of Edessa and Syriac Documents, Remains of the First Ages, The Ante-Nicene Fathers* 8. Edited by Alexander Roberts and James Donaldson. Buffalo: Christian Literature, 1886.

Wardrop, Margery, trans. *Life of Saint Nino*. Edited by George Anton Kiraz. Rreprint. Analecta Gorgiana 3. Piscataway, NJ: Gorgias, 2006.

Warner, Marina. *Alone of All Her Sex: The Myth and the Cult of the Virgin Mary*. New York: Knopf, 1976.

Watiz, "Neue Untersuchungen über die sogenannten judenchristlichen Evangelien." *Zeitschrift für die neutestamentliche Wissenschaft und die Kunde der älteren Kirche* 36 (1937): 68–81.

Watson, Francis. *Gospel Writing: A Canonical Perspective*. Grand Rapids, MI: William B. Eerdmans, 2013.

Webb, Matilda. *The Churches and Catacombs of Early Christian Rome: A Comprehensive Guide*. Brighton: Sussex Academic Press, 2001.

Weitzmann, Kurt. *Late Antique and Early Christian Book Illumination*. New York: George Braziller, 1977.

———. *Age of Spirituality: Late Antique and Early Christian Art, Third to Seventh Century: Catalogue of the Exhibition at the Metropolitan Museum of Art, November 19, 1977, Through February 12, 1978*. New York: Metropolitan Museum of Art, 1979.

Weitzmann, Kurt, and Herbert L. Kessler. *The Frescoes of the Dura Synagogue and Christian Art*. Dumbarton Oaks Studies 28. Washington, DC: Dumbarton Oaks Research Library and Collection, 1990.

Wenger, Antoine. *L'Assomption de la T.S. Vierge dans la tradition byzantine du VIe au Xe siècle: Études et documents*. Archives de l'Orient Chrétien 5. Paris: Inst. Français d'Études Byzantines, 1955.

Westall, Richard. "Constantius II and the Basilica of St. Peter in the Vatican." *Historia* 64, no. 2 (2015): 205–42.

Wiegand, Johannes. *Das altchristliche Hauptportal an der Kirche der heiligen Sabina auf dem aventinischen Hügel zu Rom.* Trier: Paulinus-Dr, 1900.

Wijngaards, John. "The Priesthood of Mary." *The Tablet* 253 (December 1999): 1638–40.

———. *The Ordained Women Deacons of the Church's First Millennium.* Norwich: Caterbury Press, 2001.

———. *Women Deacons in the Early Church: Historical Texts and Contemporary Debates.* New York: Crossroad, 2002.

Wilkinson, John, trans. *Egeria's Travels.* 3rd edn. Oxford: Oxbow Books, 1999.

Williams, D. H. *Ambrose of Milan and the End of the Arian-Nicene Conflicts.* Oxford: Clarendon, 1995.

Williams, Frank, trans. *The Panarion of Epiphanius of Salamis.* 2 vols. Nag Hammadi and Manichaean Studies 35 and 36. Leiden: Brill, 1994/1997.

Wilmart, André. *Analecta reginensia: Extraits des manuscrits latins de la reine Christine conservés au Vatican.* Studi e testi 59. Vatican City: Biblioteca apostolica Vaticana, 1933.

Wilpert, Joseph. *Fractio panis: La plus ancienne représentation du sacrifice eucharistique.* Paris: Librairie de Firmin-Didot, 1896.

———. *Un capitolo di storia del vestiario: tre studii sul vestiario dei tempi posconstaniniani.* Rome: Tipografia dell'Unione Cooperativa Editrice, 1898.

———. *Die Gewandung der Christen in den ersten Jahrhunderten: vornehmlich nach den Katakomben-Malereien dargestellt.* Heidelberg: Universitätsbibliothek Heidelberg, 1898.

———. *Die Malereien der Katakomben Roms.* 2 vols. Freiburg im Breisgau: Herdersche, 1903.

———. *Die römischen Mosaiken und Malereien der kirchlichen Bauten vom IV. bis XIII. Jahrhundert.* 4 vols. Freiburg im Breisgau: Herder, 1916.

———. "Le due più antiche rappresentazioni della Adoratio Crucis." *Atti della Pontificia Accademia romana di archeologia,* series 3, Memorie 2 (1928): 135–55.

———. *I Sarcofagi cristiani antichi.* 2 vols. Roma: Pontificio Istituto di archeologia Cristiana, 1929.

Wolf, Gerhard. "Icons and Sites: Cult Images of the Virgin in Mediaeval Rome." Pages 23–49 in *Images of the Mother of God: Perceptions of the Theotokos in Byzantium.* Edited by Maria Vassilaki. Aldershot: Ashgate, 2005.

Wright, William, trans. *Contributions to the Apocryphal Literature of the New Testament: Collected and Edited from Syriac Manuscripts in the British Museum.* London: Williams and Norgate, 1865.

———. "The Obsequies of the Holy Virgin." Pages 42–51 in *Contributions to the Apocryphal Literature of the New Testament: Collected and Edited from Syriac Manuscripts in the British Museum.* Translated by William Wright. London: Williams and Norgate, 1865.

———. "The Departure of My Lady Mary from This World." *Journal of Sacred Literature and Biblical Record* 7 (1865): 129–60.

———. "The History of the Virgin Mary, the Holy Mother of God." Pages 18–24 in *Contributions to the Apocryphal Literature of the New Testament: Collected and Edited from Syriac Manuscripts in the British Museum.* Edited by William Wright. London: Williams and Norgate, 1865.

———. "Transitus Beate Virginis." Pages 24–41 in *Contributions to the Apocryphal Literature of the New Testament: Collected and Edited from Syriac Manuscripts in the British Museum.* Edited by William Wright. London: Williams and Norgate, 1865.

Wright, Wilmer Cave. *The Works of the Emperor Julian.* vol. 3. Cambridge, MA: Harvard University Press, 2014.

Wulff, Oskar. *Altchristliche und byzantinische Kunst.* 2 vols. Berlin: Athenaion, 1914.

Yeroulanou, Aimilia. "The Mother of God in Jewelry." Pages 226–35 in *Mother of God: Representations of the Virgin in Byzantine Art.* Edited by Maria Vassilaki. Milan: Skira, 2000.

Yonge, C. D., trans. *The Works of Philo.* Peabody, MA: Hendrickson, 2004.

Zangara, Vincenza. "Una predicazione alla presenza dei principi: la chiesa di Ravenna nella prima metà del sec. V." *Antiquité Tardive* 8 (2000): 265–304.

Zanker, Paul. *The Power of Images in the Age of Augustus.* Translated by Alan Shapiro. Ann Arbor: The University of Michigan Press, 1990.

Zervos, George T. "Dating the *Protevangelium of James*: The Justin Martyr Connection." Pages 415–34 in *Society of Biblical Literature 1994 Seminar Papers.* Edited by Eugene H. Lovering, Jr. Atlanta: Scholars, 1994.

———. "An Early Non-Canonical Annunciation Story." Pages 664–91 in *Society of Biblical Literature 1997 Seminar Papers.* Evanston: American Theological Library Association, 1997.

Index

© The Editor(s) (if applicable) and The Author(s) 2019

A. Kateusz, *Mary and Early Christian Women*,

https://doi.org/10.1007/978-3-030-11111-3

Printed in the United States
By Bookmasters